ROOTS
OF
FUTILITY

∿∿∿∿∿∿∿∿∿∿∿∿∿∿∿∿∿∿∿

NORMAN A. POLANSKY

ROBERT D. BORGMAN

CHRISTINE DE SAIX

ROOTS
OF
FUTILITY

Jossey-Bass Inc., Publishers

San Francisco · Washington · London · 1972

ROOTS OF FUTILITY
by Norman A. Polansky, Robert D. Borgman, and Christine De Saix

Library of Congress Catalogue Card Number LC 72-5894

International Standard Book Number ISBN 0-87589-150-0

Manufactured in the United States of America

JACKET DESIGN BY WILLI BAUM

FIRST EDITION

Code 7235

The Jossey-Bass
Behavioral Science Series

General Editors

WILLIAM E. HENRY, *University of Chicago*

NEVITT SANFORD, *Wright Institute, Berkeley*

Special Adviser in Social Welfare

MARTIN B. LOEB, *University of Wisconsin*

Preface

Roots of Futility began not with a design but with a dream. The
dream was to help the most pitiable of the Appalachian poor, the
children. Fine-featured, doe-eyed, with sallow skin and rotting
teeth, one sees them alongside country roads or worriedly clinging
to their parents in the town. These youngsters and their families
are not touched by the government programs of road-building and
housing which benefit the more affluent. Their parents lack the
connections and skills needed to milk these programs as they have
been designed to be milked by cynical entrepreneurs in Appalachian
misery; they fare badly on relief. And so, years after the initiation of
the war on poverty, the children are still as badly off as before.

Our work went forward during a time of dreadful deterioration of life in great cities. We are not so blissfully withdrawn into
our mountains that we forget that all our futures are being decided
in the metropolises. Yet, the decline of the countryside has exascer-
bated the urban agony, and for the segment of the people with
whom *Roots of Futility* is concerned, the difference between city

and country life does not seem important. We would not have
anticipated that a research project that evolved into a study of futility
should have had its locus in the Appalachian mountains. Reared
partly in the traditions of Emile Durkheim and Georg Simmel, we
are not a little surprised ourselves. The ubiquity of alienation may
be our most important discovery.

A numbing sense of futility lies close to the heart of modern
unease. Sociologists refer to alienation, but they are not alone.
Philosophers also are preoccupied with a vision of man adrift in an
indifferent universe. Most serious clinicians tell us that they encounter ever more patients whose pervasive feelings of futility and
loneliness bespeak the schizoid quality of their personalities. How
do such feelings arise? How are they perpetuated and transmitted?
Do they reflect a dry-eyed recognition of man's fate or a neurotic
nightmare? Such seemingly abstruse questions have a practical
urgency for all helping professionals.

The theoretical issues emerged while we were studying the
problem of child neglect and marginal child care in southern, rural
Appalachia. Our effort was initiated and largely supported by the
U.S. Children's Bureau, Grant PR 1200. The bureau, however,
abandoned us by disappearing during the course of the project,
thereby giving us a taste of how it might feel to be one of the children who concern us here. Charles Gershenson, then of the bureau,
supported us immeasurably for four years or more, not only with
the mechanics of funding but also toward clarifying goals. His able
successors as project managers have been Ann F. Neel and Virginia
K. White. The research is terminating under Program Grants
SRS89-P-800-55/4-01 and 89-P-800-53/4-06 of the Community
Services Administration, Social and Rehabilitation Services, Department of Health, Education, and Welfare.

The original intention, itself not modest, was to study
what can be done to prevent the children of our study area from
needing placement outside their own homes, particularly in institutions. That issue was then especially urgent because residential
facilities are perhaps even less in evidence here than in most rural
sections. However, it did not take long in scouting the problem to
discover it was off the mark. Most youngsters who eventually land
in institutions have first suffered dreadful deprivation. This fact

was brought home forcibly to the senior author when, in the course of preliminary work, he reviewed ten records chosen at random from the files of a juvenile facility. He had never seen such distilled childhood misery.

Precipitants of placement fade into insignificance beside the childhood deprivation that precedes it. But many studies have been made of deprivation ever since "cultural deprivation" (whatever that is) hove into view. Surely we did not need still another study proving that the poor are short of money. It would be better to take the money we were paid and give it to the subjects, for each of us had shown himself and herself capable of other self-support. Knowledge may be power, as they used to say, but knowledge is not action, and all that research produces is knowledge. So, we asked, what do we most need to know that would help the helpers? Which problem is so baffling that even if there were plentiful funds, we would not know how best to spend them? Through such reasoning, we were led to the group of women who became the main focus of our curiosity, the mothers with the apathy-futility syndrome.

Polansky's Law states that research takes longer, costs more, and finds out less than one had hoped. Although the present effort is no exception, we have had our successes in pushing back the frontiers of ignorance. It is a gross oversimplification to regard child neglect solely, or even primarily, in economic terms, although it is certainly associated with poverty. In studying the role of maternal character in child neglect, we are led to evidence of pervasive infantilism; and in a primitive core we uncover the sense of futility. We see, then, how the affect of futility and behavioral apathy in a mother mean disaster for her child.

Thus, we trace the outlines of intergenerational cycles of deprivation and futility which underlie the familiar cycle of poverty. But, are these cycles or vortices? Should we take as our image the wheel or a sucking whirlpool? The child's character neurosis often caricatures what, in his parent, is no more than a charming eccentricity. The stabilized interaction of mother and child may require that the child emerge far more infantile than the mother. Hence, treatment may be more than a matter of jarring loose a static, messy family situation; it may require an initial kick strong enough to reverse a downward spiral from generation to generation. Under

such circumstances, half measures may be no better than nothing, or they may be worse. They can reinforce the slogan already emblazoned on a family's coat of arms: Nothing does any good. To other half measures must also be added misdirected social action.

In plan, *Roots of Futility* takes the reader through several preliminary studies, a major field study, and two subsequent researches which pursued specific leads. Chapter One introduces the problem of neglect as it is experienced in our area, using case illustrations. An intensive pilot study of ten "neglectful" mothers highlighted their infantilism and withdrawal. Issues of operationalizing neglect are further pursued in Chapter Two, with a review of legal definitions and their limitations as bases for research. We conducted an expert survey, using the critical incident technique to establish which dimensions of child care appear most crucial. Thereupon, we constructed our Childhood Level of Living Scale.

After focusing attention on our main problem, the role of the apathy-futility syndrome in child neglect, we turn to relevant social and psychological theories in Chapter Three. Exploring futility, we offer a reformulation of alienation as a psychological concept, relating it to universal experiences of depression and ego-splitting in infancy. Similar issues of theory recur in Chapter Four, in which, while placing our study population in sociocultural perspective, we dispose of the inclination to view Appalachian culture monolithically. Social stratification operates in the mountains as elsewhere.

Chapter Five begins the report on the major diagnostic study, which was the core of our work. It lays out the study design, sampling, psychological tests, and social work instruments by which maternal character is to be compared with child caring and the latter, in turn, to measurable sequellae in the child. The next several chapters contain the key results of this study.

Chapters Nine and Ten report digressions into phenomena whose theoretical relevance was established in the course of our work. Despite the significance of the cycle of infantilization in neglect, we found that the process of infantilization has hardly been studied systematically. Chapter Nine reports two studies of this illuminating concept. In Chapter Ten we advert to Polansky's concept, verbal accessibility, extending previous work and demon-

strating the usefulness of the concept in rapid diagnosis of the neglectful mother.

The final two chapters contain a sober reversion to the theme with which we began: What is to be done for the apathetic-futile mother? Labeled "Exercises in Futility," Chapter Eleven recounts a study of over ninety AFDC (Aid to Families of Dependent Children) cases, including an analysis of games mothers and welfare workers play. Our ideas of what is to be done, some of which are radical, are given in Chapter Twelve.

It is a pleasure to thank some of the many persons who participated in the work or who encouraged it. Shlomo Sharlin, Betty Jane Smith, and Mary Lou Wing were full-time members of the project at various times. Others who contributed their knowledge and energy as part-time workers include social workers Donald Boone, Elizabeth B. Harkins and Katherine Williams. John D. Patton served as our influential psychiatric consultant, and Jay Meddin as a noteworthy student assistant. Our project has been blessed with several attractive, amusing, and competent secretaries in the tradition started by Margaret Jewett, carried forward by Oval Ball, and ending with Sylvia Floyd.

Reaching the research populations of interest demanded more than permissions; it required shared dedication to our goals by a number of remarkable people at work in our area; we wish we could thank each. We do want to acknowledge the continuing support of Ruth Aleshire, then of the North Carolina Department of Public Welfare; Dorothy Crawford, director of the welfare program in Macon County, N.C.; Rebecca Johnson Stradley, who headed the day-care center program in Macon County, which hosted our major study; and B. H. Hartman, head of the Developmental Evaluation Clinic in Asheville, N.C. In Georgia, we have had help from T. M. Parham, then head of children's services for the state Department of Family and Children's Services, and, at a later phase, Nathan Andereck of that agency. But our biggest gratitude is to the mothers of Appalachia who participated in this research. We found all of them likeable, most of them admirable, and we salute them.

At the University of Georgia, we enjoyed the understanding support of the two administrators most involved, Charles A. Stewart,

dean, School of Social Work, whose personal attention was invaluable, and Frederick L. Bates, formerly head, Department of Sociology; we also want to thank the university Office of General Research, personified in Linda Allen and Ernie Harrison.

Some of our results have appeared in preliminary papers in a variety of places, over the years. Acknowledgement is made to the following journals and publishers for permission to adapt from these earlier publications: *Child Welfare, American Journal of Orthopsychiatry, Social Casework,* National Association of Social Workers, National Conference on Social Welfare, Columbia University Press, and Child Welfare League of America.

Finally, there are three local people whose contributions, nonspecific and not to be specified, we record with love: Nancy Finley Polansky (Appalachian-in-residence), Patricia Borgman, and P. F. De Saix.

Athens, Georgia   NORMAN A. POLANSKY
September 1972   ROBERT D. BORGMAN
                                           CHRISTINE DE SAIX

Contents

1

Poor as Job's Turkey

To reach the offices where we worked, you drive west on Tunnel Road. Guarding the eastern entrance to our city lies Beaucatcher Mountain, so named because, in the days of the horse and buggy, the route over it was long enough and slow enough to give a maiden lady a fair chance at her escort. Now, however, there is a vehicular tunnel under the mountain. As you leave its gloom, downtown Asheville and the hills beyond burst upon your eyes.

Mounting the overpass to reach our building, you face a vision so enchanting as to distract the most obsessed social scientist. For there, bathed at once in sunshine and in haze, lie the Great Smoky Mountains of Tennessee and North Carolina, row on row as far as the eye can see until they are one with the sky. Smoky they truly are, blue-grey and wrapped in their ancient mists, daring you to enter and unravel their enigmas. Warm enough for comfort, cool enough for change, the Smokies are a naturalist's paradise. It is said the area immediately around Asheville supports, as natural growth, the greatest variety of flora of any spot on earth. This is

1

the land that God remembered; even the best efforts of those who exploit and rape it have hardly damaged His spectacle.

There is no time of the year when the Smokies are not breathtaking. In the hot summer sun, the mountainsides loom still and bright, interspersed with coves that promise relief and give it. The wintry ice that skids and spraddles us across the roads enshrouds gaunt trees and trims them with glass lace. In the autumn, the leaves lend glorious backing to an occasional wisp of smoke from a hillside cabin with chimney of native stone. And in the spring, in the spring, we dare to live and love again.

Many of those who live in the mountains have been there for generations. They no longer talk Elizabethan English if, in fact, they ever did, but they do have their local expressions just as the boys in Carbondale, Pennsylvania and the old men in the Williamsburg section of New York City do. Like all peasant languages, including that of the ancient Hebrews, their talk is chary of abstractions. They rely instead on figures of speech to move the freight of meaning, some of them salty, and most of them fun. Place names tell their stories in words which we all understand. There are several Bear Wallows; there is Possum Trot.

Life has always been hard for those who live by farming in the Smokies, and, despite their reputation for reticence and courage, our farmers have not been loath to mention it. Not for the country-club set is Hardscrable Road (the signs were corrected to Hardscrabble only this year!) or Poverty Branch. Scattered through the mountains are wonderful people who leave their native farms unwillingly and struggle to return to them. Women, in these self-respecting families, work particularly hard at cleaning, sewing, and cooking. They are prodigious canners of garden vegetables and fruits. Old habits of putting by for winter survive even among well-to-do townspeople, many of whom "make their own gardens" and can for taste and pleasure, if no longer out of necessity. The men are typically competent and strong. Education is now more widespread than once it was, but even among those with little, there are few "slow leaks." They know what wood has made a chair, when a cow is ready for slaughter, what is probably wrong with a brake system, and where to invest money.

But there are others. Nestled in coves with the most gorgeous

scenery God has made is the household which has created, as
private enterprise, its own garbage heap and junk pile in its front
yard. To most of these folks, the views, the flowers, the trees mean
nothing; they are scarcely aware when strawberries glow ripe for
the picking. We find men who, for the sake of a few dollars for
whiskey, will start a forest fire in order to be called up to fight it.
Their lifetimes are lost in preoccupation with drinking, loafing,
fighting, and sex without special pleasure. As they treat the land,
they treat themselves: heedlessly and without remorse.

Out of this small minority comes human squalor which
rivals that of Gary, Cleveland, or Pittsburgh—all places where
people throng so that "you can't stir 'em with a stick." We have
not had to search hard to discover the discrepancies between the
beauty of the hills and the ugliness of how some live in them. Our
discoveries required only a willingness to trip over the available
evidence and to sprawl on the hard facts of what life is like for the
most unfortunate of southern Appalachia. Man *has* to be the most
adaptable of all the animals. How else can we account for the fact
that we intruded with our professional skills into Eden and emerged
with a study entitled *Roots of Futility?*

FOCI

This book is about work on behalf of children, but the focus
of our research was their mothers. The children who have concerned
us are getting less than their fair share of what life has to offer,
many because of poverty, some because of neglect, and some because of both, for troubles are not equitably distributed. Why do
we meet a child on AFDC (Aid to Families of Dependent Children) who is skinny, barefoot, and unkempt while half a mile away
there is another, who is also on AFDC, but infinitely better cared
for? We tried to take a fresh look at why youngsters come to live
so poorly, and we had to assume from the beginning that much of
the answer lay with their mothers. This report, then, deals with how
the personalities of a group of women, all of them living at or near
the poverty line, affected the way they reared their children.

We were particularly intrigued by one group of women who
were called to our attention by welfare personnel early in our

studies. These mothers dragged out their uneventful, seemingless affectless days in a state of slatternly immobilization. More in challenge than curiosity we were asked, "What would *you* do with such a woman?" Eventually, we came to regard these women as typifying the "apathy-futility syndrome," a pattern about which we shall have more to say later on, for mothers with this constellation constitute a large segment of those involved in child neglect. In order to treat, one must first understand. The title of this study is derived from our interest in the apathy-futility syndrome.

What are the roots from which adult futility stems? A study of mothers would be incomplete if it did not address this question and the further question: What is the impact of the mother's pattern on her children? For, if the maternal personality affects the way she cares for her child, does the child-caring associated with a particular cast of personality reflect itself in the child's development? Everyone has heard of an intergenerational cycle of poverty. Almost from the beginning, we observed what appeared to be, at least in some families, an intergenerational cycle of futility. But what are the specific mechanisms by which this dismal outlook is transmitted? From our initial involvement in the practical matter of child neglect and marginal child care, we were inexorably led to explorations in theories of personality and more general issues in child development.

Looking backward on our work and forward into this book, it is not possible to say whether we were more interested in advancing theory or in bringing about change. Lewin said there is nothing so practical as a good theory, and we believe it. All that research can do, in fields like ours, is to improve the directions by which those who do, do. We recognize no clear distinction between theoretically-oriented and so-called applied research. Good theory is the only guide to practice. Our intent has been to accumulate the kind of knowledge that contributes both to general theory and to practical work.

SUBJECTS

Our families stand apart from most of those in other research we have read in several important respects. Our work was con-

centrated nearly entirely among the poor—although this focus is
no longer as unique as it once was in studies of child development.
But our biggest divergence from most organized research was where
our families resided. We remarked that they came from southern
Appalachia. Specifically, they reside in the mountains of western
North Carolina and the tier of north Georgia counties which are
also included in Appalachia.

The folks we studied were rural people. Whatever the stereotypes, Appalachia is by no means purely rural. Embedded in the
study area, our headquarters during these researches, is Asheville,
North Carolina. This city of 70,000 has two private golf clubs,
two private mental hospitals, a suburb of expensive homes from
which all Jews and blacks are barred, and more than its share of
industrial pollution. Asheville is the upstanding American city
Thomas Wolfe called Altamont in *Look Homeward Angel*. Well,
Altamont is a marvelous place to live, but it is not rural, neither by
census definition nor in life style. Knoxville, home of the University
of Tennessee and other industries, neighbored our study area, and
we were within a few hours driving time of Atlanta, Georgia. We
had to pick and choose in our work to ensure we were dealing
primarily with rural populations.

For this generation of social scientists, our cities are "where
the action is." We believe that they contain the most explosive elements of the population. Nevertheless, many millions of Americans
live in the country, and only a few of them are wealthy suburban-
ites, writers, or retired social workers. Ginsburg has pointed out
that, in the 1960s, 30 per cent of the population was rural, but 40
per cent of the poor were (Ginsburg, 1969, pp. 177, 180). According to the 1970 census, fifty-four million persons or 26.4 per cent of
the American population were regarded as "rural farm and nonfarm" (U.S. Department of Commerce, 1970).

Because both problems and brains have concentrated in
cities, much effort has been devoted to studying the families living
in them. However, it is only prudent that attention also be given to
our extensive countryside. Much of the human burden under which
cities are staggering was recruited from rural areas. Urban health
and welfare loads are swollen with refugees from rural blight to
whom the city offered uncertainty, but an uncertainty which was

better than the pockets of desperation they left behind. Many of our mothers are from the group well termed, *The People Left Behind* (President's National Advisory Commission on Rural Poverty, 1967); probably most of them, nevertheless, are folks who prefer to stay where they are for reasons ranging from admirable to neurotic.

We were concerned with marginal child-caring and child neglect. But not all the women who helped in our studies were neglectful mothers. Far from it! We studied the *full range* of those women who made themselves available for research. We needed the competent to contrast with those who were less successful. Only a handful of the women we got to know in depth might be identified as neglectful mothers. We took mothers as they came: good, bad, and every lady very much herself.

Let us call attention to two questions we carried with us: Would our observations apply to other rural families, living elsewhere in this country? (We believe that, on the whole, they do.) Are the dynamics prevalent among mothers whose children receive poor care substantially the same in urban and suburban settings? (We suspect, from our own experiences, that they are.) However, since we have not been able as yet to provide empirical answers to these highly relevant queries, we can only encourage the reader to bear them in mind as he follows our experiences.

RECURRENT THEMES

What causes marginal child caring and child neglect? Statistically and otherwise, child neglect is doubtless a phenomenon of poverty. It is not widespread among those who are better off, even though its visibility might be greater among the latter groups. From one standpoint, this correlation hardly needs explanation. As Joe E. Lewis, the night club monologuist, used to remark, "I've lived poor, and I've lived rich. Rich is better." Money contributes to the child's standard of living, of course. Yet, lack of money cannot be the only explanation for neglect. We deliberately limited our research almost exclusively to families in straitened circumstances. Nevertheless, we found wide variations in the welfare of their children.

For the other set of factors, we chose to concentrate on the personality of the mother. We do not maintain that fathers are irrelevant in these families, or that siblings in large families do not often play important roles, for they do. But we wanted to keep our research within a manageable focus, and we have little doubt that the mother is a crucial variable.

We recognize two ways one can make clinical formulations about the women involved in child neglect: dynamically and structurally. In dynamic formulations, we assume that the mother is substantially an intact person and that her poor child-caring is a response to specific pressures. A favored example of such pressure is economic stress. But psychological pressures may be equally important. In either case, the poor child-caring results from a specific set of dynamics in which inadequacy as a mother is an encapsulated problem in an otherwise effective personality.

In the structural formulation, child neglect is not walled off from the many other things the woman is also neglecting. We regard her defect as characterological. The poor ability in mothering pervades most other aspects of her existence. Either type of formulation may be correct, depending on the case. There are definitely competent women whose mothering role is specifically invaded by conflict as there are women with generally crippled personalities whose poor mothering merely reflects their total pattern.

It makes considerable difference which type of explanation fits the great majority of cases, for this generalization should influence programs of service. For example, if child neglect is usually encapsulated and simply related to economic stress, then programs of guaranteed annual income for the poor will solve this problem. If, however, child neglect is typically part of a pervasive inadequacy in the maternal personality, then financial assistance will be an insufficient condition for the alleviation of marginal child care in the next generation.

RID HARD AND PUT UP MUDDY

Horses are still much admired in the mountains, but not many poor people own them. Most owners are doctors or businessmen or their teen-age daughters indulging in still another leisure-

time pursuit. Yet the habit of horses survives into the day of the second-hand auto and so does some of the vocabulary. If a person has been having a bad time and is pushed and abused by life, he might say: Friend, I've been rid hard and put up muddy. This study is the story of the life of many youngsters in cove communities—beautiful children with regular features, wide blue eyes, and rotting teeth.

We doubt whether the depth of rural poverty that concerns us here is familiar to most who will read this book. A few may have witnessed at some time the filth, the sounds, and the rancid odors connected with that way of life. But, we rapidly repress them, just as so many rich men of humble beginnings like to pretend to themselves they did not really mind being wet, cold, shivering, and hungry. The ego provides us all with a merciful forgetting. So, before we continue the exposition of issues and theory that provide the intellectual motifs for our work, let us remind ourselves what the task is all about.

These cases are from the notes of Christine De Saix (Polansky, 1969, pp. 81–101). As always, there has been distorting and masking to guard a family's privacy, but the essential images are true. One case history focuses on the life of a small boy, the other on a woman whose personality typifies the syndrome which dominated our work.

Joey Carter. I met Joey at the Day Care Center. He was a small, wiry, tough little four-year-old. He had been attending irregularly for several weeks but still rebelled at their "well-rounded diet." (Joey ate no vegetables and only chicken and hot dogs as meat.) He loved active play but refused to touch pencil, paint brush, or crayons. I was curious about the kind of home and family which produced Joey.

The Carters lived in a concrete block house many miles from the nearest town. Although the house was modern looking, several years old, it had never been completed. There were no steps to the front door. The wooden framing was rotting because it had never been protected by paint. Inside, the trim was unfinished, and the subflooring had never been covered—the wide cracks were filled with mud and grease.

The front yard displayed an accumulation of junk, includ-

ing two stripped cars. The front end of another car was raised by a pulley over the limb of a tree with its motor missing. The yard had never been seeded; even weeds would not grow on the hard, eroded slope to the house. To get to the door in rainy weather, the children would slide down the mud with speed and dexterity. When I visited, they laid two planks end to end so that I could edge my way to the entrance.

On the living room floor, in front of the pot-bellied stove, lay the engine from the car. Parts were strewn about, but the family stepped over them agilely, meanwhile tracking grease through the house. It seemed that when the weather was the least bit inclement, Mr. Carter, a shade-tree mechanic, transferred parts and tools to the comfort of the house.

Bright green plastic furniture showed rough wear by six children, four of them teen-agers. Springs protruded dangerously, and Mrs. Carter graciously directed me to a section which was protected by a blanket so that I would not be hurt. There were cheap end tables and a coffee table with one end resting on a concrete block to replace its broken legs. Every available surface was piled high with debris—clothing, phonograph records, comic books. Each was capped by an 8 × 10 photo of one of the children proudly displayed in a plastic frame. A fish bowl with murky water and two sluggish fish perched most perilously on one table. In fact, during my visit, it was spilled and one of the fish slipped through the floorboards causing Joey great anguish.

The kitchen floor was always wet because the water, flowing by gravity from a spring, ran constantly through the sink from a valveless pipe, often overflowing. Flies swarmed over unwashed dishes and food scraps; the dishes were left for the girls to do after school. There were no screens at the doors or the windows. Boxes of clothing which had been "donated" to the family were stacked high against windows and in a narrow hall, requiring the family to slide past them.

The house contained space for a bathroom since it had "piped water," but fixtures had never been installed and there was no septic tank. The space was used to store feed, seed, and bags of coal for the stove.

Mrs. Carter was a short obese middle-aged woman, whose

protruding stomach made her appear to be late in pregnancy. Her dress was always wet and dirty, her hair never combed, and she wore run-down, high-heeled shoes around the house. She smiled continuously, with her dark eyes almost closed. When she forgot to wear her dentures, she looked almost grotesque.

In contrast, Mr. Carter was a tall, gangling man with rugged features and large blue eyes. He seemed to enjoy company and was friendly and outgoing. His presence dominated the room. He bragged about his mechanical skill, gently bossed everybody, and seemed proud of his domain. The children stood around admiring him. He made the long trip to town several times a week, when the impulse moved him, never planning his purchases or purpose. He thought nothing of keeping the children home from school to go with him. He provided the domestic entertainment, and the boys resented leaving for school when he had a big car repair under way.

Mr. Carter received a small veteran's pension. From time to time, he worked briefly in an area plant, but only long enough to get cash to purchase parts for the car he was repairing.

The Carters had met when they were both past thirty and married after a few days' courtship. She was the eldest of a dozen children, and had stayed with her parents until their deaths. Mr. Carter's family were property owners, and his brothers and sisters were comfortably self-supporting. Many neighbors were related to him but reluctant to admit it. They had all given up on the Carters after years of trying and forbade their children from playing with Carters', who were destructive and undisciplined. When one of the Carter girls was younger, she was raped by a group of older boys from the neighborhood. The Carters threatened court action but withdrew the threat when the doctor and neighbors offered to charge the Carters with neglect and counterthreatened removal of their children to foster homes.

All the Carter males were indulged. If there were any gardening to do, Mrs. Carter did it. If there was housework to be done, the girls did it. The older boys had dropped out of school, but one girl had graduated, and the other attended as regularly as possible. From time to time, one of the elder boys left home for a short

period to work. Mr. and Mrs. Carter grieved for him and always got the youngster persuaded to return.

Joey had it doubly hard—he was the baby and he was a boy. He did not learn to walk until age two because he was constantly carried. He had not learned to talk plainly because he got whatever he wanted without speech. He slept with his parents. Mrs. Carter patted her upper arm and said: "He sleeps right here." He would fall asleep watching television and they would carry him to bed, clothes and all. The only discomfort they complained about was that he frequently wet the bed. Both Mr. and Mrs. Carter spoke of missing him since he attended the Day Care Center, and the teachers suspected that they often kept him home for company.

Mrs. Archer. For years, Mrs. Archer had baffled the county department of social services. She appeared at the office weekly to ask for clothing, and delighted in rummaging through castoffs in the store front maintained by a Junior League. She begged compulsively from everyone she met. But, the things she got had little value to her. Her loot was stacked high in a spare room of the house, while she and her children lived half-dressed in dirty, threadbare garments.

The Archer shack is located on Pone Skillet Road, which leads treacherously to the mountain top. The scenery is a naturalist's delight—there are rhododendrons, laurels, ferns, and dogwoods in profusion. A hundred waterfalls form as streams dash over rocks down the slope. On the five-mile trip up the mountain, one passes only one clump of houses. But Mrs. Archer denies relationship to these people, although the community is known as Archer Gap.

The Archer house is partially covered with imitation brick (tar-paper) siding, and the other wide bare boards have been finished only by the wind, rain and sun, which were always more liberal on the mountain top than down in the cove. Many windows have been replaced with cardboard. The yard is littered with junk from old cars and an assortment of oil cans. A triple amputee doll lies half-buried in the mud.

In the wintertime, bedroom and kitchen furniture are all moved into the living room. The family huddles around the pot-bellied stove which serves as both cook-stove and heater. An effort

has been made to insulate the walls of this room with an old piece of linoleum and corrugated cardboard boxes. All are tacked up with the printing exposed, giving a pop art effect—TOMATO SOUP, KLEENEX, KOTEX. All of the furnishings are dilapidated and dirty. There is no linen, and an assortment of dirty patchwork quilts are tossed across bumpy mattresses.

A light cord hangs from the middle of the room. Strings are attached to the chain leading to the sofa, a chair, and the bed, so that, if there were a bulb, it could have been controlled from any reclining place in the room. The Archer's boast the luxury of a pump and a spigot in the house. But no switch has been installed. The water is cut on and off by screwing the fuse in and out of its socket. A modern washing machine stands proudly in the kitchen, but is seldom used. Heating water is too strenuous a chore, and Mrs. Archer has "no faith in new fangled ideas—like cold-water soap." There is neither inside nor outside plumbing at the Archer house. In the winter they use a slopjar, and in the summer they use the yard.

Although Mrs. Archer is in her mid-twenties, she stoops like one thrice her age. Potentially a pretty young woman with sky blue eyes and strawberry-blonde hair, one sees now decayed teeth stained with tobacco juice, matted hair, a dirty body covered by buttonless, shapeless, unlaundered clothing. In the months that we knew her, Mrs. Archer never expressed any emotions. She could not recall when she cried or when she had last become angry. During the interviews, she often kept her eyes closed and her head down.

Mrs. Archer was the oldest of seven children born to parents who lived in an isolated area of another county. They were illiterate themselves and put no stock in education for their children. The older children seldom went to school because they had to walk several miles to get to the school bus. Mrs. Archer guessed she went to the fifth grade before she "aged" out.

In Mrs. Archer's memory, the family had always been supported by public welfare and got all their clothing from churches and friends. After she was married, the "welfare" moved her parents closer to town. Several of the younger children were placed in foster care; subsequently the parents consented to their adoption,

and there has been no contact with them since. One younger brother, who was left with his parents, made a career for himself in service. A sister graduated from high school, married well, and lives in what Mrs. Archer describes with hostility as a "glass house."

Like so many of the women we saw, Mrs. Archer had married a man much older than she. She could recall no details of their meeting, courtship, or marriage. He was a frail-looking man who complained of stomach problems. His hair was long and shaggy, falling across his pale face, partially hiding badly-crossed eyes.

Mr. Archer had lived all of his life in the house he now used for his family, land that had been in the family for generations. The mountains around are rich in timber, and Mr. Archer sometimes hires out near his home cutting logs for paper mills and plywood plants. But, he frequently does not feel like working. Mrs. Archer sympathizes with him, and encourages him to stay home whenever he "feels puny."

The first child born to the Archers died in infancy because "she just wasn't able to make it." One would suspect the elusive syndrome of "failure to thrive" had claimed her. The second child was an attractive six-year-old with beautiful blue-green eyes, dark curly hair, and a wiry little body. In her first year of school, she presented two problems. First, her mother really did not want her to leave to go to school; second, she took home everything she could get her hands on—chalk, crayons, paper, and even possessions of other children which attracted her. She was not stealing or sneaky; rather, she is greedy, hoarding whatever she can get, like a pack-rat —or her mother. Sue Ella frequently complains of toothache, and happily stays home from school.

Martha was four years old. Because of the isolation and deprivation of the home, efforts were made to get her into a day care program when she was three. Both Mr. and Mrs. Archer balked at her going to school, and her break away had to wait at least another year. Both Sue Ella and Martha are skilled in the art of chewing tobacco and spitting accurately into the stove from five feet away.

Two-year-old Sam is a beautiful child with blond curls and enormous blue eyes, which seem to take in everything, although

he says not one word. (Both the younger children seem shy.) Sam seemed happy only when he was nursing at his mother's breast. Whenever Mrs. Archer sat down, he was in her lap pulling at the neck of her dress to nurse and seemed to get satisfaction from fondling her body while he was sucking. Mrs. Archer never held him or cuddled him but seemed oblivious to his presence, as if he were just an extension of her own body. She cannot bring herself to wean Sam, although she says that she is "pretty well dried up." The clinic has told her to stop nursing the baby because she herself needs all the nourishment she can get, and Sam could drink milk.

On one occasion, we had arranged with Mrs. Archer to take her and the children to the Health Clinic in town. Watching her get herself and the children ready was a study in confusion. When she could not find a wash cloth, she ripped up a pair of panties which seemed to be in good repair. She washed her own face and then the childrens'. The rest of their bodies were filthy. She put on an unpressed blouse with several buttons missing and then rummaged through drawers filled with junk to find a pin. She put a clean shirt and pants on the baby but used an old dress belt to hold up the pants. Martha had been running about in a dirty night gown. Mrs. Archer pulled a pair of corduroy pants over the gown and topped this with a dirty tee shirt. Another furious search was made for a comb. When one could not be found, our worker gave her one. Mrs. Archer gave a few futile tugs to her own tangled hair, and then let each child struggle with his own. Finally, we were on the way to the clinic.

And so, atop their mountain, with majestic views in every direction, live Mr. and Mrs. Archer and their children.

TEN NEGLECTFUL MOTHERS

The case of the Archers is drawn from a group we came to know in our earliest organized study, conducted in 1966 (Polansky and others, 1968, pp. 467–475). At that stage, we believed it would be premature to design a substantial quantitative study because we did not feel sufficiently familiar with the area of research. Before committing ourselves to the theories and the instruments that a major study entails, we preferred to begin with clinical research

on a limited number of mothers at risk, whom we might get to know in depth. Accordingly, we conducted a pilot study. Necessarily preliminary, devoted to exploring, rather than concluding, it nevertheless led to insights, which later quantitative research served to clarify and elaborate.

The pilot study was carried out in two counties of western North Carolina: Macon and McDowell.[1] Women were nominated for study by the head of the welfare department in each county. Three criteria were followed in selecting a mother: that the department, either currently or in the recent past, had reason to be gravely concerned about the level of care children in the family were receiving; that the family contained at least one child around five years of age, the age on which we decided to focus in our studies; that there was reason to hope the mother could be persuaded to cooperate. We were introduced in a straightforward way as engaged in work aimed at improving the lot of children in the mountains. Of course, we had nothing concrete to offer the mother in exchange for her help, except an occasional trip to town or other small favor. Field work for the study was done by Christine De Saix and Mary Lou Wing.

Out of twelve women to whom we were introduced, it proved possible to establish a diagnostic relationship with ten. One of the mothers moved away during the study. The other became involved in a series of crises with the agency, which made our continued presence in the home not only inadvisable, but impossible to maintain. Of course, it was not easy to sustain our other contacts. Typical experiences included making an appointment and driving a long distance from Asheville to keep it, only to find no one at home. Nearly every mother was anxious in the company of a relative stranger. Yet, we did find that once contact was made and some trusting occurred, the majority enjoyed talking. It is poignant, but expectable, that for several mothers, it was a revelation to talk with someone who was totally interested in them as individuals. So, even though we made no pretense of offering treatment or anything beside the desire to "understand what it's like," some of our case-

[1] Our thanks go to Dorothy Crawford and H. Gene Herrell and their staffs in these counties for help in selecting and introducing us to these mothers.

workers inevitably became entangled and had difficulty withdrawing because of the helpfulness the mothers seemed to find in their concern. From the beginning, therefore, we confronted the issue of what the investigator owes to the "subject"—and to his research caseworker—if he conducts research on personality that attempts to probe to any depth. Consequently, there were several instances in which contact was maintained beyond the period needed for research purposes only, and some services were given.

Given the skill and persistence of two mature caseworkers converted into research social workers, it proved possible to use surprisingly sophisticated forms of data collection. They followed— not slavishly—a social history outline Polansky brought along from previous practice in a private psychiatric hospital. From history-taking interviews with the mother, supplemented by such collateral sources as the local welfare department and occasional relatives also in the picture, it was possible to compile a formal social history in each case. Eight of the ten mothers also participated in psychological testing, which included the Wechsler Adult Intelligence Scale (WAIS), the Raven Matrices, and the Bender Gestalt.

Our research was focused on the effects of maternal personality on child rearing. To study the latter, we tape recorded a long interview with each mother, following the same outline used with middle- and working-class women in the Boston area by Sears, Maccoby and Levin (1957). Sears and his colleagues compared attitudes toward discipline, feeding, and the like, as these vary between social classes. We were able to go beyond their level of research, for we had information not only about what the mother said but observations—our own and others—of what she did. Interestingly, we discovered that most of these mothers talked well about child-rearing. They were not ignorant of what is generally acceptable behavior in the larger community; they just were not practicing it.

The pilot study made us aware of the heterogeneity of conditions related to child neglect. Several homes represented chronic, low-level care. The filth and disorder were unbelievable; intellectual stimulation was so negligible that there was not a printed word in the home, not even a Bible. Yet, the mothers would not dream of leaving their children unattended. In one family, the children

usually received quite good care. However, about every three months, both parents would get drunk simultaneously and disappear, leaving their youngsters temporarily abandoned. Another home was puzzling because, superficially, the place was so well organized. Despite the fact that the husband was alcoholic and the family was living on welfare, the house was always neat and clean. But there was reason for the agency's concern. Of eight children, some of whom were grown by the time of our study, *not one* had made a success of school, job or marriage; two boys were, at that time, in trouble for delinquency. The mother's defiance came out in her inability to discipline her children. She was the only member of the family with adequate control systems. We found this form of child neglect striking in an otherwise hard-working, self-righteous woman. When marginal child caring and neglect take so many forms, so must the dynamics in the women involved. Yet, there are commonalities within the disparities, and to these we turn next.

Let us set down now some characteristics we found relatively widespread in the group, even if each does not apply to every neglectful mother. Of course, ours is not the first attempt at such characterization; similar women have also been described by Young (1964), Reiner and Kaufman (1959), and Howells (1966, pp. 1159–1164). Nevertheless, small as it was, ours was the first systematic study of a sample of women from a rural area, and certainly from this area.

Although we did not, of course, subject these women to a mental-status examination by our psychiatrist or to clinical psychological testing in the full sense, it was obvious that they represented a nosological puzzle. We were dealing with an unusual group of people.

The women complained of little, if any, subjective distress. We noted few, if any, clearcut neurotic symptoms, such as obvious phobias, obsessions, compulsions, or conversions. Likewise, we found little gross evidence of psychotic thought disorders or palpable disorders of mood. While some psychiatrists might label them "psychopathic" or "sociopathic," we were disinclined to make this value judgment. If there were such a term, our psychiatrist, John Patton, felt they might best fit such a diagnosis as "primary personality type."

Descriptively, nearly all of these women fit a syndrome Ruesch once labelled the infantile personality (1948, pp. 134–144). By this well chosen term, Ruesch meant the substantial group of patients who are not only immature, but their childishness is *itself* the major problem. They have wide areas of functioning which have never properly developed; they may be expected to be fixated at an early, pregenital phase of development. But, in contrast to the preoccupation in this book, Ruesch contributed little to understanding *why* they are as they are. What, then, are some ways in which pervasive immaturity manifested itself in the group of mothers we studied initially?

Most discussions of family pathology in urban slums mention the one-parent family. Usually, it is described as an "isolated nuclear family" eking out an existence on alien soil since it is also mobile. Geographic and social mobility were *not* at issue in our group. Seven of the ten mothers lived close either to their own mothers or to their mothers-in-law. Quite often, they lived on family-owned land, with their housing provided by the elder generation. Appalachia has had considerable out migration for decades as residents sought opportunity elsewhere. In our group, the few who had tried it "on the outside" had drifted back "to the home place."

Separation anxiety was a noteworthy feature in most of the mothers. Thus, they would set up symbiotic relationships with their children such that children were kept home from school for reasons most mothers would not accept. In fact, a number did a good job of primary mothering as long as the infant was helpless and attached to them. When her baby reached the toddler stage, the mother became discombobulated by his mobility and his emergence as a distinct personality. In her typical all-or-none fashion, she would then master her separation anxiety by detaching herself from the youngster, treating him as a sibling or even as a tiny adult, in many respects. ("Why doesn't he go to school?" "He doesn't want to go.")

Phobic reactions deriving from primordial separation anxiety also play a role in the failure to use medical facilities. If the mother does not bring her youngster to a clinic, she does not necessarily have a bias against "modern medicine." Often, she is afraid of

leaving her home grounds at all, afraid of the unfamiliar, and afraid of being looked over and found wanting. So, she avoids the clinic as she does the PTA—and, often, the church.

Ruesch originally described the infantile personality as "the core problem of psychosomatic medicine," and his observations were later confirmed by Hill (1952, p. 429). "When infantile persons fail to get along with someone, the standard remedy may be to become ill, that is, to vomit or have diarrhea or fainting attacks. . . . It would appear many of these infantile characters eventually suffer from psychosomatic illnesses. That is to say, they persistently use visceral reactions instead of verbal symbolic communication."

A number of theoreticians prefer to see all distress among the urban poor as due to environmental pressures. They do not afford a poor woman the luxury of a classical neurosis. It was fascinating to us, therefore, to contrast the calm and quiet of their environment with the psychological stress our mothers experienced. Two had stomach ulcers, a common condition among low-income folks in the mountains. One woman had suffered from asthma *until she left her mother's house*—her dynamics could not have been more "middle class." Several complained of their "nerves," and one woman had had a hospitalizable depression. We do not wish to overemphasize the psychogenetic factor in the poor health we encountered. A lifetime of drafty housing and nutritional deficiency takes its toll. But, the kind of severe emotional problems that also beset well-to-do housewives should also not be overlooked.

Relationships between wife and husband were also of interest. The lower-class pattern of serial marriage was not unknown to our group, but it was extremely atypical. As a rule, these were resigned marriages. Whatever their faults, the partners seemed genuinely fond of each other. A husband might drink, fail to provide, and spend his money foolishly, but his wife would not complain against him. There was not much bickering between husband and wife—or perhaps they would not tell us, for the general culture proscribes expressing such feelings verbally, even within the family.

Fathers made a difference to the living standards in most households, of course. A couple of husbands were, in fact, greatly upset by the mess in their homes and the poor care their children

received. More than one desertion had occurred in our group because the father became disgusted with his wife's passivity and
ineptness. But, as we saw it in this preliminary study, most husbands
operated on the level of their wives. An outsider might notice how
dilapidated the house was and wonder at the occupants' inertia.
But the poor housing often represented more than lack of motivation. By and large, these particular men lacked the skills and often
the most elemental tools for ordinary small repairs.

TYPOLOGY OF NEGLECTFUL MOTHERS

We next confronted the question whether, at this stage of
our work, subcategories of neglectful mothers were appearing. What
patternings did we find, which were beginning to force themselves
into view? To look for these, we "staffed" each case, just as one
would in a clinic or hospital.

The most impressive outcome of our involving ourselves
concretely with the problem families was the extent to which these
mothers fit the pattern of Ruesch's infantile personality. In the
traditional characterology of psychoanalysis, this indicated significant pre-Oedipal fixations, of course. However, there were variations on the central theme of infantilism. We identified four types
of infantile mothers. These we shall now list, going from the most
to the least mature personality organization.

Eruptive, with shame. This type of mother suddenly involves herself in drunkenness, orgiastic sex, or the like, with coincidental abandonment of her children. The explosiveness tells us that,
in her case, the underlying dynamic issue is the need for affect discharge, tension release, or both. Rather than projecting responsibility for her behavior, this woman often verbalizes a sense of shame.
Her actions contain a self-destructive element. Indeed, as our psychiatrist, John Patton, pointed out, the child neglect is secondary
to self-neglect. Typically, the episode of neglect can be traced to the
loss of some person or object to whom she was much attached. Her
threshing about reveals symbolic attempts to compensate for loss
of the object and for feelings of lowered self-esteem. Although
immature, this sort of mother has many strengths and is highly
treatable, given reasonably competent handling. Many caseworkers

would like to hold this mother up as a stereotype for all, but her prognosis is much better than for most.

Eruptive, without shame. Again, we may infer that the underlying dynamic is rage, but this mother uses massive doses of primitive denial to defend herself against responsibility and guilt for her actions. Here, the precipitant is likely to be a rise of frustration within the mother, due to a combination of internal and external circumstances. Because of generally low frustration tolerance, many cannot take long periods of dull living, unrelieved by excitement or bouts of self-indulgent pleasure. However, unless deterioration occurs (as it sometimes does), the periods of pleasure-seeking acting out tend to be self-limiting, and this is why the neglect is episodic rather than chronic. With this type of mother, one "picks up the pieces," uses authority, and hopes maturity will set in before disaster does. Whereas eruptive mothers engage in sins of commission, the next two types of mothers are guilty of child-rearing errors of omission.

Apathetic, without thought disorder. The low level of child care among these women is chronic. In so far as the "disease" has a "course," it is either static or turns gradually downhill. Characteristic features are behavioral apathy and a deep sense of futility which they also use defensively if one tries to penetrate their withdrawal. However, these mothers may function well intellectually. At first, in fact, they seem to lack motivation rather than competence—but this often proves illusory, for competence also has suffered. The relationship to their children includes the failure to draw clear boundaries; it may be termed symbiotic. (This group is substantially the one we shall later describe as manifesting the "apathy-futility syndrome.")

Apathetic, with thought disorder. The distinguishing features of this type, contrasted with that above, are the incapacity to sustain complex, logical thought, the incapacity to deal with abstractions, and the markedly poor judgment shown in handling money. With this type, too, there is usually no clearly precipitating event. The helplessness of this mother may come to light only when someone who formerly covered for her dies, or deserts her. What we see, then, is not a reactive depression but the sudden revelation of extensive ego weakness. The neglect is likely to be chronic and

reversible (if at all) only via tedious and heroic interventions. We noticed, by the way, that the more apathetic mothers especially seemed to need always to have a nursing infant. We also became aware that child neglect is characteristic of a substantial group of mothers of extremely low intelligence.

2

When Is a
Child Neglected?

As must already be clear, our research was not conducted with scholarly equanimity. Nor do we pretend that it was. The lives of some youngsters are more than distressing—the onlooker is appalled, shocked, and disgusted. Yet, if a researcher is to do any good, his thoughts must be harnessed to his feelings.

The mission originally was to review child-welfare services in the mountain area in order to select priorities for new services. From a preliminary scouting of the problem, the most pressing unmet need was the arrangement for children to be removed from their homes, or protection for those who were about to be removed. It next became clear that to study placement of children would be to focus on an effect rather than on its cause. In our area, the majority of those in placement or in need of placement are victims of child neglect. Hall County, in northeast Georgia, serves as an ex-

ample. As of February 7, 1966, it had 429 youngsters receiving child-welfare services. Of these, 251 had been referred for neglect. Child placement in a foster home or—as things may eventually work out—in a mental or correctional institution, often culminates after years of neglect, whether glaring or insidious.

So, child neglect as a cause of placement became one theme around which our research polarized. From studying neglect, we were led to a maternal figure often implicated: the mother with the "apathy-futility syndrome." She became the other focus of our research. But studying the neglectful mother required first identifying neglect. To put our research into its more general context, we now discuss the significance of child neglect as a social problem, the legal and scientific issues involved in identification of the neglectful parent, and the measurement techniques which we devised.

STATISTICS

According to Oscar Wilde, statistics draw a straight line from an unwarranted assumption to a foregone conclusion. Nonetheless, sheer numbers of cases inevitably affect our feelings about the importance of any social problem.

Taking a broad view of child care, any child so poor as to be eligible for relief deserves concern. Our largest program, indeed the public's first line of defense against inadequate child-caring, is Aid to Families of Dependent Children (AFDC). By now, this system is enormous, with about 4 per cent of all American children included at any one time. As of February, 1970, there were over five million youngsters on AFDC and nearly two million adults. The monthly cost was over 350 million dollars. For the fiscal year ending June 30, 1970, the cost nationally was almost five billion dollars.[1] Beyond essential financial assistance are all the various child-welfare "services," dedicated to helping with blindness, deafness, retardation, emotional disturbance, child abuse, and child neglect. As of March 31, 1969, there were estimated to be 700,000 children receiving such help through public agencies with another 250,000

---

[1] These figures are from the National Center for Social Statistics, Social and Rehabilitation Service, Department of Health, Education, and Welfare.

under the care of private organizations. 249,000 were in foster care, and 74,000 in institutions for dependent, neglected, and emotionally disturbed youngsters (National Center for Social Statistics, 1969). On any given day, then, there are between five and six million youngsters receiving financial assistance and around a million under care receiving specialized social services of all kinds.

We found it difficult to get trustworthy figures regarding child neglect since states differ in their accounting systems, and some do not report centrally at all. Neglect is often reported as one element in an unholy trinity: neglect, abuse, and exploitation; or neglect, abuse, and abandonment. These are the classical reasons for protective services. Neglect undoubtedly predominates as the basis for agency intervention. Jeter's survey in 1961 (1963, p. 79) has been widely cited. She reports that the most important problems presented by the 377,000 children served by public agencies in 1961 were neglect, abuse, and exploitation. "For the children in foster care served by public agencies, the predominance of neglect, abuse, or exploitation is shown again. . . . Forty-three per cent of these children had neglect, abuse, or exploitation as a principal problem."

Child abuse as a social event stirs repugnance and anger in the public. One wonders, therefore, how frequent abuse is relative to neglect. It is just as well that such curiosity not be taken too seriously. Not only are official statistics hard to come by, but there is every reason to believe that the bulk of neglect and abuse goes officially unreported. Gil has done the best documented study of the nature and incidence of child abuse in the United States. He considers that the six thousand to seven thousand incidents *reported* annually are, as a group, more representative of cases involving severe physical injury to the child than those where the pain received was not accompanied by noticeable physical damage (Gil, 1970, p. 138).

For what it is worth, we did succeed in establishing that, in at least one state, North Carolina, 2,258 youngsters were regarded as having been neglected in the year ending June 30, 1970, compared with 195 cases of child abuse. If all those insidious conditions we term *marginal child care* were added to the picture, the disproportion of neglect over abuse would be greater.

Our impressions of the significance of child neglect in southern Appalachia are in line with those of experts who have surveyed it nationally. Thus, Kadushin said (1965, pp. 30f) : "The fact that neglect and abandonment show up as constituting one of the principal factors associated with the separation of children from their families would indicate that the neglectful parent is, to a considerable extent, representative of the population at risk for separation services."

Here, then, is a problem that overloads our facilities when we attempt to deal with it now and that leaves marks requiring massive repairs in years to come. Now that there are, relatively speaking, fewer true orphans, as parental life spans have increased, and fewer children warranting placement for sheer survival, since we have social security and AFDC, a high proportion of children require placement because of the unfitness of their homes. Our ignorance of how to treat neglect effectively and cheaply makes it a suitable subject of research for that reason alone. Glowing reports to the contrary, the typical case is tedious, expensive, and relatively unsuccessful. Following an exhaustive review of available literature on the phenomenon in this country, Norman and Nancy Polansky concluded (1968): "The formal policies of social agencies in this field are sanguine to the point of being fatuous regarding the potentiality for change in a large proportion of the parents involved. The fact is that most hard-headed observers report little success with the methods of aggressive casework (or unaggressive psychiatry) now being practiced. This is true even when an adequate attempt at treatment is made, something which is possible in only a few areas of the country." And, over the long haul, as we remarked earlier, the inmates of detention and treatment institutions—children, adolescents, and adults—represent the sequellae of chronic neglect—sometimes physical, sometimes emotional, often both.

DEFINING NEGLECT LEGALLY

One way neglect may be operationally defined is by reliance on court action. In addition to its social and psychological concomitants, neglect is a criminal offense. Occasionally, it is punished by imprisonment of the parent. So, one way to identify child neglect

is to study instances in which formal charges have been filed or, even more strictly, the parent has been adjudicated neglectful by a court of law. Sheridan, for example, used the latter criterion (1956, pp. 91–93) in surveying the intellectual abilities of a sample of English mothers.

From a scientific standpoint, however, adjudication is not a satisfactory method of determining what we have in mind. Only a small proportion of cases is taken to court, either because of professional treatment considerations or because of reluctance to take extreme action in a poorly defined area of social work practice. Moreover, the laws in most states provide broad judicial latitude. Neglect statutes teem with adjectives and adverbs—properly, improperly, necessary, unfit, inadequate—which compel interpretation. Legal standards tend to be established empirically as courts make difficult judgments about specific situations. Hence, *common law,* rather than *statutory law,* governs in most cases.

Although state laws are generally vague about standards of child care that constitute legal neglect, they tend to be more specific about areas of parental responsibility. The areas of concern codified in our laws are of interest here for two reasons. First, they have inevitably strongly affected the agencies dedicated to child protection. Second, they undoubtedly reflect the thinking of the general community. What, then, are some of these areas?

(1) Statutes of all states specify a concern for *provision of physical necessities,* such as food, clothing, shelter, medical care, and, sometimes, sanitation and cleanliness.

(2) Statutes are usually concerned with *parental supervision of the child.* This means attentiveness to his physical safety as well as control of his whereabouts and activities which might constitute a threat or annoyance to the community.

(3) Frequently mentioned is *protection of the child against exposure to illegal and immoral adult activities,* such as criminal behavior, prostitution, gambling, or alcohol or narcotics addiction.

(4) Nearly all states require *school attendance* for children between specified ages.

(5) Most states prohibit *exploitation* of the child in such activities as street begging, exhibiting physical oddities for money, or entertaining audiences for pay, except under specified safeguards.

(6) *Child labor* is prohibited in all states, and hours of employment and types of work are regulated for youngsters of specified ages. However, responsibility for compliance here is typically placed on the employer rather than on the parent.

(7) Concern with *emotional or psychological neglect* is implied in legal proscriptions of inadequate supervision, exploitation of offspring, or the like. However, as of 1963 only Idaho and Minnesota explicitly recognized emotional neglect (Kadushin, 1967, p. 215). Of course, the consequences of emotional neglect are far more difficult to demonstrate than those of physical neglect. Iron deficiency may be readily shown, but deficiencies in ego functioning attributable to parental failure are harder to prove to everyone's satisfaction. Probably for this reason, neither social workers nor the general public have yet strongly supported legal intervention in cases involving emotional neglect (Boehm, 1964, pp. 453–464). At the time we did these studies, moreover, correlation of physical with emotional neglect had not been demonstrated. In fact, it was widely believed the two had little to do with each other.

In most states, neglect is treated under both the juvenile (or domestic-relations) code and the criminal code. North Carolina, for example, maintains that parents charged with neglect are subject to proceedings under either or both types of law. Of course, there are important consequences of which court is involved. In the adversary proceedings of the criminal court, rules of evidence are typically conscientiously adhered to, and the rights of parents are much in evidence, just as the focus of the disposition is on them. Not infrequently, the criminal court ignores the question of where the children are to live while their parents are incarcerated.

In a recent case in a North Carolina mill town, the police found two babies, aged 6 and 18 months, alone in an unheated shack. Their soiled diapers were literally frozen to their skins. One policeman sought the parents, found them intoxicated in an illegal tavern, and ordered them to return home and care for their infants. When he checked a few hours later and found the children still abandoned, he filed a formal complaint against the parents while others on the force arranged for them to stay with the maternal grandmother until the case was heard.

Both parents were sentenced to prison for child neglect. Three months later, the grandmother appeared at the welfare department, pled inability to care for the infants, and turned them over. Welfare department and prison officials persuaded the parents to sign permission that the children be placed in foster homes, since no court action had been taken regarding them. Some months later, the parents were paroled and reclaimed the babies, which they had a legal right to do. The welfare department immediately filed a petition in domestic relations court asking custody of the children on the grounds of physical neglect. However, this court refused the petition saying this could not be proved in the short time they had been with the parents since the latter returned from prison!

Juvenile court versus criminal court is an issue with adumbrations to a host of others. As with many other social issues, gestures toward a treatment approach are weighed against reliance on punitive, deterrent action. The question of jurisdiction also places in opposition children's rights with parents' rights. Maas and Engler (1959, p. 31) quote a juvenile-court judge whose outlook is not different from that of many rural people: "God gave the parents children; it would take something very strong to take them away. Yes, I am quite reluctant to set myself up as judge of someone's fitness to raise children." The other attitude maintains that all children have inherent rights to "care and protection," and when parents fail to provide these, it is up to the state to intervene on their behalf since the community as a whole stands in place of the parent. The puzzle is how to avoid invading the privacy of all parents while, at the same time, insuring the safety and future of an occasional, mistreated child.

When it comes to the identification and measurement of child caring, the adversary proceedings of the criminal court yield dichotomous definitions. One is, or is not, adjudicated neglectful. Partial neglect is not recognized. This classification system violates our observation that child-caring falls along a continuum rather than into two discrete categories. The point at which Judge Black draws the line differs systematically from Judge Smith's, and the evidence Judge Smith regards as germane also differs from Judge Black's. In an area as complicated as this, we believe it is unques-

tionably sensible of our legislators to leave room for the exercise of judicial wisdom, whenever it exists. But scientifically, the arrangement is not satisfactory.

Finally, whether explicitly or implicitly, neglect as a legal entity carries implications of wilfulness on the part of parents. Estimating deliberateness among the parents at risk, who display little foresight about most of their activities, is extremely hard. This classical legal dilemma is further obfuscated by the fact that it involves not sins of commission but sins of omission. Child neglect, in other words, intimates parental fault. But, if the parent is living no better than his children and wants to keep them with him, the general attitude is that his progeny and heirs may be unlucky, but they are not neglected.

There are also down-to-earth reasons for dubiousness about official statistics on child neglect, which we have encountered in our work, but which are not commonly mentioned in the professional literature. We have yet to find a parent who regards a neglect complaint as a compliment or a favor. In areas, like Appalachia, where everyone is more or less armed, there is an understandable reluctance to trade buckshot with local citizens whose control systems leave much to be feared. Furthermore, parents vote, but minor children do not, and an unpopular decision on a neglect petition might cost a judge more votes than responsible removal of such youngsters would ever gain for him. Political calculation begets a genial toleration for the misfortunes of other people's children, which a young caseworker may find infuriating, but a courthouse habitué displays as warm compassion for insulted parents.

We have been at pains to review the legal definitions of neglect because they introduce some of the concerns we face in attempting a scientific assessment. We did not expect that lawyers, whether in court or legislative chamber, would give us the measurement we needed. But, in view of the extensive research that has been done on child development and child welfare, we expected that there were instruments available which, with slight modification, could be fitted to the studies we had in mind. Much to our amazement, not only were there no "generally accepted" instruments, but there were no instruments calculated to measure the grossly low level we had in mind at all. Thus, in order to approach

the study of the neglectful mother, we had to develop what we now call our Childhood Level of Living Scale.

MEASURING ADEQUACY OF CHILD CARING

The pitfalls inevitable to a legalistic definition of child neglect emphasize problems the social scientist has with so value-laden a concept. An obvious strategy was to redirect attention to a neutral term, suggesting objective appraisal. We therefore shifted from trying to identify child neglect, as such, to working on a less loaded concept called *adequacy of child caring*. Obviously, child neglect represents poor, inadequate parenting. We also coined the expression *marginal child care* to refer to care that is poor, but not so extreme as to warrant our calling it neglect.

The shift in terms was helpful. It formalized the notion that we were concerned with a continuum, rather than with a dichotomy or with a series of distinct categories. But, a host of measurement issues still had to be faced and choices had to be made in order to settle on a (hopefully) feasible and valid technique for ranking mothers. Some of these issues are of sufficient general interest to detail here.

We needed to analyze the vantages from which data might be collected. Adequacy of child care is a complex variable; not surprisingly, observations potentially relevant to deciding how well a child is being cared for come from many places. Data also vary in regard to how direct the observations are or how much inference is required. But, fortunately, even though the observational problem is complicated, there are a finite number of ways to go about it. Basically, one can determine what the mother is providing for her child, or he can examine the child and draw conclusions from that. Everything else is variation on these themes. Let us list the permutations.

Child's current condition. Should a child have a correctable physical defect about which nothing is being done, the conclusion is obvious. Similarly, if he arrives in school dirty, tired, and listless, we are certainly justified in assuming all is not well at home. The physical, emotional, and intellectual character of the child tell us what his life is like, albeit in a general way.

Sequellae in the child. A youngster's present condition often suggests how he has been treated in the past. For example, we are inclined to regard most chronic juvenile delinquents as reflective of long-term parental failure. However, presumption of neglect implies that we are working from a well-established cause-effect relationship between parental handling and control systems in the personality. It also requires ruling out plausible alternative explanations— for instance that the delinquency does not reflect brain damage or that it has not occurred in a relatively normal child who lives in a delinquent subculture.

Child's own report. Besides examining the youngster, one can, of course, ask him about the life he is leading. Self-reports are valuable, but subject to distortion. A naive younger child probably will not exaggerate the comforts in his home, but we have known an older one to defend his family's honor by covering up how badly off he was. In view of the dynamics inherent in neglect, the custom of some judges of asking the youngster to elect whether or not to remain at home is ridiculous. It is the rare product of a withdrawn woman who does not cling all the harder to her. Indeed, it might be a sign of emotional health in the family if a child is *able* to ask to be removed! (See Chapter Three.)

Direct observation of child-caring. These data undoubtedly are most credible from a scientific standpoint. Unfortunately, it is seldom possible to get a systematic picture of how the child is being cared for by direct observation. What we usually have are anecdotal reports from neighbors, relatives, or the police of striking episodes they have observed which may, or may not, be representative. At times, we do have direct observation by social workers and nurses who have seen the mother attend her children while visiting the home. But, any attempt to accumulate systematically sampled behavior records on child-caring practices only serves to remind us of the degree to which marginal child-caring and neglect are insidious and *terribly* private stories.

Parental reports of care given. Some of our best-known studies of child-rearing practices rely on interviews which collect mothers' descriptions of what they do. As with reports from youngsters, it is likely that the bulk of what an interviewer is told is valid. Most of the women we encountered are reasonably truthful. They

are often oblivious enough that they feel no need to distort. Yet, some parents who offer indifferent care, who punish impulsively and the like, paint a rosy picture. As we learned in the pilot study reported in Chapter One, regardless of what such parents practice, they know what is generally preached.

Available amenities. We can estimate how a child must be living from an informal inventory of his family's household possessions. For instance, if a social worker is called in to care for a family temporarily abandoned by the mother and finds no food in the house at all, she fears the worst about the diet on any other day. Absence of heating arrangements, bedding, furnishings, window panes—these are visible signs to any intelligent adult. In the study of a primitive tribe, such possessions might be called artifacts. It may seem invidious to count a poor family's artifacts, but it is one way to estimate their living standards.

Parental character. By "character," of course, we refer to aspects of personality which are enduring; no value judgments are implied. One must doubt whether a woman who is chronically depressed is giving her child adequate care, even though a mental hospital may have seen fit to discharge her. We can infer certain probabilities, even without detailed observation of her behavior. Parents with histories of instability, criminality, or sexual acting out are also worrisome. But, projecting the living standard of her offspring from a woman's promiscuity requires correlational studies we still do not have and are unlikely nowadays to obtain. All we really know, therefore, is that parents with severe character disorders make poor role models for their children.

We speak of these vantages for data collection with familiarity because we have used them all at one time or another in our research. Each has its strong and weak points. Information easiest to obtain is sometimes of least certain meaning.

It is necessary to distinguish a directly observable fact from a conjecture, on the one hand, or a prediction, on the other. The aim, after all, is to guess whether or not what is presently going on is harmful to the child or will ultimately harm him. There are surprises in making such predictions. Using our own CLL Scale, Hepner and Maiden (1971, pp. 219–223) have recently found that, among rapidly growing children, the child's nutritional status

was more related to the *cognitive/emotional* aspects of mothering than to the family's per capita income, per capita expenditures on food, or actual caloric intake! They concluded that "adequate mothering" is protective to the child under the combined stresses of rapid growth and low quality feeding. Apparently, except in extreme cases, we cannot even draw a direct line from the food provided to the child's nutritional status.

The more relationships that are established and tested between factors that can be measured and ultimate effects on children, the better inferences we can make. For this reason, among others, we were led inexorably to "basic research" from a very practical problem. Of course, the association which has interested us most is that between the maternal character (the apathy-futility syndrome) and the level of care her children are receiving. But, for the reasons given, at this stage of history, there can be no completely satisfying measure of adequacy of child care.

Having reviewed the *ways* in which data may be obtained, let us turn to the next issue. Along which dimensions ought one to look? One way to answer this question is to draw on the collective wisdom of fellow professionals as it is codified in formal statements. Here, for example, are criteria for protective service workers set down by the Children's Division of the American Humane Association (American Humane Association, 1966, p. 25).

It is presumed that physical, emotional, and intellectual growth and welfare are being jeopardized when, for example, the child is: (1) malnourished, ill clad, dirty, without proper shelter or sleeping arrangements; (2) without supervision, unattended; (3) ill and lacking essential medical care; (4) denied normal experiences that produce feelings of being loved, wanted, secure, and worthy (emotional neglect); (5) failing to attend school regularly; (6) exploited, overworked; (7) emotionally disturbed due to constant friction in the home, marital discord, mentally ill parents; (8) exposed to unwholesome and demoralizing circumstances.

The resemblance between this listing and our earlier recounting of facets which recur in legal definitions of neglect is hardly coincidental. Both reflect community norms; both represent con-

ventional wisdom. It is an interesting exercise to review the Humane Association criteria to see how many represent immediate and pressing danger and how many involve future predictions. But theirs is not by any means a senseless listing. In the final analysis, we always have to do the best we can in a given state of the art.

EXPERIENCE SURVEY

The social scientist's training inevitably pushes him toward narrowing both his research questions and his measuring instruments. We share that training and accepted the limited focus of instruments available to quantify parental behaviors. Yet, here we were concerned with scaling maternal adequacy. This is a broad concept, and it demands a complex measurement, reversing our usual inclination.

There were other reasons why the instruments already available did not fit our needs. We were interested in more than surface data, based on more knowledge than one-shot interviews, for instance. But the biggest reason we felt constrained to develop our own scaling technique lay in the group we proposed to study. Our concern, in this research, was with people who were rural, who lived in the mountains, and whose socioeconomic status was low. We needed an instrument which would detect variations within a group which were hardly even sampled in, for example, studies of families whose children were in University schools set up to demonstrate advanced methods of teaching.

Developing our own technique led to the obvious question: What dimensions does it pay to measure? Even a broad-gauged approach cannot include everything. We do not know, of course, but we would hazard a guess that whether one's nursery is blue or cream is less significant than whether one's mother is calm or explosive. The number of variables that might conceivably affect the outcome of a child's life is infinite. So, we have to ask not only which dimensions are relevant, but also which carry the most weight.

There are two ways one can answer these questions. If there is a body of theory in which the investigator has confidence, he can choose his dimensions from within it and organize his measurements *theoretically*. But in an unexplored field, there is no choice but to

proceed *empirically*. That is, the investigator measures everything he can think of and uses a process of trial and error (formalized as factor analysis) to tell him which variables overlap each other, which correlate most with the criterion, and so forth. Our area of study was far from unexplored; therefore, we proposed to use a combination of theory and empiricism in developing our instrument. Based on our preconceptions and the Freudian framework in which we operate, there were a number of dimensions we were sure to have included. The problem, therefore, was how to force ourselves beyond our own biases.

We decided to conduct an *experience survey* as the next exploratory study in our research program. Such a survey is a systematic but nonrigorous study. Its aim is to exploit the wisdom which has already accumulated among specialists practicing in a given field which they, themselves, have not had occasion either to analyze or to try to articulate (Selltiz, Jahoda, Deutsch, and Cook, 1959, pp. 55–59).

The survey we conducted had certain characteristics because of the needs of our work. For example, it might have seemed "scientific" to present informants with a list of dimensions of child care to rank in importance. However, this procedure would have effectively blocked their producing *new* facets for us to consider. We could have asked them, "What comes to mind when you think of child neglect?" But since the term *neglect* already has so many connotations, they might associate our abstraction with their conceptions. In building an instrument to measure child care, we were in far greater need of concrete items which are readily observable in order to operationalize the concepts we had already.

Our solution was to conduct the survey by means of Flanagan's (1954, pp. 327–358) Critical Incident Technique. As Alfred Kahn says (1960, p. 70), this technique "merits special attention as a fruitful type of method in a formulative-exploratory design." The advantages of Flanagan's method are: (1) It frees the observer to report facets of the phenomenon which he finds most important —or, at least, most salient. (2) It calls for concrete descriptions of events the observer has experienced himself.

In our research, the chief purpose of the experience survey

was to forward construction of the instrument to measure adequacy of child caring. However, by selecting samples for study and, in effect, replicating a first rural study with a sample from metropolitan Atlanta, we were simultaneously able to throw light on two substantive questions as well. These questions were: (a) Do professionals from rural areas view child neglect differently from those in an urban area? (b) Does the occupation of the outside observer affect the dimensions salient in viewing neglect?

Let us now collate results from the two interlocking studies. Data were collected in twenty-five rural counties of western North Carolina and northern Georgia, yielding interviews with fifty-seven welfare workers and thirty-eight public health nurses, for a total of ninety-five.[2] After the data from the first study had been analyzed, an opportunity was found to repeat the study in an urban area. We were eager to do this because, throughout our work, we have had the impression that much that we were finding was similar to experiences in cities.

The area of the replication was metropolitan Atlanta, including DeKalb and Fulton Counties. Atlanta was geographically convenient to us. It has the additional advantage that, in its general ethnic and religious make-up and regional outlook, it has much in common with our rural areas. The urban sample included seventy-eight persons in public social work and welfare positions and fifty-one public health nurses, for a total of 129. All of those interviewed were persons in regular contact with low-income families with children.

In order to elicit what we termed "negative incidents," the following was read to each subject interviewed, after a brief introduction to the purpose of the study: "Could you give me an example of some specific thing that parents were or were not doing to a child which made you *very concerned* for the child's welfare?"

The term *neglect* was specifically avoided to minimize our collecting stereotypes. Rather, we defined our critical incidents in terms of concern-evoking behavior. The informant (or *observer* as Flanagan terms him) responded with case illustrations which we

[2] Mary Lou Wing and Jay Meddin interviewed rural sample; Schlomo Sharlin conducted urban replication.

recorded verbatim. Typically, each gave two or more incidents. We found that the practitioners could relate easily to this mode of questioning.

Indeed, using Flanagan's technique, the collection of data is easy to design and easy to conduct. The crunch comes in trying to analyze it. Given all these narrative incidents, what patterns emerge? How may they be coded?

As in any coding operation, we needed to establish rules for unitizing. We made the basic unit an idea descriptive of acting or failing to act to fulfill a child-caring function. The coding unit was usually a grammatical clause. Units were to be coded as specifically, or concretely, as the observer's statement permitted. With major headings, subheadings, and the like, the code we evolved encompassed nearly two hundred categories. Intercoder reliability was tested in applying the code to our interview protocols, and, after training, it peaked out at 92 per cent agreement.[3] As always, training toward intercoder agreement led to clarification and elaboration of the categories identified.

SALIENT DIMENSIONS OF CHILD-CARING

We noted earlier that "adequacy of child-caring" is multidimensional, a fact which has to be borne in mind in trying to measure it. The results of the experience survey support this view. The fantastic number of ways a child may be neglected or mistreated are testified to by the long list in Table 1. And this table, be it noted, is not a complete listing of all the ideas encountered. It contains only those mentioned by at least 5 per cent of either the rural or the urban informants in our study.

The percentages in Table 1 do not cumulate to 100 because the categories are not mutually exclusive. Moreover, replies occurred at varying levels of abstraction and were so coded. Thus, if the observer expressed concern that the child lived in a house with broken window panes (code category IA6b), this reply would count under this specific heading and, of course, under each of those under which it was subsumed. However, if the same observer also mentioned lack of running water, he would still be counted only once under the

[3] Coders for these data were Mary Lou Wing and Elizabeth Harkins.

more general heading of mentioning inadequate housing. In short, each percentage, at whatever level of abstraction, is an undupli-cated count of the observer's mentioning something codable under that heading, a counting of observers, not of mentions.

From Table 1, we note that 95 per cent of those working in rural counties described at least one condition falling under In-sufficient Physical Care, Protection, or Health Care; the percentage of those answering similarly in the Atlanta area was almost the same—94 per cent. From the next line in the table, however, we see that whereas half of the rural welfare workers and nurses men-tioned inadequate housing in some form, only a quarter of those in the city did so, a difference which is statistically significant at beyond 0.1 per cent.

In this instance, the discrepancy appears to be based on real differences. If one bases one's benign impressions of rural living on glimpses from a speeding car, it is hard to believe that rural slums are even worse than those in cities. Rural people do not have the protections offered by strict housing codes, nor do they have land-lords against whom to file complaints of violations. According to Leon Ginsburg (1969, p. 181), of West Virginia: "Data from the 1960 census reveal that 27 per cent of rural housing was substan-dard at that time, compared with 14 per cent of urban areas."

Although poor housing was the most salient for our rural informants, emotional neglect was of greater expressed concern to those from Atlanta. A substantial number of other items differed between settings, but most of these involved tiny fractions of the observers. Wherever they work, those we interviewed found chil-dren insufficiently fed, in unsafe surroundings, with poor medical care, and so forth. The poor parental models depicted by the figures under category III (Inadequate Nurturance of Control Systems) are salient to half or more of the workers from both geographic areas. In short, those dimensions of inadequate parenting which proved salient in the city were generally similar to those which proved salient in the mountains.

In addition to comparing rural with urban viewpoints, our sampling permitted us to study the influence of profession on views of concern-evoking behaviors in parents. Responses by welfare workers were compared with those by public health nurses, in the

Table 1

SALIENT DIMENSIONS OF INADEQUATE CHILD CARE

Code Category	Percentage of Observers Mentioning Category		P
	Rural (N = 95)	Urban (N = 129)	
I. Insufficient Physical Care, Protection, Health Care	95	94	.001
A. Inadequate housing	50	23	.01*
1. Isolation or remoteness of location	6	0	
2. Overfrequent moving (instability)	7	6	
3. Severe overcrowding	16	15	
4. No electricity	6	2	
5. No running water	14	2	
6. No protection against cold, rain, or snow	24	5	.001
a. Cold and dampness mentioned	8	1	.001
b. Broken, unrepaired windows or doors	6	0	.02
c. General rottenness of construction	8	1	.01*
7. Scantiness and dilapidation of furniture	10	1	.02
B. Insufficient or inappropriate feeding	58	45	.01
1. Sporadic failure to provide food at all	14	12	
a. Lack of food in house is mentioned	7	2	
2. Partial failure to provide food	33	22	.10

	Group 1	Group 2	p
a. Grossly inappropriate food given	2	6	
b. Malnutrition diagnosed medically	8	3	
(1) Resulting in death	5	1	.05*
c. "Failure to thrive"	8	6	
3. Irresponsibility about when and what children eat	10	8	
C. Failure to provide safeguarding			
1. Lack of sanitary facilities	71	65	
2. Exposure of children to disease-transmitting conditions	7	2	.05
a. Chickens and barnyard animals wander through house	33	6	.001
b. Eating and cooking utensils unclean	5	0	.01
c. Flies and vermin present	9	0	.02*
3. General unsanitary conditions	46	2	
a. "Filth," "dirt," "sweepings" present	22	33	.05
b. Dirty rags and clothes lying about	7	8	.01
c. Children remain unwashed for long periods	23	1	.05
(1) Come to school dirty	7	26	.05
4. Hazardous conditions	8	2	
a. Junk, broken glass where children play	23	2	.05
5. Child abandonment by both parents	6	0	.01*
6. Abandonment by at least one parent	6	22	
a. Mother has deserted	9	5	.01
b. Father has deserted	22	16	.10
7. Inattention to safety of the children	27	41	.01
a. Children left alone brief periods, but danger	8	21	.05
b. Tragedy due to parental inattention cited	5	7	.02

Table 1 (Cont.)

SALIENT DIMENSIONS OF INADEQUATE CHILD CARE

Code Category	Percentage of Observers Mentioning Category		P
	Rural (N = 95)	Urban (N = 129)	
c. Relatively young child is left to supervise the others	9	14	
d. Children permitted to "wander" with inappropriate freedom	7	8	
e. Lack of parental judgment about danger	15	7	.10
D. Unsuitable clothing and coverings	43	26	.02
1. Not enough clothing to protect against cold	7	6	
2. Clothing is filthy, never washed	10	10	
3. Clothing unmended or ragged	5	0	.02*
4. Child has been found with literally no clothes	5	4	
5. No shoes for child	3	9	
6. Inadequate blankets	9	1	.01
7. No sheets or bedding	6	2	
E. Failure to provide for rest	14	1	.001
1. Too many huddle in one bed	5	1	.05*

F. Failure to provide needed medical care	60	69	
1. Refusal or resistance to taking child for care, after urging	29	13	.01
2. Failure to take child for medical care—motive unclear	19	15	
3. No follow through on prescribed treatment	12	22	
4. "Insufficient concern" to report illness to helping persons	0	9	
5. Professional had to get child to facilities	5	4	
6. Failure to provide expectable home medical care	7	7	.001*
G. Failure to plan family size	8	10	
II. Child Abuse	38	27	
A. Violence against child	27	22	
1. Child tied and beaten	6	0	
2. Bruises from beatings observed	3	5	
4. Deep cuts or broken bones from parents' action	6	4	.01*
B. Sexual molestation or exploitation	20	7	
1. Father or stepfather-daughter incest	8	2	.01
3. Failure to protect child from sexual abuse by other adults	6	3	.05
III. Inadequate Nurturance of Control Systems	83	81	
A. Exposure of child to parental "immorality"	63	48	

Table 1 (Cont.)

SALIENT DIMENSIONS OF INADEQUATE CHILD CARE

Code Category	Percentage of Observers Mentioning Category		P
	Rural (N = 95)	Urban (N = 129)	
1. Mother has illicit relations children can witness	4	5	
2. Mother's "affairs" are probably known to children	30	4	.001
3. Father frequently drunk in children's presence	28	12	.01
4. Mother frequently drunk in children's presence	25	20	
5. A parent is addicted to narcotics	7	2	
6. Parental acts of violence are witnessed by child	16	12	
7. Exposing child to frequent verbal conflicts	6	9	
B. Exposure of child to parental infantilism			
1. Child witnesses impulse-buying and/or poor management of money	67	50	
2. Parent shows selfishness in spending money	9	10	
3. Other comments about failures to be an adequate behavioral model	16	10	
4. Constant use of obscenities by parents	56	41	
5. Non-support, refusal or evasion of work	6	1	.02*
C. Lack of guidance	9	13	
	34	40	

1. Inattentiveness to children's delinquent behavior   14   18

   a. Acceptance of stealing   6   8

   b. Acceptance of prostitution   5   4

2. Impulsivity or inconsistency in discipline   6   12

3. Child's (resultant) uncontrollability mentioned   12   12

D. Oversevere discipline   10   15

1. Unrealistic expectations of the child   4   8

2. Slapping, screaming, and hollering remarked on   2   8

IV. Emotional Neglect   19   41   .01

A. Nondemonstrativeness   4   5

B. Gross insensitivity to child's feelings   7   12

1. Indifference to child's seeking reassurance   0   5   .04*

C. Gross interference with child's chances for socializing   5   8

V. Failure to Provide for Cognitive Stimulation   36   52   .10

A. Vocabulary limitations   4   8

1. Child unable to talk age-expectably   4   7

B. Child not in school   25   46   .02

1. Parents keep him home for own reasons   9   9

2. Parents appear not to care whether he misses   4   32   .001

---

* Signifies Fisher's Exact Test was used. Otherwise, P was based on the Chi-square test based on Z cells only. All tests were with raw frequencies, of course.

mountains and in metropolitan Atlanta. Once again, we found more agreement than divergence between the two points of view; substantially the same things are salient to both professions.

There were, however, a number of differences which seem worth pointing up since they illustrate so well how one's professional preoccupations determine one's slant on a serious social problem. Thus, nurses were significantly more aware of failure to provide needed medical attention in both the rural and urban settings than the welfare workers. (See Tables 2 and 3). But the welfare workers were more conscious of child abandonment, which requires them to take action; of inattentiveness of the parent to a child's delinquent behavior; and of children exposed to parents' immorality and acting out. A striking difference between the groups is visible in the last line of Tables 2 and 3, namely, nurses are much more conscious, as a group, of the fact that failure to limit family size may itself be a form of "neglectful" behavior by a woman.

These surveys were made in the late 1960s. Yet, *not one* welfare worker in the mountains and only a handful of those in the city referred to failure to use birth control as an aspect of poor parenting.

CHILDHOOD LEVEL OF LIVING SCALE

In our research, we were interested in pursuing hypotheses regarding the relationship between maternal personality and level of child-caring. In order to study this relationship, it was necessary that the two concepts be independently defined and measured. Otherwise, our research would be circular. We shifted, therefore, from thinking about the mother and father to concern with the style of life their children were experiencing. Of course this was affected by what the parents did, but it was, in fact, a somewhat independent issue, just as "What is?" is different from "Why is it?"

Using what we had learned from reviewing the literature, from our pilot study, and from our experience survey, we were ready to construct what we termed the *Childhood Level of Living Scale*. The term *level of living* is itself indicative. It was taken from the rural sociologists who invented it while conducting studies among the very poor (Collazo-Collazo and Ramsey, 1960; Belcher,

Table 2

Nurses' vs. Welfare Workers' Views of Child Neglect in Rural Setting

Code	Category	Percentage of Nurses (N = 38)	Percentage of Welfare Workers (N = 57)	P
IC6.	Abandonment by one parent	8	31	.02
IC7.	Inattention to safety of the children	16	53	.01
IIA.	Violence against child	11	39	.01
IIIA.	Exposure of child to parental "immorality"	42	79	.05
IIIC1.	Inattentiveness to children's delinquent behavior	5	21	.05
IF.	Failure to provide needed medical care	82	44	.02
IF1.	Refusal or resistance to take child for care, after urging	42	19	.05
IF3.	No follow through on prescribed treatment	24	5	.02
IG.	Failure to plan family size	31	0	.02

1951, pp. 246-255). If one is studying a population where everyone falls into the lowest category, the usual measures of socioeconomic status are too coarse. In our case, we already knew that
the problems of neglect and marginal child-caring are closely linked
with poverty. Therefore, we planned to confine our research to the
population at greatest risk—the very poor. Like the sociologists, we
needed a measurement technique capable of making discriminations below the reach of most scaling devices. For, even in a group
of families who are all on AFDC, there may be marked variations
in living standards. Whereas Sears, Maccoby, and Levin (1957)
might have been interested in whether a working-class mother was
more or less permissive than a middle-class lady with respect to how
her child eats, we had the more urgent question: Is there food in
the house at all?

The Childhood Level of Living (or CLL) Scale is designed
for use by a worker who has, or is acquiring, a reasonably intimate
knowledge of a family from repeated home visits and from direct
questioning of the mother. To a large extent, it provides a way of
objectifying and quantifying knowledge and impressions the worker
is gaining about the family anyhow. The scale consists of a large
number of items. Nearly all of these items are direct statements
which are to be checked as true or false. For instance: Water is
piped into the house; at least one of the children sleeps in the same
bed as the parents; mother follows through on rewards.[4]

Of course, a major issue in measuring adequacy of child-
caring is the age of the child. Failure to dress a baby may be "neglectful," but dressing a ten-year-old is infantilizing. In short, in
devising the CLL we had to gear ourselves to a specific age group.
Therefore, our scale was designed to apply to youngsters aged five
or thereabouts. Only a few items appear age-linked in using the
scale. Items dealing with adequacy of housing, for instance, seem
pretty universal and applicable to adults too.

There were 316 items in the original CLL Scale, and these
were used in our first major field study in which it was employed.
From item analyses, however, it was determined that many could

---

[4] In addition to the authors, former staff members Betty Jane Smith
and Mary Lou Wing contributed significantly to developing the CLL Scale.

be dropped because they were nondiscriminating. For example, we encountered only one house that did not have electricity. The final scale, therefore, consists of 136 items only, and this measure forms the basis for most findings based on the CLL reported in this book. Subsequently, a further shortening was accomplished by cluster analyses when we came to train AFDC workers in the use of the scale in a later phase of our research program. This shortened version—totalling eighty-nine items—appears to sample the same content universe as that covered by the complete scale, albeit with loss in precision.

The 136 items in the full CLL Scale were next grouped by a combination of rational and empirical judgments into twenty-one subscales. These may be organized, in turn, into two major parts, as follows. Part A—Physical Care: (I) Comfort, (II) Safety, (III) State of Repair, (IV) Hygienic Conditions, (V) Feeding Patterns, (VI) Safety Precautions, (VII) Disease Prevention, (VIII) Use of Medical Facilities, (IX) Clothing, (X) Housing Composite, (XI) Sleeping Arrangements, (XII) Regularity of Provision for Rest, (XIII) Grooming, (XIV) Home Comforts. Part B—Emotional/Cognitive Care: (XV) Cultural Artifacts, (XVI) Parental Play with Child, (XVII) Promoting Curiosity, (XVIII) Consistency in Encouraging Superego Development, (XIX) Level of Disciplinary Techniques, (XX) Providing Reliable Role Image, (XXI) Providing Reliable Evidences of Affection.

Thus, from the CLL Scale we could derive a total score, a score for physical care alone, or a score for cognitive/emotional care alone; or we could correlate specific subscales against other factors to answer precise research questions.

There was, however, a surprising degree of consistency among the scores on various subscales and with the total. For example, in our major field study (Chapter Five), the correlation between physical care and cognitive/emotional care scores was substantial—on the order of $+.75$. Since all aspects of the CLL Scale intercorrelate, it is meaningful to speak of an *overall* CLL score. The overall score became the most important operational definition of adequacy of child caring for the purposes of our series of studies. For the convenience of fellow researchers, a complete copy of the scale, along with directions for its use, are given as Appendix A.

Table 3

Nurses' vs. Welfare Workers' Views of Child Neglect in Urban Setting

Code Category	Percentage of Nurses (N = 51)	Percentage of Welfare Workers (N = 78)	P
IC6. Abandonment by one parent	10	29	.02
IIIA. Exposure of child to parental "immorality"	31	59	.05
IIIA6. Parental acts of violence are witnessed by child	2	19	.01
IIIC1. Inattentiveness to children's delinquent behavior	8	24	.05
V. Failure to provide for cognitive stimulation	31	65	.01
VB. Child not in school	22	62	.01
VB2. Parents appear not to care whether he misses	16	42	.01
IA3b. Presence of more than one family in small quarters	16	1	.01
IB2c. "Failure to thrive"	14	1	.01
IF2. Failure to take child for medical care—motive unclear	27	6	.01
IG. Failure to plan family size	18	4	.02

Above we have considered some of the elements involved in the legal definition of child neglect. Although an argument can be made for the necessity of reliance on judicial wisdom in handling such cases (Gill, 1960, pp. 1–16), use of the law as our criterion introduces difficulties. These include complications in estimating parental wilfulness; political pressures operative on prosecutors and judges in rural areas; and the arbitrary dichotomization of a dimension which is probably a continuum. Hence, for our studies, the term *neglect* was replaced by the more neutral, objective concept, *adequacy of child-caring*. The latter refers to the level of living the child is experiencing; it has more to do with what the mother *does* than with what the mother *is*. In short, it is a dimension relatively independent of maternal personality, at least theoretically, and therefore permits comparison between the youngster's standard of living and other variables in the family—including, of course, the mother's personality.

Based on preliminary work, including an extensive experience survey of persons working in our area, a Childhood Level of Living (CLL) Scale was developed. This scale became the major tool for discriminating among children as to the adequacy of care they were receiving, thereby making comparable differentiations among their mothers. We turn now to look at a significant dynamic problem prevalent among the mothers whose children have relatively low standards of living. Their mothers are widely thought to be victims of feelings of futility. So, let us now lay the theoretical groundwork for examining maternal personality; let's have a look at futility.

3

Desolation

~~~~~~~~~~~~~~~~~~~~~~~~~~~

Familiarizing himself with rural women whose children are victims of inadequate care was quite an experience for the senior author. Like many in social work and allied professions, he had put in his years among the poor, but this experience was long behind him. Most recently, for instance, he had been psychotherapist and head of social service at a private mental hospital. Many of the patients were wealthy, although not all were. They came from substantial homes with maid service available and serviceable cars to drive. It is a bit difficult to define just what dress is appropriate for admission to a psychiatric hospital, but whatever it was, they wore it. Their relatives were also articulate folks, competent despite their emotional problems, and well-groomed. Cleanliness is the opiate of these people. Many were from southern Appalachia.

To contact the women of interest in this research, he began at the county welfare department in a small mountain town. Sitting among office furnishings best described as grim, he asked to be introduced to a sample of the women who were presenting the most

frustrating treatment puzzles to the workers. The staff, ranging from the beleaguered to the serenely indolent, were happy to oblige, for this middle-aged professorial type, soon found himself thrust among people whose housekeeping standards appalled his family heritage for three generations back. Their hair was stringy and matted; they looked unclean; and they smelled as though they wore the same clothes continually for both social and sexual intercourse. Many related with a suspiciousness so pervasive it blocked idle curiosity. And at the end of each home visit, the guide was asking with ill-concealed delight, "Just what would you suggest I *do* with Mrs. Jones?" So much for generalizations about "the Appalachian culture"!

Fortunately, these inadequate mothers proved to be people, too. It is not necessary to renounce one's background as a middle-class professional, nor to undertake advanced training in cultural anthropology in order to have a conversation with one. If the researcher is alert and combines straightforward speech with competent skills in interviewing, these women respond. Gradually, the differences in dress and demeanor fell away. The mothers whom the welfare staff were finding hard-to-reach looked more and more familiar; they were the sisters of richer patients in the nearby mental hospital, who were hard-to-treat. The character problems, the extreme infantilism, were the same.

What became incongruous, then, was not that Polansky was probing the psyche of one of these girls but the setting in which he was doing it. He missed the protections and prerogatives of his own office. He was unable to conceptualize what our clients were coping with. But psychiatric sophistication might have just provided him with labels and with better justifications for our clients' failures.

A few of the mothers seemed mentally retarded; a scattering suggested gross psychiatric problems; but the majority appeared within the not-quite-normal limits we associate with character disorder. And of these there seemed, as a first approximation, to be two groupings—discernible, but not completely separate. The first group was the impulsive women, lacking controls. These women typically are in excellent contact; they relate, they are active, and they manipulate, so the worker can countermanipulate. They make worrisome clients, but one feels one has a chance with them.

More difficult, seemingly impossible, were the women who are withdrawn, immobilized, unrelated, who remain passive and defeat one by sheer evasion. Because they are so hard to treat, the second group came to fascinate us.

APATHY-FUTILITY SYNDROME

The syndrome is, of course, our own invention. To those with comparable training, it is not unfamiliar. However, to keep from being trapped and prematurely limited by standard nomenclature, we chose to put together our own picture of what we saw in concrete terms. Our definition included women who exhibited the following traits.

(1) A pervasive aura that nothing is worth doing. These women do not set up goals or pursue them with energy or purpose. They are unresponsive to attempts to mobilize themselves.

(2) An emotional numbness which is sometimes mistaken for depression. It is not so lively as depression.

(3) Absence of intense personal relationships beyond forlorn clinging, even to her children.

(4) Expression of anger passive-aggressively, especially in defiance of authority figures.

(5) Lack of competence in many areas of living, often visibly associated with the fear of failure—an unwillingness to invest energy to acquire skills.

(6) Non-commitment to positive stands and low self-confidence, which contrast with persistence in stubborn negativism.

(7) Verbal inaccessibility regarding important feelings and difficulty in facilitating the thinking through of problems by talking about them.

(8) An uncanny ability to infect those who try to help with the same feelings of futility.

The characteristic affect in the apathy-futility syndrome is the deep sense of futility, accompanied by massive inhibition, giving rise to a far-reaching anesthesia or numbness. Behaviorally, there is generalized slowing and straining toward immobility. Cognition is constricted, rigid, and impoverished, and such distortions as occur are likely to be due to excessive concreteness and stereotyping

rather than efflorescences of fantasy. Impoverishment in relationships is accompanied by reticence, especially in speech. Below, we
shall discuss at length the significance of what we have termed
verbal inaccessibility, which leads to the eventual limitation of intellectual development, and our strategy for treatment (Polansky,
1971).

Since women with the apathy-futility syndrome otherwise
make use of relatively primitive defense mechanisms, it is not surprising that many are prone to ill-defined bodily complaints. Of
these, some have physical bases, others seem pure conversions. But
the majority are truly psychosomatic, combining emotional and
physical factors. To have realistic troubles, to be poor, and live in
an isolated shack is still no protection against neurosis. Trouble is
not fairly distributed, not even randomly. Quite the contrary!

The image we have drawn is readily recognized by those
who have worked not just with child neglect but more generally
among the very poor. The image seems at first a caricature of the
"beat down" mountaineer of either sex. Colleagues who have been
at work more recently than we in urban slums and ghettos tell us
they know the pattern well. It is worth emphasizing, therefore, that
the apathy-futility syndrome is an *extreme* form of what is commonly seen among the poor. It is not unknown among the very rich.

A facet of the apathy-futility syndrome critical in treatment is the ability to disarm the helping person by infecting him
with the same sense of futility. Many of us leave the presence of such
a person finding it hard to go on to the next client.

We commented that the apathy-futility syndrome often encountered among mothers involved in marginal child care appears
to be an extreme form of a type common in low-income groups.
The sense of futility is as familiar as the expression: "You can't
fight city hall." It is often asserted that the inertia pandemic among
the very poor is an intelligent, or at least an expectable, reaction to
the hopelessness of their lot. Thus, Jeffers writes (1967, p. 122),
"Among parents in general, but probably to a greater extent among
parents who are poor, much behavior that is called apathy is better
understood as 'knowing the score.'" Child neglect, like many other
social ills, is related to poverty. One might conclude, therefore, that
the reason we saw so many apathetic-futile women was because of

the objectively hopeless circumstances in which they live. Let us label this approach the sociological approach.

However, hopelessness is not characteristic of situations but of people. Not all of the poor are "beat down." Some remain active, ebullient, and goal-seeking. Why do some poor mountain women become apathetic while others continue to work and provide surprisingly well for their children? To answer this question requires a knowledge of personality dynamics. Let us label this approach the psychological approach.

Taken in its purest form, each approach involves an untenable assumption. Hartmann has said (1958, p. 46) that psychoanalysis presumes "average expectable environmental conditions." Sociology, presumes an average expectable person. The purpose of such assumptions is, of course, convenience in making formulations, for they permit the theoretician to assume wide areas of discourse can be treated as constant, that for his purposes, other things being equal, *ceteris paribus* can be accepted. But in the real world, life is not so amenable. Personality and environment vary.

Our investigations were limited to low-income families. Our attention was directed toward this group because they are the population at greatest risk of marginal child-caring. However, an effect of this sampling was to cut off our chances of observing the play of social factors since they were, for practical purposes, held constant. Psychological forces were highlighted instead, and there is an emphasis on personality theory in our research. At the same time, we were cognizant of the importance of social realities and processes as they affect child care. One process which seemed germane to apathetic-futile reactions among neglectful mothers was alienation.

ALIENATION

If societies, like persons, pass through phases of growth and decay, then ketabolic processes have been prominent in ours in recent years. Ofttimes, we seem to be breathing psychological smog, immersed in social pollution. Our common uneasiness takes many forms: erosion of craftsmanship; casual dishonesty; purposeless violence; and the disappearance of amiable hypocrisies among

people that ease our lives. (See Reich, 1971.) More and more, the average man finds himself alone in a coldly indifferent universe that does not lend even the dignity of meaning to his suffering. He is described as alienated.

Alienation is an appropriate term to describe our social psychological pollution, even though the word has been popularized and corrupted in sloganeering. The kernal of insight it invokes is at least as old as Karl Marx's analysis of the effects of capitalism on a typical industrial worker. Marx predicted that the worker, divorced from realistic power of decision over his labor and the disposition of what he has produced, would separate himself from any psychological investment in the system. In effect, he would be alienated. It is no longer possible to take seriously the proposition that the whole working class in our country is alienated, but there is a germ of truth in Marx's formulation, however vague. What does alienation mean, more precisely?

Melvin Seeman in 1959 (pp. 783–791) analyzed five major usages of the term *alienation:* powerlessness, meaninglessness, normlessness, isolation, and self-estrangement. Powerlessness refers to one's feeling that one cannot determine one's satisfactions or one's fate by one's own efforts. This situation was postulated of the industrial employee spotlighted by Marx; his notion was later generalized to the army, to the university, and to other bureaucracies by Max Weber (Gerth and Mills, 1946, p. 50). Meaninglessness implies uncertainty whether one can estimate the effects of one's actions: doubt that one really "knows the score." Normlessness derives ultimately from Durkheim's notion of anomie; as later elaborated by Merton (1949), it combines the notions that there are no clearcut standards for behavior with the idea that such standards as there are are not to be followed in order to achieve success. Especially as applied to intellectuals, isolation implies standing apart from the values commonly adhered to in one's culture. (As Woody Allen says: "My parents' values were God and wall-to-wall carpeting.") Finally, self-estrangement is a notion which somewhat eludes Seeman but which is all too familiar among clinicians. Self-estrangement involves treating others as means to one's own ends, rather than as persons to be loved in their own right.

In any population, Seeman's conceptually distinct phenomena tend to be intercorrelated. That is, the processes in the individual which underlie alienation are likely to become visible in several, or all, of these forms as we shall show below. A wideranging cast of the characters who dismay us are thought of as alienated nowadays. They include the criminal (organized and disorganized), the exploitative developer, the social climber and dropout, the disillusioned intellectual, and the mentally ill (Schleifer and Teale, 1964; Lewis, 1967). They also include the apathetic, neglectful mother.

Yet, in all the formulations about deviance which invoke the concept of alienation, one is aware of a vagueness, a logical slippage, as if we had a clever figure of speech which was, nevertheless, inept for precise prediction. We perceive an inability to account for important individual differences, already visible in Merton's influential paper. Why should one lower-class youngster withdraw from the anomie of his neighborhood into becoming a drifter while his buddy tries to emulate Al Capone?

The loss of precision stems from the fact that an essentially psychological conception has been inserted into sociological formulations in an unclear way. These confusions in the use of the term are affirmed in a recent book by the Danish sociologist, Joachim Israel. Israel too (1971, p. 5) notes that the word *alienation* has had two usages, "one referring to sociological processes and one to psychological states." However, as a sociologist, he offers no psychological formulation, but instead recommends that the term be dropped in favor of others. We are unhappy with this solution because some phenomena associated with alienation are real and important. These phenomena struck us as potentially relevant in understanding the apathetic-futile reaction and kindred pathologies in our mothers.

Although our interests are more in application than development of theory for its own sake, work among the very poor in our mountain area convinced us of the necessity for advancing theory in order to encompass what we were uncovering. It remained, therefore, to develop a psychological explanation of the phenomena subsumed under alienation, which would be compatible with both

our research results and our previous backgrounds in practicing
social work and psychology.

The route to understanding alienation lies through exploring
feelings of futility to their primordial roots. The experienced clinician immediately associates the affect of futility with the schizoid
personality. Besides withdrawal and other inappropriate social behavior, the most distinguishing diagnostic mark of the schizoid is
his firm grasp on futility. In reviewing the thinking significant to
our problem, we were drawn repeatedly to Fairbairn's (1952)
psychoanalytic investigations of the schizoid position. These have
subsequently been clarified and extended by Guntrip (1969).

The analysis of alienation begins with accepting the fact
that there are schizoid elements in each of us. We are accustomed to
the notion of a schizoid personality, but it is more accurate to
recognize a schizoid spectrum along which everyone can be scaled.
One's position on the spectrum depends on the extent to which
schizoid elements dominate in his personality. Schizoid characteristics include ways of acting, feeling, and relating stemming from
defenses that arise during an early developmental crisis. Since such
crises are universal, the issue is not whether a person has encountered schizoid problems, but how he has resolved them. What, then,
is this developmental crisis? And which outcomes lead to the withdrawal and hopelessness we associate with schizoid personalities?

No one knows the newborn's mind. But undoubtedly, the
overriding concern of the organism is survival. The infant needs
air. He also needs other ingredients from the maternal breast:
water, without which the internal environment cannot function;
and food, to energize life processes. Usually when we talk of "deprivation," we mean psychological deprivation or what is loosely
called cultural deprivation. Cultural deprivation is serious business,
but it is not a matter of life or death. For the neonate, loss of maternal care results in mortal fear, for it portends death by starvation
or death by desiccation. It must be from such primordial beginnings
that we get the terror experienced by many patients of finding

themselves alone and unloved. The dreadful vulnerability we associate with loneliness was not, in its beginning, imagined. We
clung to our mothers for life itself.

Yet, the mother to whom we desperately cling also becomes
the target of angry feelings. No mother is so sensitive and ever-
available that her infant never experiences hunger or neglect, even
it it is only momentarily. Therefore, the greater our need of her,
the more prone are we to become angry. Almost from the beginning, the relationship to the mother involves a violent, primitive
mixture of love (or need) and anger. The early developmental
crisis, therefore, centers around the fate of the bad feelings toward
the mother. These may have two pathological outcomes. As Guntrip (1969, p. 24) points out, one reaction is rage, "the problem
of hate, or love made angry." When anger toward the mother is
compounded with love and enormous need, it leads to depression
and may endure as a depressive core within the personality.

Anger is not, however, the most primitive reaction to maternal deprivation. An even more primitive response to undepend-
able feeding is to become hungrier and hungrier, empty, and
desolate. Fairbairn and Guntrip have phrased it shrewdly: This is
the schizoid problem of "love made hungry." It accounts for the
otherwise puzzling observation that children who have been
markedly deprived cling desperately to their mothers. The desolation of love made hungry leads to overwhelming craving to possess
the mother utterly, to devour her. But such overwhelming needfulness would destroy the object of one's needs.

The dilemma of the schizoid stance is unpromising. Not to
love is to perish in loneliness; to love is to destroy the person one
desires. To preserve the object one must flee her. The young organism seeks to extricate himself from the intolerable admixture of
emotion into which his mother and his greed have thrust him, and
he does this by erecting a defense. He detaches himself from his
mother and his need of her, and he numbs himself against despair
and desolation.

Futility, then, is not an ultimate feeling state, defying further analysis. Nor is it a hard-eyed insight into man's fate. It is an
affect which accompanies and is partially caused by a defense. We
have this feeling ultimately because of a hunger waxed so greedy it

·seeks to grind up the source of all supplies, and because of a massive inhibition of affect, or numbing, we counterpose against the terrible emotions we have generated. One consequence of affect-inhibition is the ghastly sense of emptiness. ("I feel all dead inside"; "I am a flat person, only two dimensions.") The other consequence is a bleak feeling that nothing will do any good, and this feeling, too, is due to self-imposed numbness, akin to death. But how could the child know that in slamming the door on anger and depression, he is also inadvertently canceling his chance at all the other emotions—like joy, humor, and love? How can one feel better if one will not feel at all?

If futility is the pervasive schizoid affect, detachment is the critical defensive maneuver. What can we say about this mechanism? First, it is a phase of probably the most primitive defense of all, splitting in the ego. Splitting is implicated in such familiar operations as denial, dissociation, and displacement. Kernberg (1967, p. 663) has put his finger on the crucial transaction. Initially, the infant has difficulty in "putting it all together," in integrating, and this difficulty is an inability normal and expectable in the very young ego. But, in splitting, we see an instance of a general principle Rapaport (1967, pp. 530–568) identified. The ego converts into activity something which it has passively experienced. The child takes what was initially an incapacity to synthesize and molds it into an active, deliberate process of holding things apart in his mind. He keeps an idea from a related idea, a feeling from its object, and whole lines of thought from consciousness. In this sense, we understand disenchantment or detachment to be derived primordially from splitting.

As with other related mechanisms, detachment is not necessarily pathological. It can be used to help cope with inescapable realities. If the person we have loved dies, or while living withdraws her love, it is helpful to be able to give up, as it were, and to cease to occupy ourselves with her. Only when we are suddenly face to face with an old passion which we thought we had long since quenched are we forcibly reminded that detachment is a defense. For we may be visited with a sudden surge of longing, anger, and anxiety that witness the continuing vigor of feelings long repressed. Similarly, Cumming and Henry (1961) recognize the functional

utility of what they call disengagement in aged men and women losing their ability to participate socially and increasingly preoccupied with ceasing to be.

SCHIZOID REMNANTS

We assume that bad feelings toward one's mother are universal, that every infant, without exception, must deal with the painful mixture of good-mother–bad-mother emotions which Klein (1952), for one, postulates to be instinctive. It is part of man's fate that he begins with the potential for emphasizing either of two stances deriving from these bad feelings: the depressive position and the schizoid position.

Let us summarize the possible outcomes of the original conflictual feelings toward the mother.

(1) The outcome most hoped for, and which does occur to some extent in each of us, is the resolution of bad feelings toward one's mother, or at least their marked abatement. This resolution occurs when the child is sufficiently reassured that he will, in fact, be fed before it is too late. Then, the strength of the hunger drive abates, and he passes on to other developmental tasks. Some prefer to regard this outcome as "normal." Although it is to be hoped for, there is nothing "natural" or inevitable about resolving bad mother feelings. Even with a loving and competent woman, digestive disturbances in the infant can disturb the process; so may illness in the mother or a family catastrophe which coincides with a crucial phase of the infant's development.

(2) Another outcome is that hunger unmet leads to anger, the anger leads to guilt and is then turned against the self—the depressive stance. The guilt and depression would not exist, of course, unless there had been a relationship formed, so some aspects of development must have already proceeded "normally" for depression to occur. An ability to form meaningful relationships survives. Unfortunately, these relationships are often ambivalent, and the person with this pattern finds himself growing intensely angry even as he starts to love.

(3) The most pathogenic outcome, as we noted, is to have one's hunger go substantially unfed and intensify into emptiness

and greed. Greed leads to the desire to devour the loved person; consequently, there is a fear of loving. From the strongly schizoid core in the personality come numbing, apathy, and avoidance of people with whom one might become involved.

Sociological discussions of alienation are colored by a fantasy. Alienation is seen as a descent from Eden. The unspoken assumption is that man is naturally loving, goal-directed, and optimistic, unless prevented from being so by the intervention of some ugly social process. Is this really so? The Freudian view of man's fate is far more grim than that assumed by Durkheim or Merton. Is it not highly expectable that one may emerge from infancy with a lifelong undercurrent of depression or withdrawal and sometimes both? Often, the *best* we can hope for is to have fought successfully to overcome these dread weaknesses within ourselves.

People commonly have markedly schizoid and depressive cores within their personalities. We postulate that some traces of depressive and schizoid remnants are present in each of us. During periods of illness, weakness, or defeat they come to the fore. Any one of us is a candidate for despair or for detachment and futility as defenses against this dismal emotion. No wonder so many people are alienated from specific social institutions, and others can only be seen as totally alienated.

Let us pause to review where we are. In the course of offering a psychological explanation of alienation, we identifed it with a defense mechanism, detachment. We noted that this defense is not always unhealthy and also that it has its roots, in turn, in primitive splitting. We have also demonstrated the psychological roots of futility. Futility is the affect which, for a variety of reasons, accompanies the primitive splitting and numbing which may be one outcome of the child's bad feelings toward his mother. It comes from severe deprivation, whether real or as *experienced* by the child because of his own physical limitations.

However, to rest our analysis of futility here would be outright reductionism. We would have taken a number of penetrating insights of sociologists and claimed them for Freudian ego psychology by a simple act of translation into a new set of concepts. If a schizoid patient we are seeing is, in fact, living under Hartmann's "average expectable environmental conditions," the theory we have

described is reasonably adequate for steering his treatment. But it is not adequate as a basis for understanding futility, for there is every reason to believe that the world one faces long after one's basic personality is formed still has powerful effects and may, in fact, modify one's underlying makeup.

ROLE OF SOCIAL PROCESSES

These influences by the environment do not work as directly, as much on a one-to-one mirroring basis, as sociological theorists presume. If feelings of futility could be directly articulated to a debilitating environment, we would hardly need psychological theory. Common sense would suffice. We seem to have a situation in which social processes have their consequences mediated through structural differences among people, sometimes with surprising results.

Take the man with a markedly depressive core. Such a person thrives on busyness. Although he may complain of overwork, he adores having people clamoring for his services, for this reassures him that his early guilt is misplaced; he is not so unlovable as he fears. He is happy in a work situation that is rigidly structured and makes demands. Loose ends in his life expose him to the devils that await from within. So, hard work helps hold this man together.

Similarly, from our work in mental hospitals in this country, we know the needs of patients with loose ego boundaries. What used to be termed "spontaneous remissions" were often due to a regime in the hospital which countered inner looseness with clear external structuring. The patient recompensated seemingly without specific individual therapy. Who knows how many primitive and potentially explosive personalities are being held together by the authoritarian regimes in foreign countries? Although we believe in democracy, we are not convinced that every nation is ready for it. Sometimes, a nation acquires a form of government which is not a reflection of its basic personality structure (Kardiner, 1945) but a kind of compensation for it! They may not deserve it, but people get the kind of government that they need. So, social environments have effects, but they are not always the effects we first anticipate.

By the same token, later social support may combine with

internal efforts and compensate for psychological difficulties emerging from the earliest years. Of the many, many people who emerge from childhood with depressive or schizoid tendencies, relatively few remain severely handicapped. The process of adaptation then, clearly must not end with infancy. Consistent loving and care in later childhood undoubtedly help to counter the basic mistrust to which Erikson (1950) alludes, and healing continues into later life. The question, clinically, is whether the person can survive despite his character neurosis or whether he suffers from crippling symptoms.

We are inevitably affected by the morale of the group of which we are a member. High group morale buffers each against his own defeatist tendencies; our feelings of futility are less likely to emerge and take over when they are consistently disconfirmed by the attitudes of those surrounding us. However, a hollow void within exasercbated by a society that does not agree on what should be permitted, and which does not believe in its own future, leads to a wide-ranging alienation. Alienation as a pervasive state reflects the compounding of schizoid elements within the person with an anomic situation without. Each of us carries the seeds within him.

If society is to be blamed, then, it should be for failure to protect the individual against the wasteland within, not for creating it. Defenses, after all, are not direct reflections of reality, but reactions, sometimes of an extremely unrealistic, immature infant, to how he experiences the world. Detachment and futility are defenses which constantly threaten to become pathological; they usually lend nothing to the enjoyment of life. The issue, therefore, is whether a woman growing up and living in a mountain cabin has had one of these uncomforting modes of adjustment reinforced by all she experiences later or whether it has gradually dissipated as she discovers the world is not so unpromising as she had thought it.

CONSEQUENCES IN THE MATERNAL ROLE

Among neglectful mothers, we have noted, are a scattering with palpable, well-defined psychiatric conditions, such as mental retardation and psychosis. But, of those with diffuse character disorders, the predominant types are women with symptoms we have

grouped into the apathy-futility syndrome and impulse-ridden mothers.

We have sketched above a theory regarding the outcomes of infantile bad mother feelings. The schizoid stance has an obvious relevance to the pattern of passive, negativistic withdrawal. But how may we understand impulsivity? Is it, in fact, related to the apathetic-futile reaction?

This question is an empirical one to be answered by nature rather than theory, and we did not have the answer until we did some of our research. However, we did know to begin with that, at least in the opinion of some colleagues, the two patterns are not always mutually exclusive. The implication was that if you took a sample of inadequate mothers and examined them from a variety of angles, you would find some who combined withdrawal with acting-out and who had other features in common. We did this study, and its results are reported in Chapter Seven. But, meanwhile, what can we infer from theory?

Clinically, there are two dynamic threads to be followed in our approach to the impulse-ridden mother. One of these threads has to do with the failure to develop an adequate control system; there are a variety of reasons this may come about. The other thread on which we would like to focus at the moment relates impulsivity to a depressive core within the mother, which is *another* pathological outcome of bad mother feelings. It is typical, although not universal, that neglect by the impulse-ridden mother is *episodic* rather than chronic. It is likely to be interspersed with long stretches of competent care. We get the impression that the woman involved can survive her routine for only so long before she has to break loose in search of excitement and fun, whether in drinking, promiscuity, or some other type of activity. During the periods of frenzied pleasure-seeking, child care and housekeeping deteriorate.

It is as if there were something driving such a mother, as if she were momentarily hypomanic. Attempts to block an escapade are met with anger and recrimination, like the teen-ager who says, "You never let me have no fun." Under these conditions—and they do *not* apply to every impulsive mother—the impulsivity must be seen as a kind of reaction-formation against chronic depressiveness (Kaufman, 1963, p. 201).

We may hypothesize from theory, therefore, that the apathetic-futile mother and the impulsive mother, on the average, are likely to be related. They should have elements in common because both are living with substantial remnants of the same conflictual events in earliest childhood, both are likely to be fixated at an infantile level. But, of the two, the impulsive should be somewhat more advanced. If this is true, we would expect it to reflect itself in measures of cognitive-intellectual functioning and other evidences of maturation.

Of course, this whole line of theory presumes that the inadequate mothering is a reflection of early life experiences and fixations. As we have also noted, if the poor mothering is embedded in an otherwise competent woman, we would be led to conclude that, at least in her case, the inadequacy reflects a specific psychological conflict, rather than pervasive incapacity due to early character distortions.

CONSEQUENCES FOR CHILDREN

We have made much of our study of the maternal personality, but the research program, as a whole, was motivated by our concern for children. What are the effects in the next generation likely to be? We discovered that research previous to ours offered a sketchy basis for differential predictions. On the whole, results reported are nondiscriminating. Inquiry into the etiology of delinquency or drug addiction or mental illness has turned up substantially similar answers. As compared with youngsters who are presumably normal, these children have mothers who are less mature, less sensitive to their needs, and more preoccupied with their own problems. They are just not "good" mothers.

We postulated that infantile elements in a mother will reflect themselves in inadequacies in the child's level of living. We hypothesized further that these inadequacies would have demonstrably deleterious effects on a child's growth and development. In effect, we evolved an image of what we called the intergenerational cycle of infantilism on which a host of other social problems might be seen to rest including—at least in part—the cycle of poverty. The hypothesis that infantilism in the mother gives rise to infantil-

ism in her children accords with the nonspecific effects reported in the literature. We were ambitious to go beyond the general model and relate specific patterns in the child to identifiable elements in the maternal personality. The results of this effort are given in Chapter Eight.

Finally, we are in general agreement with others that the child's total environment, his subculture as well as his immediate family, plays a role in the formation of his personality. This influence should be true with regard to the sense of futility and other phenomena subsumed under alienation. Therefore, in addition to the impressions we were forming from case studies, we did several organized explorations into the effects of social structure and process on feelings of futility. These studies provide a good backdrop against which to view our other researches, so let us turn to them next.

4

Futility in a Cultural Context

The area identified as southern Appalachia has had flexible boundaries over the years. For example, the most comprehensive multi-university study of the area was published in 1962 under the title, *The Southern Appalachian Region: A Survey* (Ford). Those investigators listed twenty-two counties in North Carolina and twenty in northern Georgia. A recent extended delineation was made by the Department of the Interior, and we chose to conform to it on the occasions when a definition was relevant to sampling in our research. Under this definition, our study area included twenty-eight counties in western North Carolina, totalling 823,000 persons on the 1970 census. Southern Appalachian Georgia now numbers thirty-five counties with a population of 815,000. Thus, our study area (western North Carolina and northern Georgia) embraced approximately 1.6 million persons, about a quarter of those in all of

southern Appalachia. Those under 18 constituted 45% of western North Carolina in 1960; the comparable figure for northern Georgia was 38%; the total population under 18 was close to 700,000.

Although our research ranged into both states, our headquarters was in Asheville, North Carolina, and our observations are mostly about that section of the country. In both states, we were involved with predominantly *rural* counties, as planned, but not all residents were farmers. The median county in our western North Carolina sample had 63 per cent of its population classified as rural *nonfarm;* the median in Georgia was even higher—69 per cent. The Carolina mountaineers have traditionally had a high rate of natural increase, one of the highest in the world, with families of north European stock running as high as twelve, fifteen, and even more children. Yet the population there did not grow as rapidly as that in the state as a whole. The reason for the *relative* decline was a constant outmigration of young adults seeking better jobs and living conditions elsewhere. To an extent, therefore, those who remained with the land were a residual group, which may have had implications for the cultural values and the personality types predominating. But in the decade of the 1960s, the movement out of the mountains and into the cities slowed. Several of our most rural counties, far from losing population, had the highest proportionate increases during those years.

We had the impression that the people who live in these mountains are geographically stable and relatively poor. These impressions are strongly supported by data from the 1960 census (which were applicable while our fieldwork was under way). America has been known as a land of immigrants, but immigration has not taken place to the mountains for generations. None of the sixty-three counties studied had more than 1 per cent of its population foreign-born, and only a few had that much. (A more typical figure is one per thousand.) Indeed, in the median mountain county studied, 90 per cent of the residents had been born in that county. By the 1970 census, about 15 per cent of western North Carolina residents were black; 10 per cent of those in north Georgia were black. Whereas in the coastal regions of Carolina, as well as in

south Georgia, blacks are heavily rural, those in the mountains are likely to be found in or near the towns.

Because they are the population at greatest risk of child neglect, our research was directed toward families in the lowest income brackets, many on public welfare. Even the average self-supporting mountain family is relatively poor by national standards. The 1960 census reported a median *family* income for the whole *state* of North Carolina of $3,956. Twenty-one of the twenty-eight western counties had median incomes below the state's norm. Put another way, the per capita income of our Carolina mountaineers was about half that of the United States as a whole and about three-fourths that of their state. There is excellent statistical justification for regarding this area as deprived. Income in the north Georgia mountains is roughly on a par with that of the rest of the state of Georgia—but per capita income for all of Georgia was 10 per cent lower than that of North Carolina in 1960.

Reflections of these income and ethnicity figures will be visible in the latter half of this chapter, where we report research using social class as a variable. On a socioeconomic scale devised for rural areas, it was found that at least half our samples of students were categorized lower class by parental income and education, and the median social class in the Negro samples was significantly lower.

HISTORICAL AND CULTURAL PERSPECTIVES

Later in this chapter, we will show that the society of southern Appalachia is far from monolithic. It contains strata which divide the population in important ways, psychological as well as economic. Yet, compared with many other parts of America, this region is marked by stability and homogeneity on such characteristics as nativity, religion, race, and even spread in income. Mountain people are tolerant toward other Caucasians and readily accept foreigners into their families. But basically, this is WASP country.

Western North Carolina was settled before the American revolution. It was populous enough to have been "split down the middle" by the Civil War. As always, the reasons for migrating

there varied, but the strongest motive was the search for opportunity. Land could be acquired in the rugged hills either for free or cheaply. Many of the earliest settlers were English. Some had come to the plantations farther east as indentured servants but had subsequently jumped bond and fled to the mountains. Others with wives and children left debts and failure near the coast to try again in a new region. A few were already wealthy when they migrated. They established huge timbering and farming operations using black slaves, the same as their contemporaries who operated plantations in the coastal plain.

Other mountain families are of Scottish or Scotch-Irish origin, and a large segment of this group reached the mountains only after having settled originally in eastern Pennsylvania. But, feeding their land hunger, they made their way as far south as Asheville during colonial times. Among the Scottish, loyalty to original land and clan has survived in numerous middle-class families during their two centuries in America. By such festivals as the Highland Games, which are held annually and attract hundreds of participants and spectators, they celebrate their nostalgia for Scotland.

There has also been a surprisingly large infusion of other northern European blood, particularly the Germans whose remarkable fecundity has sent them everywhere (Wittke, 1939). Thus, one may unexpectedly encounter a seemingly exotic name, in an upland cove, which is obviously teutonic in origin (for instance Giezentanner or Ochsenreiter); others have gradually anglicized the spelling of their surnames for simplicity's sake (for instance Buhn altered to Boone). In so settled a population, surnames themselves become of interest. A whole settlement may consist of families with only two or three surnames; we recently read a list of the graduating class in a small uplands high school, and, in a class of less than forty, we counted six students with one surname and five with another. Usually, these youngsters are cousins, near or once or twice removed. Finally, some local families have an Indian ancestor somewhere, although such ancestry has not yet become prestigeful. Most markedly Indian are the Cherokees living here because their great-great-grandfathers survived the bloody relocation of the whole tribe to Oklahoma in the latter part of the 19th century.

One learns to be wary about imputing sentiments to such hard-lived frontier types. Southern Appalachia is definitely in what is known as the bible belt. Many persons adhere to fundamentalistic religious sects. Yet, there was a long period during which organized religion was not much in evidence. The lower-class Englishman who had jumped his indenture was unlikely to carry with him a devotion to the established church. With the population living in isolated clumps, there were impediments to maintaining religious observance and it gradually died out. By and large, therefore, the rural mountaineers were, in effect, *re*converted to organized Christianity during the revivalism of the latter part of the 19th century. An amused scepticism toward preachers is still widespread, and there are numerous well-respected men who refuse to attend church. Although there is undoubtedly a streak of *fatalism* in the culture, it is hard to tell whether it results *from* their religious forms, as has been maintained, or has influenced the direction which religion takes for them.

Similarly, the practical difficulties and expense of arranging schooling for children, along with the concreteness of effort that it took to survive, led most poorer families to place a low premium on "book larnin." It was not unknown for a family which had once had at least functional literacy to lose it after a generation or two in the mountains. Even hard-working families who were relatively well off might be able to arrange no more schooling than a few months for a few years for most of their children. Except for obvious occupational advantages, education is not valued by most of the population. Many poor families do not urge their youngsters to complete high school. The Scottish Presbyterians take pride in the fact that their ministers have always been required to be educated men, in contrast to other denominations whose standards were loose in this regard. To this day, it is important that a person known to be educated not sound too much that way in informal conversation, or he will be thought "uppity."

We can, then, make a few generalizations about the culture of southern Appalachia, and we will return to that theme below. Our main conclusion, nevertheless, is that our study area is not unusual. Each of us has lived in southern Appalachia for years prior to beginning these investigations. The senior author is married

into a family which has been here for at least a century and a half. But in some university reports we had difficulty recognizing our area. There are noteworthy exceptions like Caudill (1962) and Weller (1965), but much that has been written is either romanticized or exaggerated to make a predetermined case. The life style, the hardships, and the neighbor-watching we found in numerous cove communities were the common lot of all rural dwellers in Europe and America until two or three decades ago. Indeed, there are astonishing resemblances between the mountains and the Jewish *shtetl* of Poland around 1890 (Zborowski and Herzog, 1952). In short, many patterns specifically attributed to southern Appalachia strike us as survivals of the universal peasant culture whence most of us sprang.

As far as the major issue of our research is concerned, we are aware that standards of child-rearing vary between groups, but we have heard of no place where the neighbors hang a medal on a mother for leaving her infants cold and hungry. It is nearly impossible to find a woman who will admit she intentionally did such a thing. Child neglect is deviant behavior, here as elsewhere. It may serve some unconscious purpose in the mother, but it is not sanctioned.

We have not found most of the families we were studying inordinately quaint or strange; those who are so are also so regarded by their neighbors and childhood classmates. A number of local expressions survive, delightful and colorful turns of speech, but we found no one speaking Elizabethan English as the common stereotype has it—not, at least, that of Elizabeth I. If one needs a quintessential hillbilly for one's research, one must track him down. The stereotyped mountaineer is no longer typical of our region. He has been homogenized out of visible existence by retail chains, television, and the red-blooded American preoccupation with dollar-chasing. The situation here is reminiscent of Israel. The kibbutz has captured the international imagination, but kibbutzniks are no more than 5 per cent of the population.

To repeat, the local culture is no monolith. There are isolated people, there are poorer people, and there are black people. All are experiencing the world in various ways, ways different from the majority's. Southern Appalachian culture has some special

features derived partly from its history of settlement and very much from its peculiar economic situation. But basically, it is now part of the great American culture.

REGRESSIVE THEMES IN APPALACHIAN SUBCULTURE

To treat southern Appalachia as exotic is exaggeration, but it does have distinctive elements. Its divergences are emphases, trends, and themes, rather than sharp breaks with the general American tradition. Moreover, the traits that typify Appalachia are most characteristic of its lower socioeconomic segment, its poor and poorly educated people. The middle and upper-middle classes are relatively indistinguishable from the country-club sets well known in other American small towns. But, what are some distinctive themes in this subculture of the American?

The themes of distinctive Appalachian culture which we labeled regressive (using the term in clinical context) are not, by any means, the only noteworthy mountain values. Personal honesty, fastidiousness, courage, and loyalty are all in the local tradition. But our research, after all, is into child neglect and the roots of futility. Naturally, we highlight those cultural traits which have most bearing on these problems, traits which reflect values which are pathological or pathogenic. Below, we list the traits separately for expository reasons, of course. Psychoanalytically, however, they appear to be phenomena of the oral phase, theoretically closely interlocked.

(1) Penis worship and infantilizing the male. The relationship between the sexes contrasts noticeably with that in ordinary middle-class families. The father is accorded much *pro forma* status. If he is a weak person, it requires much manipulation and insincere deference by his wife to sustain his image. She is not above using his authority, real or supposed, to her own ends. Thus, if she withholds permission for a child to receive shots "until I ask his father," she may or may not be covering her own reluctance.

As a general rule, although the male may play with his children, he has minimal responsibility for their physical care; this is woman's work. Indeed, in working-class families, most housework is done by the wife. The man of the house typically feels that he has

fulfilled everything that might reasonably be expected of him if he works reasonably regularly and brings home his pay, or most of it. A mark of lower-class origin is a wife who tends the lawn for the family. This habit is nearly, but not quite, as tell-tale a sign as the ubiquitous habit of parking the family car on the front lawn. There is much talk of how hard Appalachian men work, for example cutting timber a few months at a time. But the labor performed is not impressive to those familiar with the sweaty efforts, year by year, of coal miners or factory workers on piece rate in cities. The mother may hold a full-time job, prepare the family's main meals, spend her weekends cleaning and washing, and still regard "making" a garden and putting up preserves for winter as forms of recreation.

The mores with respect to rearing male children are reminiscent of such groups as American Indians and the peasant cultures of a few eastern European countries. While the boys in an upland cove are free to hunt and roam, their sisters are busy with chores, beginning with the care of younger siblings at age five and even four. Indeed, in most dilapidated families, it becomes impossible to fix an age at which regular work demands on males are made, certainly not before their late teens. Associated with the pattern is usually a close tie between mother and son which makes separation difficult for either. If the son marries a "good old mountain girl," she will have been similarly indoctrinated, and the pattern of motherly and sisterly indulgence is carried over into later life, continuing the relative infantilization. In short, males are privileged characters, but their indulgence is not clearly to their benefit in the long run, for one way to ensure that your son cannot leave you is to keep him weak and infantilized.

(2) Separation anxiety, conformity, and the fusion fantasy. We found repeated evidence of separation anxiety as a cultural theme in so many versions that we were astonished it had not been previously stressed. (All the more refreshing is the recent book by Looff—1971, especially Chap. 4.) It explains, for instance, families settling so closely together that they crowd the available ancestral land. The mother's separation anxiety is mirrored in her children's fear and guilt about leaving her. Even among competent and successful people, it is common to observe old family dramas on the

issue of "Who is most special to mama?" expressed in spats and jealousies well into middle age. We cannot know how applicable these formulations would be to all those who outmigrated, but they are highly visible in the group at issue here.

In the literature on southern Appalachia it has been fashionable to extol the independence of the typical mountaineer family. Such statements often neglect evidence to the contrary. Armed force has not been required to compel these counties to accept federal grants; many lower-class persons are willing to accept relief. The defensive function of counter dependent strivings is also overlooked. As a reaction formation against tremendous passive-dependent longings, males often feel called upon to overplay their masculinity as bravado. Yet, the conflicts around orality take their toll, just as among Jewish mamas' boys. High on the hills in a objectively pressure-free countryside dwells many a gastric invalid and cardiovascular cripple. Girls, out of the same reaction formations, stress fortitude and reticence—although grumbling and self-pitying are far more frequent background noises in most poor families than the literature would lead one to expect.

Independence of thought is also read into stubbornness and clinging to traditions. We would not so characterize it if we found the same rigidity in a patient. Some of this "independence" is suspiciousness and comes from a general fear of anything new or strange; it is also a phobic reaction, reflecting, among other things, fear whether one will be able to cope with the unexpected, fear whether one has the extra psychic energy and skills. Moreover, the independence (or counter dependence) toward outsiders exists alongside great conformity among the "good old boys" within the community. This conformity applies to style of talking. If a youngster goes off to college, whatever knowledge he acquires there had better not be reflected in his speech patterns, certainly not when talking with his old friends. Dress habits are similar. A local industry once brought in an outside managerial expert as president. He was having more than the normal difficulty gaining acceptance until one of his subordinates took him aside and explained that his clothing was wrong: his coats and pants matched. When he began to mix the clothing from two intact suits, he was regarded as appropriately dressed for work in a plant—regardless of his role.

Education as a means of leading children to differ from their parents or of acquiring skills which lead them away from home is devalued. Similar pressures toward uniformity are found in the political machinations in rural counties. A high percentage of the population is chary of expressing any opinion lest it offend a neighbor or friend; in most settlements, people speak with vague near-unanimity on any issue. The typical county is completely controlled by a single faction, which holds all offices. Such "courthouse gangs" and their hangers-on are treated seriously and with respect in their home counties. The average resident has no ambition to defy the gang; rather, he would like to benefit from whatever personal connection he happens to have with it. In a number of counties, for example, relatives of local politicians, who held substantial properties, were regular recipients of public assistance in the old days. In their internal organization, such factions operate like boyhood gangs. They have a ringleader, superficially outgoing, tough, and manipulative, surrounded by a collection of satellites eager to do his bidding in exchange for scraps of patronage. This social organization, based on personal fealty and capriciousness, continues among the members until they are large-bellied and white-haired; it is not something they are expected to outgrow. Nor do they.

Hellmuth Kaiser (Fierman, 1965) has advanced a conception which seems particularly apt to these social expressions of separation anxiety. Kaiser speaks of the *delusion of fusion* as a defense universal among neurotics. In the fear of outsiders and outside influences, and in the pressures toward unanimity within the mountain culture, the fusion-fantasy seems clearly operative. As long as others closely resemble you in all ways or can be thought to, so long as those you love remain close, it is possible to maintain the fantasy they and you are as one person. The ultimate aim of the *fusion fantasy* is to defend against separation anxiety. Below, we discuss the impact of this mechanism on patterns of communication.

(3) Inexpressiveness. Ball (1965, pp. 885–895) has written of what he calls "the analgesic culture" of the mountains, and his phrasing is well-chosen. Natives of Appalachia place a value on inexpressiveness, even on maintaining a relatively bland facial expression, for example. Tears are not encouraged, of course, especially among men; the emphasis is on "keeping a stiff upper lip."

This custom is in marked contrast to the pattern in such another peasant group as the Jewish *shtetl* of Eastern Europe. According to Zborowski and Herzog (1952, p. 335), "that a child should cry when he is hurt or unhappy is a matter of course. No one will say: 'Be brave and don't cry.' . . . Grown men are not expected to weep as often or as freely as women and children, but, for them too, tears are in order during certain rituals or as an accompaniment to pleas for help, either for themselves or for their community." Even the expression of amusement is stifled as if, in keeping down tears, these families had inadvertently also bottled up their abilities to experience pleasure and joy.

Even in their physical artifacts, Appalachia manifests an antibaroque culture. Traditional mountain clothing is plain in construction and generally dark-hued. In contrast to Italians or Greeks, there is little emphasis either on ceremony or on pageantry for its own sake, for the decoration of life. In fact, the somber concreteness and utilitarian quality of living may be related to the impatience with "ideas" and intellectualism in general.

(4) Fatalism. The attitude, "What will be, will be" has been noted as an important cultural theme in the mountains by a number of previous writers, and our observations concur with theirs. The culture contains a strong sense of fatalism, a feeling that many matters cannot be helped, so why contend with the inevitable? Of course, this stance is not unique to our locality. It is ubiquitous in all peasant groups—people whose lives are markedly influenced by the vagaries of sun, wind, and cold. Yet, when we operationalize fatalism as felt powerlessness, it proves to an extent a class-linked attitude, even in our mountains.

What is the function of this value in the lives of our people, for it can interfere with their taking action when action might be in order. Perhaps it is no accident that the fatalism is most acutely remarked by helping personnel—social workers, public health nurses, community specialists—who are concerned with bringing about change. In line with our emphasizing the oral elements in the culture, we see first that "fatalism" is used to justify inactivity and yielding to passive longings. Secondly, fatalism provides an aura of maturity and respectability to primitive negativism. Finally, fatalism is used as a defense. If one toyed with the notion something

might be tried to help a dying relative, one would be faced with the threat of guilt for not having gotten him that help. But, as long as "nothing can be done," one has a shield against both guilt and failure.

This analysis, of course, deals only with questions outside the role of religious belief. Fatalism is commonly ascribed to the mountaineers' respect for the supernatural. But, this conclusion overlooks the fact that many coreligionists do not share the same sense of powerlessness. Nor, as noted, is religion very significant to the majority, especially among the very poor.

VERBAL INACCESSIBILITY AND SOCIAL CLASS

Nonverbalism was earlier listed as one of the distinguishing features of women with the apathy-futility pattern. In that context, nonverbalism was treated as an issue in the structure of individual personality. But reticence has also been remarked as a trait generic to the mountain subculture as a whole, namely, the stereotype of the taciturn mountaineer (Schachter, 1962). Not only did they decline to discuss their affairs with outsiders, they were quiet even within the family.

We became interested in this issue for several reasons. From the standpoint of practice, pronounced nonverbalism could dictate modifications in treatment approaches. At the same time, we did not find the reluctance to talk universal. Some neglectful mothers, seen in the earliest pilot study, were highly voluble. And, finally, we carried into the present investigations a theoretical interest in verbal communication, which the senior author had pursued in research and clinical work for over a decade (Polansky, 1971). The theories were organized around his concept, verbal accessibility.

Verbal accessibility (VA) is defined as the readiness of a person to talk about his most important attitudes and feelings and to engage in discussions of them with another person. VA is not the same as volubility; it is possible to be highly vocal while still revealing little about oneself, as in circumstantiality. From observations, the following questions came to mind: (1) Are the mountaineers generally low in VA, namely, are they verbally inaccessible or are there marked variations on this attribute within their population? (2) If there is variation, is it possible to identify segments of

the population in which the inaccessibility is most marked? (3) In
the event systematic covariations are identified, how shall we explain them?

Although we were unaware of their work when ours was
under way, ours was not the only group in the region with these
preoccupations. David H. Looff, child psychiatrist from the University of Kentucky Medical School, was concurrently conducting
substantial clinical research in eastern Kentucky. The congruence
of his observations, made independently from our own, is the more
impressive, scientifically, because the ignorance of each of the other's
work seems to have been mutual; at least he does not cite our occasional publications. Above, we mentioned Looff's identifying
separation anxiety as a significant dynamic problem in many
families. He also devotes an entire chapter to questions of regional
nonverbalism. In the present context, Looff observes (1971, p. 77),
"The striking phenomenon is that the silent families exist side by
side with others who are quite able to express feelings and ideas
sensitively in words. The silent stereotype simply does not hold true
for all."

He goes on to discuss some clinical phenomena related to
nonverbalism, as well as the effects of early language deficits on
children's progress in school. "Many Eastern Kentucky families,
particularly in the lower and working classes, set sparse speech
models for their children (1971, p. 79, emphasis added)." We had
similar speculations on the presence of class-related differences and
are able to confirm Looff's impressions with some systematic data
from our locale farther south. These data were partially reported
by Polansky and Brown in 1967 (pp. 651–660), but that study was
subsequently augumented and the analysis extended.

These studies specifically disregarded the conception of
southern Appalachian culture as monolithic. Instead, they examined
the effects of such variables as socioeconomic status, sex, race, and
degree of isolation of one's community on the measured VA of
samples of adolescents.

SAMPLING AND MEASUREMENTS

Data were collected from 180 adolescents attending high
schools serving largely rural and semirural populations in the

mountains of western North Carolina and north Georgia. The subjects were chosen to be under the statutory school age of sixteen to
secure representative sampling and averaged slightly under fifteen.
Samples were drawn from: (1) A small manufacturing town whose
high school serves the surrounding countryside. Two white samples,
thirty in each, were drawn from this school, roughly the upper
third and lower third socioeconomically within this small town.
Each sample contained equal numbers of boys and girls—fifteen of
each. (2) An isolated "cove" community, all white. (3) An isolated
farm community which was also "lily white." (4) An Appalachian
county with a large black population. Two samples of thirty were
drawn from the then-existing all-black high school. These were divided into higher and lower socioeconomic groups although, in
actuality, the distinction was between lower-lower class and upper-
lower class in the black group.

Data were collected in each school by instruments lending
themselves to paper-and-pencil group testing and individual interviewing. Socioeconomic status was assessed with a scale devised by
McGuire and White (1955), whose standards are appropriate for
rural populations. Their weighted index involves occupation, source
of income, and education. The youngster's status was determined
by rating that of the head of his family, usually his father. The
higher the score, the lower the socioeconomic status.

Verbal accessibility was approached through three operationally independent measurements. These included: (a) direct questioning of the subject, which we labelled his *Self-Avowed VA;* (b)
indirect measurement through tapping relevant attitudes on a scale
for *Orientation toward Verbal Inaccessibility;* (c) situational test
of *VA Measured Projectively.* Each of these measurements will be
described below as appropriate for reporting results. Each measure
was relatively independent of the others within the limited range of
subjects sampled.

SELF-AVOWED VA

Self-avowed VA can be measured in straightforward fashion.
The subject is given a list of potential targets of verbal communication, for example, mother, father, best friend same sex, best friend

opposite sex. Next, he is given a particular topic one might discuss. He is then asked whether he would talk about this particular topic with each of the possible communicatees, and his answers, negative and affirmative, are recorded. In our study we used such items as: Whom do you, or would you, talk to about whether you can do things as well as most of your friends? Whom do you, or would you, talk to about what you think about the rules your parents make for you? Whom do you, or would you, talk to about whether you like the way you look?

There were sixteen such items, each tapping a potentially charged, determinant attitudinal area. There were also seven communicatees for a maximum of 112 affirmative responses. The score was simply the percentage of possible affirmations. Jourard (1961, pp. 315–320) and Rickers-Ovsiankina (1961, pp. 872f) have used this technique in written questionnaires. Our data came from interviews.

Results for the various subsamples studied are compiled in Table 4. After an overall median for all 180 subjects had been determined, we computed the percentage in each subsample scoring it. The mean socioeconomic score for each subsample is also given in Table 4. Descriptively, a score of sixty-seven or higher delineates the lower-lower class; a score below fifty-two represents lower-middle class. Except for the town high group, all samples were predominantly lower class.

The outstanding discovery, using the direct, self-reported VA scores, is the consistently low scoring of the children from the two isolated, rural communities. Of sixty children interviewed in both a mountain cove and Georgia farms, only two boys reported themselves above the overall median on VA. Within the town sample, the lower-class group scored relatively lower than the middle-class one.

However, on this scale, there were two findings which were inconsistent with results on our other measures. First, the typical superiority of girls over boys is not *self*-reported. Instead, girls' patterns fit their subgroup's. Secondly, the black children *report* themselves very open, but this openness is *not* borne out by indirect measurement, as we shall see below. Indeed, we wonder whether self-avowed VA is not heavily affected by what the subject feels to

be the prevailing mores in his immediate group. Such a public attitude may reflect conformity pressures and imply more uniformity in the group than exists. In short, are those in the isolated communities, the purest Appalachians, really "silent-turned," or do they

Table 4

PROPORTIONS ABOVE THE MEDIAN ON
SELF-AVOWED VERBAL ACCESSIBILITY
(N = 180)

	Negro Low	*Negro High*	*Cove Community*	*Farm Community*
Boys	87%	93%	13%	00%
Girls	80%	93%	00%	00%
Mean socioeconomic score	71	59	66	62

	Town Low	*Town High*
Boys	47%	60%
Girls	53%	67%
Mean socioeconomic score	67	36

think they *ought* to be? The answer to this question has significance, of course, for how they may be treated psychologically.

ORIENTATION TOWARD VERBAL INACCESSIBILITY

To measure the existence of values inhibitory to talking about feelings, we used an instrument scaling orientation toward verbal inaccessibility. Originally developed with Jaffee (1962, pp. 105–111), the scale contained values having to do with keeping

one's thoughts to oneself, antiintrusiveness, and antiintrospective-ness. We used a written questionnaire with the usual format of declarative statements which one might score "strongly agree" to "strongly disagree." Effects of the response set were evaded by so wording items that only acceptance of some and rejection of others could lead to a high inaccessibility score. Examples of items are: "If somebody is interested in me, I'm willing to hear what he's got to say." "People can change their old habits if they try hard enough." "The really smart guys keep their opinions to themselves." "If you want to do things right, it's good to learn from the advice of other people."

The higher the score, the more the subject is taken to be oriented toward verbal inaccessibility. Odd-even split-half relia-bility of this instrument was +.79.

In contrast to their self-avowed VA, on this indirect mea-sure, the black youngsters reported values inhibitory to expressing feelings. The mean score for the 120 white subjects was 26.2; that for the 60 black, 29.6. (Difference significant beyond .01 by t-test.) Perhaps because their general ethnic situation outweighed small socioeconomic differences, no class difference was found within the black subsamples.

Data from the 120 white subjects were then analyzed for the effects of social class and sex differences, utilizing a two-way analysis of variance. Adolescents from the relatively lower socio-economic background were oriented more toward inaccessibility, and this difference was significant at .05 by F-test ($F = 5.056$; d.f. 1 and 116). Girls' values were more oriented toward openness than were the boys', a difference also significant at beyond the 5 per cent level by F-test. The sex difference, by the way, extended also into the black samples. In other words, on this less direct test of attitudes relevant to VA, girls were the more accessible, despite their responses on the self-avowed measure. In fact, as a general rule, wherever we have found a difference between the sexes with respect to verbal accessibility that was statistically significant, it has always shown the females more open. Geographic isolation of one's community did not play a consistent role in these results. The mountain cove community was again inhibited, but the Georgia farm community was not.

Thus, we may conclude the following. Youngsters disadvantaged because of race were more oriented toward inaccessibility; the whites most disadvantaged socioeconomically were also the most inhibited. In every subsample studied, girls held values favoring openness more than did boys.

PROJECTIVE TEST OF VERBAL ACCESSIBILITY

As a further means of studying the VA phenomenon, we made use of a projective technique. In the group testing sessions in which the attitude scales were administered, the subjects were also asked to complete an incomplete sentences form. The form was adapted from Rotter and Willerman (1947, pp. 43–48) by Nooney and Polansky (1962, pp. 33–40). The rationale for this measure of VA rested on the observation that the relative openness of communication evident in incomplete-sentence responses may be as noteworthy as the need-content expressed. Hence, by asking the subjects to complete an incomplete sentence form during other testing, we were, in effect, administering a situational test of their VA. Completions were judged on a five-point scale. Criteria for a *high* rating were: "There is personal relevance, with relatively strong affect expressed. References are to self, parents as objects of attitudes. Negative affect expressed is strong; there is risk-taking; body- or competence-image may be questioned, with pain expressed."

Coding of protocols was done blind. Intercoder reliabilities (rho) of +.85 and +.84 were achieved from two independent samples of data. However, split-half reliability of the 16-stem form was only .67 in this restricted range. This is far beyond chance, of course, but probably only adequate for comparisons between group means. On the projective measure of VA, a higher score represents greater verbal accessibility.

Once again, class differences within the black sample were not significant. Again, the white adolescents scored significantly more accessible than did the black (means were 29.9 and 27.2, P < .01 by t-test). Sex and class differences within the white samples are represented in Table 5.

White youngsters in high SES (socioeconomic status) groups

Table 5

MEAN SCORES ON PROJECTIVE VERBAL ACCESSIBILITY TEST

Sex	Socioeconomic Status		Total
	High	Low	
White Boys	29.7	27.1	28.5
White Girls	32.7	29.7	31.2
Total	31.2	28.4	—

are more open on the projective test of VA than blacks; they are also more open than whites of lower status. Difference between means was significant at beyond the 1 per cent level by F-test, based on two-way analysis of variance. The girls proved more accessible than the boys, with the difference between means also significant beyond .01. On this measure, too, the scores were consistently in favor of the girls throughout the subsamples.

The average socioeconomic status of the subjects from the town lower group was comparable to those of the groups of white adolescents from the isolated communities. Hence, we may ask whether relative isolation is a factor distinguishable from class, as such. Using the estimate of the standard error of the difference between means derived from our analysis of variance, t-tests demonstrated the town lower sample to be significantly more verbally accessible than each of the isolated white groups. A similar difference was also found on the self-avowed measure of VA. Hence, in two of three measures, isolation was linked to more pronounced reticence.

VARIATIONS WITHIN APPALACHIA ON VERBAL ACCESSIBILITY

Let us summarize the findings of our study. Partly because we were still exploring unfamiliar territory, we used three different methods for measuring VA among adolescents. Two measures were indirect: the first, a projective test indicating how open the youngster made himself to *us;* the second, a scale of values and attitudes. The third measure relied on self-reports of VA. The latter measure

is, of course, susceptible to distortion from an ingratiating need to give affirmative responses to the interviewer, and this factor may have operated in the black subsamples. Scores on the incomplete sentences test might be depressed due to functional illiteracy, although we had hoped to overcome this problem by choosing our subjects from the ninth and tenth grades in high school. The lack of skill in written expression might reflect generalized nonverbalism, of which verbal inaccessibility would be only one aspect. So, each measurement had its advantages and disadvantages for our purposes.

From the results on the indirect measures of VA, youngsters from the advantaged families in the white population are significantly higher on VA, despite the constricted socioeconomic range sampled. Our finding is in accord with a tentative observation also reported by Looff (1971, p. 79, emphasis added). "Many eastern Kentucky families, *particularly in the lower and working classes,* set sparse speech models for their children." Although they reported themselves open on the self-avowed measure, the black children from the segregated high school scored consistently lower than the white children on both indirect measures of VA. But, this difference can also be seen as class-linked, since blacks also averaged lower on the measure of socioeconomic status.

The evidence suggests that where class is held constant, youngsters from isolated rural communities are more reticent than those from places "in the mainstream" in our mountains. Looff has aptly labelled as the "consolidated school syndrome" the mutism and withdrawal of children who come from isolated communities when they are brought into contact with strangers if their own tiny mountain schools are eliminated in favor of countywide arrangements. The variation in VA may be one source of culture shock for the youngsters—but it must play less of a role than their separation anxiety.

Finally, we find that girls appear consistently higher on VA than do boys. Looff, once again (1971, p. 87), mentions this phenomenon, citing the local expression that "talk is women's work." However, a sex difference extends far outside our region (Polansky, 1971, pp. 231f). Even in the Jewish *shtetl* we have been contrasting to the American highlands, it was said that men are supposed to be

more silent than women in any case (Zborowski and Herzog, 1952, p. 302).

Earlier in this chapter, we commented that the subculture we know as southern Appalachia is far from monolithic. Data regarding VA bear this out. But, if those from poorer families are not open about their feelings and those from isolated coves even less open, why should this be? What is the explanation?

One explanation that has been offered is that the poorest families have a sparse language code and pass this on to their children. We find this explanation too glib. Why does the lowest stratum have such a code and maintain it in the first place? Obviously, we need an explanation more dynamic than one that "culture acculturates."

We have proposed a theory to account for group forces inhibiting free expression of individualized feelings. Coincidentally, the same forces operate to discourage development of what Bernstein (1962, pp. 221–240) has called *elaborated* speech as the mode of communication in that culture. This theory derives from the fusion-fantasy hypothesis of Hellmuth Kaiser (Fierman, 1965). Paradigmatically, we may say: (a) Separation anxiety, with its accompanying sense that one is ultimately alone in a potentially meaningless universe, is a feeling with which everyone has to come to terms; however, its remnants remain more pronounced where there is childhood deprivation. (b) One way of dealing with separation anxiety is through the defensive maneuver Kaiser has termed *delusion of fusion*. In this defensive fantasy, one sees oneself as *psychologically at one* with significant others, as if separation had never occurred. (c) Cultural forces interact with individual psychology to support, or to penetrate, defenses. Any defense felt necessary by a high percentage of those in a culture is likely to be valued, rationalized, and supported by the culture as a whole. (d) We hypothesize that the greater the general deprivation and insecurity in which a group lives, the stronger will be the need to maintain the fusion-fantasy. Group cohesiveness and uniformity of attitudes will be emphasized in such groups because they tend to support the delusion of fusion. (e) Expressions which emphasize highly personalized and individualized feelings are disruptive to the notion that all are as one. The same phenomenon is true for vocabulary

elements facilitating fine distinctions among attitudes. (f) Hence, we hypothesize that in a culture or in segments of a culture in which large numbers feel chronically threatened, there will be group pressures against the expression of personalized feelings and attitudes. Members of such a culture will be trained to express emotions in vague and stereotyped fashion, and reticence about feelings will be sanctioned.

Our theory provides an explanation for the emergence of restricted codes of speech and argots among such groups as ghetto youngsters and hippies; it also accounts for their preference for nonverbal forms of communication (for instance through touch and physical embrace). Nonverbal communication has the advantage, for sustaining the fusion fantasy, of being comforting and yet nonspecific in what it conveys. The theory also leads to a deduction that pressure toward uniformity is greater in the lower socioeconomic groups. This deduction would accord with the observation of conservatism and intolerance among the working class in present-day America.

POWERLESSNESS AND SOCIAL CLASS

Recurrent mention of the Appalachians' fatalistic outlook on life made us curious about this theme within their culture. Was this value truly ubiquitous in the region, or did it depend on an individual's position in the social structure? This question was of considerable importance to us because the attitude is, in some respects, incompatible with those needed to bring about change in casework.

The gist of the fatalistic orientation is the feeling that what will be, will be, regardless of one's wishes and efforts. Therefore, we decided to use an available instrument for measuring felt powerlessness. This scale was adapted by Jaffee (1959) from the original version of Rotter and Seeman (1959). Powerlessness is seen, in sociology, as one aspect of alienation, and Seeman (1966, pp. 354–367) has continued work with this concept. Rotter, a psychologist, has since rephrased the issue (Battle and Rotter, 1963, pp. 482–490) as a question of individual differences in accepting responsibility; he speaks of "internal versus external control of reinforcements" as a dimension of personality functioning.

Felt powerlessness was measured by a paper-and-pencil test adapted to the sixth-grade reading level. A Likert-type format was employed, with the subject indicating agreement or disagreement with such statements as: "I think we will always have wars between countries no matter what we do to try to stop it," "A man who gets a good job is just lucky to be at the right place at the right time," or "I feel I have little influence over the way other people act."

Odd-even split-half reliability in the present study yielded $r = +.72$. Unlike the results with respect to verbal accessibility, there was no consistent difference between the sexes on this variable. Therefore, results were subjected to a two-way analysis of variance to study the effects of class and ethnicity. The results are given in Table 6. On this measure, the higher the score, the greater the reported felt powerlessness.

The white adolescents scored lower on felt powerlessness than the black ($P < .01$ by F-test); the difference between classes was also significant at beyond .001. Indeed, inspection of the table will show that there was really no class-related difference within the black group, and since they are, overall, about equal to the lower half of the white group in socioeconomic status, the effect found could be explained solely on the basis of social class.

Once again, we detected a variation in a cultural value systematically related to stratification within the mountain society.

Table 6

MEAN SCORES ON FELT POWERLESSNESS

| Race | Socioeconomic Status | | Total |
	High	Low	
White	32.6	38.1	35.2
Black	38.4	38.3	38.4
Total	34.1	38.2	—

Felt powerlessness, with its probable relationship to fatalism, was more characteristic of the disadvantaged groups in the society—the blacks and the poor whites—than the nondisadvantaged groups. These results are in accord with what one might expect on the basis

of common sense. If a youngster is poor and his family of low pres-
tige, it is no wonder that he believes himself more at the mercy of
forces beyond his control than does someone from a more successful
family. Emotions, however, are not usually so rational nor in such
one-to-one reflection of external reality. We shall end the chapter,
therefore, with some observations on possible psychological meanings
of powerlessness.

POWERLESSNESS, HELPLESSNESS, AND DEPRESSION

Thoughts about the theoretical status of alienation are
equally relevant to powerlessness. Powerlessness has objective refer-
ents, but once again, one may appropriately ask how this sociological concept might be viewed psychologically. To the clinician,
the psychological equivalent of powerlessness is helplessness; the
emotion of helplessness, in turn, is associated with anxiety and depression. We shall address the latter relationship here.

Rapaport has left us a cogent statement of the relevant issues
in his discussion of Bibring's theory (Rapaport, 1967, p. 763). The
accepted theory had been that "the conflict is one between the ego
and the superego and involves oral fixation, ambivalence, incorpora-
tion, and aggression turned round upon the subject." In short,
depression resulted from an experience of oral deprivation and a
chain of psychological consequences which followed this frustration. The affective states accompanying depression were said to be
ego inhibition and loss of self-esteem. To these states, a third might
be added, helplessness, but in this line of theory, all three states
were "caused" by the dynamics of the depression.

Bibring saw the relationship another way. He wrote (Rapaport, 1967, p. 760): "Depression can be defined as the emotional
expression . . . of a state of helplessness . . . of the ego, irrespec-
tive of what may have caused the breakdown of the mechanisms
which established self-esteem." He sees depressions as reactivations
of the infant's state of helplessness, its lack of power to provide for
oral supplies necessary to its life. In short, in his radically new concept, the general dynamic of depression is helplessness: helplessness
"causes" depression. The transaction is within the ego. Whenever
the ego finds itself unable to carry out its aspirations—and these

will obviously differ, depending on the level of development about which we are speaking—then depression results. Thus, at the oral level, "depression follows the discovery of: (1) not being loved; (2) not being independent" (Rapaport, 1967, p. 765). At the phallic level, depression is a consequence of fear of being defeated, of being ridiculed for shortcomings, and of impending retaliation.

A third relationship might be added. Following Kaiser, Enelow (1960, pp. 153–158) speaks of people who become depressed when they have to make a decision. The act of commitment reminds them that they are not really fused with one another but alone and independently operating beings. In this reaction, one detects a kind of motivated helplessness in which immobilization is calculated to ward off depression. One might say that in this context, helplessness is used as a defense against depression.

We have, then, three permutations on the association between helplessness and depression: (1) helplessness as an aspect of depression, where depression results from transactions between the ego and other psychic institutions; (2) helplessness leading to loss of self-esteem and consequent depression, a transaction within the ego; (3) helplessness as a defense against depression. We have associated the important psychological state of helplessness with the sociological concept of felt powerlessness and the latter, in turn, to the cultural theme of fatalism. Let us return from these theoretical formulations to our observations.

We know that the children who are economically deprived report the greatest sense of powerlessness. From evidence to be presented later, we have reason to suspect that the deprivation extends even to oral supplies, so there is support for a link between powerlessness and depressiveness, even though the *direction* of the linkage remains indeterminate. But here we come upon another observation. Powerlessness is linked to fatalism—and those with this orientation may have an undercurrent of depressiveness, but they are *not* depressed! It is as if the giving up, the resignation, were accompanied by a deep relief. For fatalism has many advantages, chief of which is permitting oneself to come to terms with justifiable ego aspirations. If nothing can be done, there is no need to struggle toward defensive independence; if everything is beyond one's power to change, why feel guilty over an untreated illness in a child? We

see, then, that fatalism can be used as a defense against depression.

It remains significant that fatalism is most characteristic of those in the lowest socioeconomic class, for this segment of the population is at greatest risk of marginal child care and child neglect. Resignation may hold down anxiety and depression, but it does so at the cost of motivations which might be harnessed to bring about improving one's life, whether in accepting casework or through other means.

5

Design of a
Diagnostic Study

The broad perspective on our research has now been set down. Instead of child neglect, we are dealing with the issue of relative levels of child care. Care ranges from excellent to adequate to marginal, and neglect represents an extreme on this complex dimension of vital supplies.

We have also described the countryside in which we worked and the nature of its people. The average Appalachian is best seen as a variant of the average American. Appalachian culture is best described as a subculture rather than as an exotic or alien culture in our midst. Most local values have much in common with those of other small towns or rural areas of America. Although we find it useful to highlight a number of common themes in the subculture, it is not monolithic. Most people are relatively poor compared with the national average income, but there are social strata and these

affect *Weltanschauung* and behavior. Fatalism and verbal reticence are often attributed to the region as a whole, but we have shown that they are most pronounced in the lowest socioeconomic group.

Whatever their theoretical fascination, the latter findings were discouraging to us as practitioners. The population at greatest risk of marginal child care is in the lowest income category, and from these results it appeared that this group might be most limited in its abilities to accept casework help. However, we were encouraged when we recognized that women are characteristically more verbally accessible than men, important, since they appear so fulcral to raising children's living standards. Also, we recognized extremely important variations within any segment of the population. We are now ready to explore these individual differences in depth. The next several chapters will be devoted to describing a field study which was conducted over a period of two years. Let us begin with the aim of this study, and then proceed to its methods.

PURPOSE OF FIELD STUDY

The intention in this research was to identify and understand the mothers whose children are receiving the poor care in order to find leads as to how to help them improve the care. Having identified the marginal or neglectful mother, we had such questions as: How does her style of mothering fit into the rest of her personality? Is marginal child care an isolated problem or part of a pervasive pattern? How did she become the way she is? Does her mode of child-caring have a perceptible impact on her children? What handles in the situation might be grasped to help her improve?

The logic of our study was simple. We obtained a sample of low-income families from the same mountain county. Of course, we might have improved our chances of demonstrating significant relationships if we had made our sample more heterogeneous, but as a matter of efficiency, it seemed important to concentrate all our efforts on the group of greatest interest—the low-income, rural mothers. Next, the sample was divided into *relatively* "high" and "low" groups in terms of the caliber of care offered children. This division was done with the aid of an objective and quantitative

device, the Childhood Level of Living Scale. (See Chapter Two.)

The sample consisted not of mothers as individuals, but of *mother-child pairs*. In practice, we began by locating a group of four- and five-year-old youngsters who fitted our criteria and then studying their mothers too. In order to answer the sorts of questions we raised, we needed to know both mother and child well. It was understood from the beginning that we would require information about both mother and child resembling that in a case history or psychiatric social work study, rather than that which is typical in surveys in the child-development literature. Moreover, we proposed to supplement our own skills and knowledge with psychological testing and collateral information whenever it could be readily obtained.

POPULATION STUDIED

During our pilot studies, we met two remarkable women who were already at work helping disadvantaged families in the mountains. Their generosity of spirit and competence made it possible for us to reach the mothers and children included in this study. Dorothy Crawford, a social worker, was director of what was then known as the county welfare department in Franklin (Macon County), North Carolina. Crawford, in turn, told us of the program which had gotten under way through the efforts of Rebecca Johnson Stradley, who was supervising the Year-Round Head Start nursery-school program for Macon Program for Progress, the local OEO agency.

By a combination of energy, skill, and ingenuity, Stradley succeeded in establishing a program whose coverage was most unusual. Her nursery schools were located in four different centers throughout this rural county. She used space which she had rented, begged, and wheedled from reluctant landlords for the purpose. She had also done an impressive job of recruiting eligible children, including making arrangements to bring in those living in the most isolated parts of the county. Stradley had spent much time with parents who were reluctant to involve their children. These children are often missed by such efforts and may be most in need of supple-

mentary stimulation. As a consequence, the day-care aspect of Macon Program for Progress offered a sample of low-income, rural families which was unusually representative.

Subjects for the study were chosen from among the children then currently enrolled. The criteria were that the child be four or five years of age at the time the study began and that he come from an intact family, namely, a father was at least nominally in the home. The next step was to secure the mother's cooperation, which often required permission from the father as well. A person from the day-care–center staff, often Stradley herself, went with our research caseworker (Christine DeSaix or Betty Jane Smith) and introduced her to the mother as someone known to the day-care center. The project was presented simply as one in which we hoped to learn more about children from the mountains—how they live and how their mothers feel about things—in order to plan better programs for them. Beyond that, the caseworker was on her own in meeting suspicions and in appealing for cooperation with the study. Nearly every mother approached participated at least to some extent, although a few moved away or withdrew their children from the program for other reasons just as we were beginning contacts with them. Several evaded or refused us. But, the general level of success of DeSaix and Smith in eliciting participation in so extended a study was remarkable to the rest of us.

The final sample, therefore, was of sixty-five mother-child pairs about whom we had substantial data. Nearly all these families had incomes below three thousand dollars per year; none exceeded five thousand dollars; only three were currently on AFDC. So, we had a sample unusually representative of the "self-supporting poor," in our section. Both in its makeup and in the nature of the data collected, ours is a unique sample.

DATA

Information was obtained in three parts:

(1) Each mother was seen by one of our social workers for a series of five to eight interviews. During these conferences, data were collected regarding child-rearing practices and style of family living. A social history on the mother was also obtained. Information

gained directly from the mother was supplemented, whenever possible, by the knowledge of the day-care–center staff or those in county social welfare who knew the family. It became the social worker's responsibility to sustain the mother's contact with our study and to pull together these various sources into her own final judgments about the mother.

The social workers' data took several forms. First, a social history was written about each mother, just as one does in making a referral for psychiatric evaluation or in a child-welfare study. Second, it was necessary to reduce complex observations to standardized, coded form, and it seemed better to us that this procedure be done by the worker herself, rather than by another person making judgments from narrative protocols. Thus, using the child in each mother-child pair as "focal child" for purposes of this study, a Childhood Level of Living Scale was completed on each case. We also needed an exhaustive, standardized description of each mother's personality, and this description was obtained by the research caseworker using our Maternal Characteristics Scale (see Appendix B); we also used a Global Scale for rating verbal accessibility. Finally, we needed a sample of each mother's verbal behavior, specifically her own detailed description of some of her child-rearing attitudes. For these purposes, each mother completed a tape-recorded interview, also with the research caseworker.

(2) Both mother and child were seen for a psychological evaluation by our psychologist, Robert Borgman. Family permission was needed for testing the child, and this permission was generally forthcoming without difficulty. Only three out of sixty-five children were not tested. It was more difficult, of course, to arrange for testing the mother. We needed to have her come to a central place (our office in Franklin) where there was sufficient privacy to permit minimally constant testing conditions, and the trip was threatening to some. The testing itself aroused fear of the unknown, worries about one's adequacy, and anxiety about being "seen into." For all these reasons, testing the mother was not broached until she had established a relationship with her research social worker, whose reassurance, and companionship (and transportation) facilitated her coming to the office to see the psychologist. Most mothers were not overly anxious, but dealing with those who were required alert,

on-the-spot casework, of course. Of the sixty-five mothers in the study, fifty-five completed the testing. Ten did not, and seven of these were known, from other observations, to be well below average in child-rearing standards and other indications of personality intactness. In reviewing our results, therefore, we must bear in mind that correlations between psychometrics and other observations were systematically depressed by this further foreshortening of the range at the "lower end."

Evaluation of both mother and child was done with a standard clinical battery of tests, the sort one expects to find in a mental-health clinic. Because the use of such a battery for this sort of sample is unusual, we will devote a separate section to its rationale and the procedures used later in this chapter. However, in terms of the design, the testing was done "blind" by the psychologist—*without knowledge of the social worker's findings*—to preserve the independence of the psychological testing from other data obtained.

(3) The child was available for direct observation in the day-care center. Such observations are, of course, extremely complex, so again we faced the need to reduce available information to objective, quantifiable terms. Fortunately, we learned of Fanshel and Borgatta's Child Behavior Characteristics Scale (CBC) through David Fanshel of the Columbia University School of Social Work. This instrument, still under refinement at the time, was being developed to help foster mothers observe and "rate" children in their care. Its appeal to us lay in the use of concrete items of behavior readily understood and judged with minimal inference by persons without extensive training. (Indeed, we followed this criterion in nearly all the rating instruments we employed.) Based on factor analyses, groups of items in the CBC were combined into indices.

Each child was also rated with respect to his verbal accessibility and on two other dimensions of interest. The ratings on the CBC and other dimensions were made by the staff of the day-care center. Our research social workers explained the instruments and their meanings to the staff, but the ratings were theirs, and thus also were independent—at least to a large extent—of other data collected.

The person who knew the most about each mother-child pair was the research social worker. Therefore, all her judgments

are mutually contaminated, strictly speaking. However, even for her, many factual items were not subject to distortion by the halo effect or the like. The psychologist, as noted, was given none of the caseworker's knowledge about each mother prior to testing her and scoring the test results; similarly, the caseworker was kept ignorant of the results of the psychological testing until all the mother's data had been scaled and the history written. The day-care–center staff gave information to the social worker, but the reverse flow was minimal until data were in and set down. Therefore, ratings of children by the center staff were made in ignorance of the judgment the research caseworker might have been forming about the mothers. In short, it was not possible to maintain laboratory-type conditions of research in such a setting as ours, but we tried to preserve the independence of key measurements, especially where this procedure was essential to the pursuit of an important, substantive issue. The confidentiality of all information was closely guarded throughout, and we know of no leaks.

PSYCHOLOGICAL TESTING OF CHILDREN

The test battery utilized with the children consisted, basically, of the Stanford-Binet and a few, short projective tests. The Stanford-Binet was employed because it is most appropriate for children in the age range in which we were concentrating, namely, four- and five-year-olds. We were, of course, aware of the thinking regarding the desirability of "culture-free" testing (see next section), but after discussions with fellow researchers in this country and abroad (in Israel and Greece), we decided to stay with the Stanford-Binet in this study. We found no other consistently recommended test for young children which offered precision in scoring. Equally important, we were reluctant to utilize a psychological test which was not already well-known to the person doing our testing in so extensive and expensive a study. Borgman had evaluated comparable youngsters for the State Department of Public Welfare in North Carolina for years before joining our project, had consistently utilized the Stanford-Binet, and recommended it in this instance.

The overall results of Borgman's testing are of interest. The

children's IQs ranged from 65 to 119. The mean IQ for boys was 89, that for girls, 93, and the mean for the total group 91, which is at the lower end of the range termed "normal." Although these scores are somewhat below the average of 102 reported for five-year-olds in the United States, they closely resemble those found in a recent study of 188 Head Start pupils in St. Louis (Oliver and Barclay, 1967, pp. 1175–1179).

Another procedure was designed to assess the child's sense of attachment to his family and an attachment score was computed using a method suggested by Weinstein (1960). Each child was asked seven questions: "Who do you like to go places with the best? Whom would you tell if you were sick? Whom would you go to if you were hungry? Who treats you the best? Who makes you the happiest? Whom would you want to visit you when you grow up? Who makes you do things you don't like?" Two points were given for mention of a parent and one point for mention of other kinfolk, such as a sister or a grandparent. Each child's attachment score was the sum of the points his replies received.

PSYCHOLOGICAL TESTING OF MOTHERS

Doubts have been raised about the validity of psychological tests when applied to persons from lower socioeconomic strata. (Eells, 1951; Reissman and Miller, 1958, pp. 432–439). These doubts center on the claim that most widely-used tests are not "culture free"; the socially deprived person, not having been exposed to the same life experience as the middle-class subject is placed at a disadvantage so that his inherent ability is not fairly represented by the test results. Moreover, participation in the act of testing imposes demands by which they may be unmotivated. They must be willing to concentrate on lengthy tasks without immediate reward or even reassurances. They must also be able to use verbal communication and abstractions comfortably. Such demands are thought to be foreign to the life style of the very poor, who are thought to be action- rather than word-oriented, nonintrospective, unimaginative, and needing immediate rewards for their efforts.

We had our doubts whether the traditional clinical test battery was appropriate to the women in our study. Yet here, too,

we were faced with no trustworthy alternatives. We were intrigued by the Raven Matrices, for example, but at the time of our research, they had not been well standardized, and their precision in scoring was open to serious question. We also faced the logical problem of deciding when a test is truly "culture-free." In principle, one way to find out would be to administer the test to a variety of groups and demonstrate that it yielded the same average score and distribution in every group. But, this procedure would be evidence of the test's being "culture-free" only on the assumption that all the groups were identical on the trait to be measured. How credible is this assumption? We do not know.

So, we abandoned hope of finding a satisfactorily culture-free test at the time we needed it, and preferred, once again, to rely on tests with which our psychologist was intimately familiar and which he had used with comparable groups of women. Whether the evaluations proved valid depended, as in testing the children, on whether our findings yielded correlations with other indices in the study which were reasonable in the light of theory and clinical experience—construct and concurrent validity.

We, who have worked in social agencies serving low-income people, have sometimes been dismayed by the effects of rigidly administered psychometric procedures. If the clinician insists on using the traditional techniques laid down by the test authors (and scrupulously followed by graduate students), all too frequently, the client is upset and becomes resistant to the whole procedure. We believe that regardless of its orthodoxy or the past research supporting it, a testing procedure which makes the subject overly anxious or negativistic is unlikely to prove valid.

Hence, we followed the principle that results are more likely to be useful when test administration is fitted to the population being studied. This procedure raises a meaningful question: Can the unorthodoxly administered tests be given the same interpretation they would be given if orthodox procedures had been followed? This is a fair question and we cannot answer it. Our attention was directed, rather, to comparisons within our *own group,* all of whom were economically and socially disadvantaged to greater or lesser degree. We were looking for relative differences. Comparisons with results of other research could be made later.

The tests employed were, as noted, familiar ones. We used the Wechsler Adult Intelligence Scale (WAIS), the Thematic Apperception Test (TAT), and the Rorschach. Besides the work already done on these tests, our judgment was that, *suitably modified,* they would be more useful than newer alternatives. For example, the Illinois Test of Psycholinguistic Ability seemed too cumbersome to be tolerated by persons of limited attention span, so why adopt it?

The rules below were followed in adopting and adapting our tests. (1) The aim was to avoid losing the subject's involvement by keeping the session as short as possible while still obtaining varied information. The testing session, then, was designed to last less than an hour, during which the subject took several tests, albeit in abbreviated form to keep up her interest. (2) Instructions were as concrete as possible. Rather than leaving the subject at a loss by asking her to make up a story for the TAT, we simply asked her to "tell me what you see here," followed by a set of nondirective probes tapping topics of interest to us. (3) We moved to reduce those phases of traditional procedures that subjects are prone to regard as threatening or which make them feel inadequate. Thus, we did not question the subject's response to an item on the WAIS unless it was necessary to clarify it for scoring; neither did we routinely conduct inquiries about each Rorschach response or push for "elaboration." (4) We geared the order of presenting tasks to handle potential anxiety. Thus, in the WAIS (Wechsler, 1958) (of which we used only the five subtests correlating most highly with the total score) we offered two performance subtests first (block design and picture completion) permitting the mother to remain relatively silent at first. Only then did we follow with the three verbal subtests (comprehension, similarities and vocabulary). Subjects were next asked to take the Gray Oral Reading Paragraphs Test (1955 edition). Since most did these tests fairly well, they regained their sense of adequacy. Next came six TAT cards selected as least complex in terms of the elements in the pictures. Finally, all ten Rorschach cards were presented. And, in the Rorschach, each subject was simply asked to tell what she saw, what each card looked like to her. She was not urged to give additional responses, nor was inquiry pushed unless it seemed impossible to score a res-

ponse without further clarification. Later, the Rorschach tests were scored by the method of Phillips and his associates (1959, pp. 267–285). Despite the limited inquiry, we met with at least 80 per cent agreement for the presence-absence of each type of Rorschach score on each protocol.

We ended with a testing program which resembled the familiar clinical battery but which deliberately deviated from it in mode of administration. We felt we were faced with the choice of adhering to standard, orthodox procedures (which have their obvious advantages) or modifying the methods of administration to reduce complications which might multiply our refusal rate. We opted for a mode of testing which, although unconventional, was not capricious, that is, the deviations instituted were maintained systematically within our own study.

There remains the issue of the comparability of our data to those of others. Later, we shall show that our Rorschach scores yielded associations, most of which are highly expectable on theoretical grounds and are in line with the work of Phillips, whose scoring system we utilized so heavily. But what did we learn about intellectual ability?

The estimated full-scale IQs of these women ranged from 54 to 105. The distribution was symmetrical and roughly normal in shape, with a mean of 79, and a median of 78. In short, half these mothers would be regarded as of borderline intelligence or lower in the current nomenclature of the field. There was no significant discrepancy between the verbal and performance scores, each measure correlating highly with full-scale IQ ($r = .92$ and .86, respectively). Interestingly, the mean IQ of the mothers runs 12 points lower than that of their children, a finding which is in accord with the hypothesis of cumulative deficits in functioning.

Once again, there seems little question that the method of testing intelligence yielded a valid *rank-ordering* among the women. In other words, the testing succeeded in identifying relative degrees of intelligence. We may question how seriously to regard the depressed *absolute* score, namely, depressed as compared with the standardizing population. Similar average scores have been obtained in other studies of disadvantaged men and women (Borgman, 1969, pp. 301–304; Chansky, 1967). Our own opinion is that

a lifetime of deprivation does lead to decrements in problem-solving ability and the like, which is what we mean by intelligence, and that the low median scores cannot be explained away by testing error alone. But, although this assertion is not mere arm-chair speculation, we cannot support it with "hard" data.

6

Psychic Maturity and Maternal Competence

∿∿∿∿∿∿∿∿∿∿∿∿∿∿∿∿

A major issue, perhaps the key to the whole research program, was this: Which aspects of her personality distinguish the mother whose children are receiving relatively good care from those whose living standards are poorer? The sample of families under study was far more homogeneous socioeconomically than most similar study samples are. Therefore, with many social factors held constant, it became feasible to concentrate on variations in maternal makeup.

The standard of care her child is receiving, as measured by the Childhood Level of Living Scale, is taken as an index of a woman's success as a mother. Ability and success, however, are not the same. It is the exception rather than the rule that "all other things are equal" in the real world. Still, if the CLL score were to show expectable correlations with other features of the woman's

personality, we might accept it as a fair indicator of her ability, as well.

Based on preliminary work, as well as general personality theory, we began this major field study with a broad, but definite hypothesis. The hypothesis was that adequacy of mothering is related to overall level of ego functioning, or *psychic maturity*. What does the latter phrase imply? The mature person has at his disposal a *wide range* of operations. He can permit himself to become deliberately primitive from time to time, for he senses that his childlike phase is subservient to the adult parts of his personality, and he can overcome it when he needs to. Such controlled self-primitivization is often inherent in creative work; it is essential to empathetic understanding by a therapist. In well-integrated persons, it remains "regression in the service of the ego." We understand psychic *immaturity* in terms of relative primitivity of ego functioning in form as well as content. Immature persons are justifiably chary of even momentary regression from whatever level they have been able to attain. Intuitively, they question how easily they will be able to shake off a childish stance should they adopt one. The play is too close to their reality. Other immature persons are even more severely limited; childlike functioning is all that is available to them.

There are many ways to look at final data after testing a woman's intelligence. We wanted more than a descriptive number. Intellectual development implies the ability to differentiate the environment cognitively and then to synthesize one's experience of it to facilitate problem-solving. Our view is that intelligence is a force for adaptation.

To assess differentiation and integration of verbal concepts, we administered three subtests of the Wechsler Adult Intelligence Scale to our subjects. These subtests were the three showing the highest correlation with full-scale IQ: comprehension, similarities, and vocabulary. Perceptual-motor functioning was tested by the

two performance subtests also correlating highest with the full scale: picture completion and block design. The results were then projected to yield three IQs: verbal, performance, and full scale.

Some characteristics of the obtained distribution on the fifty-five women involved will be recalled from Chapter Five. The median full-scale score was 78, with the range from a low of 54 to a high of 105. For reasons discussed earlier in the book, we had thought that the performance subtests might yield "fairer" estimates of functioning than the verbal. Nevertheless, the mean performance IQ was only three points higher than the verbal IQ, a difference that did not approach statistical significance. Yet, despite the constricted range of scores, both on IQ and Childhood Level of Living Scale, there were consistent and meaningful correlations between the facets of the CLL and the verbal, performance, and total IQ scores.

The various correlation coefficients obtained ranged from .31 to .53. The cognitive/emotional facet of the CLL correlated more highly with intelligence than did the physical care score. Similarly, the verbal IQ score correlated better than did the performance score. One can speculate about whether these differences were "real" or reflected shrewdness while being interviewed. Either explanation is plausible. But, the differences between rs were not great, and the overall finding is more important: There was a consistent, significant, and moderate correlation between maternal intelligence and the social worker's independent rating of the standard of living of the child. If psychic maturity is reflected in intelligence tests, our hypothesis was supported.

We turn next to an issue of great practical importance. Obviously, when the cultural context is held constant, the mother's intelligence can be shown to influence the fundamental quality of her child's life. Is it possible to pinpoint a score below which the mother seems unable to learn the skills and make the judgments required for minimally adequate care of her youngster? Since the CLL yields continuous scaling, it was not possible to answer this question from our results. One would first have to seize on a CLL score and declare it to be minimal, and this choice we did not make. We know that the bulk of the mothers tested fell between the IQs of 72 and 85, roughly the borderline range. Almost all those testing higher than 85 were offering above-average child care—thirteen

of fifteen did so. Of those testing 71 or lower, nine of eleven were
below average on the CLL. However, the best information on this
issue comes from another study by Borgman (1969, pp. 301–304)
of fifty women referred to him for psychological testing by child-
welfare workers. When the IQ of Borgman's women drops as low
as 60, the mothering is almost always thought inadequate, even by
the tolerant standards held for children on AFDC.

We have come upon a number of cases of inadequate child
care in which the worker seemed either to underestimate or to be
unaware of the mother's severe intellectual limitations. The effort
to treat everyone as an individual, equal before God to all others,
may blind us to the pronounced variations in ability which also
exist. Our data serve to remind the practitioner that even though
intellectual ability is by no means the sole determinant of a woman's
caliber of mothering, intelligence does play an important role.
Indeed, in numerous cases, low maternal intelligence is the critical
factor. Probably, however, it is an asymmetrical variable, that is,
having a mother who is very bright is not as much a guarantor of
good fortune as having a very dull mother is a guarantor of disaster.

PERCEPTUAL ORGANIZATION

The WAIS yields data relevant to style and competence of
cognition. To study the formal properties of perception, we turned
to the Rorschach. We were fortunate to have available the system
for scoring developed by Phillips and his colleagues (Phillips, 1968;
Phillips, Kaden, and Waldman, 1959, pp. 267–285). The advantage to us of his system is that it is founded in the developmental
formulations of Werner (1957) and therefore is directed to the
theoretical issues that most concerned us.

Lack of perceptual differentiation of the environment is
thought to be reflected in Rorschach protocols by form-subordinate
responses (namely X or XF). The mothers scoring low on the CLL
frequently showed these responses ($P < .05$ by chi-square test).
Functional integration responses (Fi), however, reflect synthetic
operations. With respect to this Rorschach variable, we found a
trend ($P < .10$) for the mothers whose children were better off to
give these responses. Both these results are, of course, in accord with

the hypothesis regarding the relation of psychic maturity in general and competence in mothering.

We also examined the protocols for another of Phillips' signs, specifically, the index of primitive thought, which is thought to reveal the kind of leakage, or illogical associations, and the like one associates with thought disorders. However, on this variable, we found a seeming reversal: the mothers who were generally competent showed *more* primitive responses (P < .05). Separate analyses showed that the association was largely due to the relation of this kind of response to the aspect of the CLL dealing with cognitive/emotional care of the child. It was as if mothers giving primitive responses were also better able to empathize with their children's feelings. Such an explanation fits into the concept of maturity as involving a greater range of feeling than does primitive functioning—but our result in this instance was not anticipated and requires further verification.

CONCEPTION OF ROLE AND MORAL MATURITY

Along with its other good features, we associate psychic maturity with flexibility. We do not mean ability or inability to commit oneself, but, as Kounin (1941, pp. 251–282) demonstrated years ago, rigidity and all-or-none reactions are marks of primitivism. Therefore, we look for flexibility in sizing up other people's motivations and in assessing interpersonal situations, in general. From flexibility should follow the capacity to discriminate among people and institutions with whom one has had contact and to vary in feelings toward them. These traits bear an obvious relationship to mothering, so we were anxious to explore their associations to the Childhood Level of Living.

One source of relevant data was the tape recorded interview. This interview was conducted by the social worker, usually in the home, near the end of the history-taking process—that is, after several visits. Most of the interview followed an outline adapted from that used by Sears, Maccoby, and Levin (1957) in their study of child-rearing practices. However, we introduced several questions geared to evoke expressions of feeling. One group of open-ended queries had to do with the mother's recollections of her own

school years: "What did you think of school? Tell me about a teacher you liked or disliked. Tell me about your favorite subject in school." (Quite a few of our subjects had been unwilling scholars and were free to say so as adults.)

Responses to these questions were coded to yield a score for differentiation of feeling toward the early schooling experience. Vague statements of value judgment or flat assertions of like or dislike without elaboration were regarded as most primitive. Given a higher rating were comments about specific aspects of school or people whom the mother liked or disliked. Judged most mature were responses in which the mother articulated her relationship to the person or school situation she had mentioned, going beyond the statement of an attitude to a more complex description.[1]

The electronically recorded interview was also used to assess the maturity with which the subject conceptualized her maternal role. These data came in response to three questions: "Let's talk about mothers—tell me anything you want to say about them. What kind of mother did you think you wanted to be when you were growing up? How did you want to be like or different from your own mother?" Once again, in judging the replies, unelaborated value judgments ("I wanted to be a good mother.") were rated most primitive. Considered more mature were mentions of specific concrete behaviors and even vague generalizations; replies in which specific actions were thought of, coordinated through use of an abstraction or an organizing idea were judged most mature. Once again, we have an index, this time of the level of organization of the conception of the maternal role. Data from the interview clear enough for scoring were available on fifty-seven women.[2]

We were of course interested in the mothers' conceptions of their own roles, but in the present connection, our concern was with the formal qualities of the replies rather than with their content. The two indices, differentiation of feeling and level of organization in conception of mother role, were each correlated with the CLL

[1] Intercoder reliability for the scoring of differentiation of feelings was $r = .90$, for an N of fifty-eight.

[2] Intercoder reliability for scoring of conception of the maternal role was lower, in this instance $r = .74$, and so final scores were decided by resolving disagreements between the coders—De Saix and Donald Boone.

Scale. Both indices derived from the interview yielded correlations in the direction predicted by our hypothesis. The more competent mothers gave more differentiated pictures of their early school experience; they also articulated a more organized conception of the maternal role. Once again, we may say that the hypothesis of a relationship between psychic maturity and success in mothering is supported by the data.

Psychic maturity was also studied with respect to moral development. In assessing this development, we were, of course, not judging a woman's behavior by whether or not it conformed to standards we might value or to those to which lip service is paid in the culture, for instance, abstention from extramarital sex relations and intoxicating liquors. Rather, we followed a conception of moral development similar to Piaget's (1948). According to him, maturity is characterized by recognition of mutuality in which the rights and needs of others are considered along with one's own needs and rights. The mature person recognizes reciprocity, an appreciation that rights are relative.

To assess "moral maturity," the woman's six Thematic Apperception Test (TAT) stories were scored according to the degree of mutuality and sophistication evident. Conflicts which the subject had introduced into her stories were examined to see how they were resolved. If the mother, in effect, denied or failed to deal with a conflict after having introduced it, we scored the response as most primitive. Seen as less primitive were responses indicating simply that the conflictual state of affairs would continue or that the hero of the story would commit delinquent acts or otherwise perpetuate the conflict by his behavior. Judged more mature were responses involving realistic compromise between contending parties, an expectable change in one of the opponents, or the suppression of immediate gratification in the interest of long-range gain.

For example, one of the housewives scoring higher on the CLL told a TAT story about a mother who was "trying to say something to a child which the child does not want to hear." The story concluded with the mother's saying, "I'm sorry you have to hear this. I sympathize with you, but you must listen." Another adequate mother presented a story of a girl who was unhappy because her mother made her work so much and forbade her playing

with other children. She concluded the story, "The mother will be more understanding and let her go play, and the child has to learn responsibilities when they're big enough." Contrast these resolutions with the obdurate fantasies of a couple of inadequate women. "The woman and her husband were having trouble. They were both drunks. He was that way and she followed him." This story ended that the woman "committed suicide or maybe she ended up in a women's institute." Another tale concerned the girl who could not play with other children because "Her mother didn't want to cut her loose from her apron strings." This story ended with the daughter's slipping out, "getting in trouble and having to get married." In the latter tales, we find little notion of give and take toward the possibility of mutual change to bring about a resolution. Of course, an inability to conceive of resolving conflicts through negotiation and mutual yielding is not confined to performance on projective devices such as this one. The inability frequently operates as a deterrent in casework. Such women have difficulty even in conceiving of casework as possibly useful.

The intercoder reliability of scoring the TAT protocols for conflict resolution according to the standards described was .81. The measure was then compared with overall adequacy of child care as evidenced by the total score on the CLL. A correlation (r) of .42 was found, significant at beyond the 1 per cent level. Thus, mothers whose TAT stories indicated moral maturity, defined as awareness of reciprocity and mutual change, were also likely to be offering their children adequate care.

EGO WEAKNESS

The results recounted thus far were consistent with each other and with our overall hypothesis. Structured and relatively unstructured tests, having to do with the qualities of perception, cognition, and thought, showed expected associations with the CLL of the focal child. The mothering behavior correlated with verbal responses to the tests. Marginal child care, as we observed it, seemed typically to be part of a pervasive pattern of the subject's character. One naturally asks, therefore, how long she has shown unadapta-

bility. Could one have predicted inadequate mothering already in her teens, or has she been primitivized later by life's vicissitudes? Of course, those most strongly committed to environmental change as a solution prefer the latter hypothesis.

Drawing this time on information in our social histories, we constructed an index which we termed the EDO—literally, the Education-Dating-Occupation index. For example, remaining in school and achieving more than an eighth-grade education implies at least some persistence in a teen-ager. Working outside the home, typically before marriage, also shows an ability to leave the shelter of the parental household and to report regularly to work. The EDO index included the following: (a) education beyond the eighth grade; (b) engaging in some extracurricular activity while in school; (c) having premarital dating experience with at least one other boy prior to the present spouse; (d) having held at least one paid job for a year or more. These items may seem minimal cutting points for measuring adequacy among suburban teen-agers, but they did have meaning among the low-income rural women in our study. Only four of the sixty-five interviewed, for example, had ever engaged in a school activity beyond the usual class work. Given the shyness, lack of mobility, and age at marriage of many of these women, it was common to have married the first boy one had dated.

The score on Education-Dating-Occupation index was compared against the CLL, using a median test. We found that if the mother had a positive rating on at least two of the EDO factors, she was likely to be above average in her score on mothering ($P <$ .02 by chi-square test). Although the association is not strong, it indicates that marginal mothers were already less competent and outgoing than their peers in adolescence. One possible use of these results is in the realm of prevention. Even for a mother who is presently performing adequately, if her EDO score is low, her standards of child-caring are probably vulnerable. She is more "at risk of child neglect" than the young mother whose history shows lifelong ability to cope.

How did these women come to differ so much in ego strength? One looks naturally to the mother's own family of origin —to the maternal grandparents. Outsiders may lump all of these

folk together as "hillbillies" or the like, but to us, their neighbors, important differences exist within the group, many of which are family traditions which are stubbornly maintained.

History information was used to assess the adequacy of each maternal grandparent. The grandparent was rated inadequate, according to our simple scheme, if he had an educational level which was unusually limited (illiterate or less than third-grade), or if he was reported to have shown psychosocial deviance (for instance criminality, psychosis, alcoholism, extramarital affairs, multiple marriages, or desertion). In a number of instances, the mother's own report was supplemented with information picked up collaterally, often as general knowledge in the community. The relationship of the EDO score to the assessment of the maternal family of origin is summarized in Table 7.

Table 7

EGO-STRENGTH AS RELATED TO ADEQUACY OF THE
MOTHERS' OWN PARENTS

	EDO Score		*Total CLL Score*	
			Above	Below
	0–1	2–5	Median	Median
Both Parents				
Adequate	6	18	17	7
One Parent				
Adequate	5	12	7	10
Neither Parent				
Adequate	14	3	5	12
	(N = 25)	(N = 33)	(N = 29)	(N = 29)

The association between the variables in Table 7 was significant at beyond .01 by chi-square test. The girls from families where at least one parent was adjudged adequate had higher EDO scores than did those with both parents inadequate.

Finally, one might ask whether the relationships sketched are

transitive. If mothers low in EDO came from the inadequate family backgrounds, does the family of origin also predict the CLL? Yes. There is a regular relationship between the adequacy of the maternal grandparents and the woman's score on the Childhood Level of Living Scale, and this relationship is significant at the 3 per cent level by chi-square test. Mothers offering poor care came from the poorly organized families.

There has been much concern, in recent years, with the *cycle of poverty*. Socially handicapped parents are thought to rear their offspring so that they, in turn, become ineffective parents, and the pattern is continued into the next generation. Our results in this geographically stable, substantially homogeneous mountain group are in accordance with this hypothesis, but they go beyond it. The cycle of poverty does not apply to all the poor indiscriminately. Rather, it is most strikingly at work among those who are *both* disadvantaged *and* lacking in ego-strength.

CHOOSING A MATE

Despite their obvious importance, fathers are little discussed in this book for reasons already stated. Yet, it is not out of pure whimsy that we now subsume the issue of the father's capability as a provider under our general examination of maternal maturity. The most important single act a girl takes affecting the lives of her children is choosing—or, if you prefer, accepting—their father. Our earliest pilot studies of neglect suggested that if one overlooks surface manifestations, married couples in our studies were usually well matched with respect to their basic psychological maturity. The husband may be the more obsessive of the two, the wife more hysterical, but childlike men pick out childlike women. The similarity in psychosexual stage is undoubtedly part of what we mean when we say we feel *simpatico*.

Our research offered us the chance for a partial test of this observation. We did not, of course, attempt anything as ineluctible as measuring psychogenetic development, but we did attempt to operationalize the general ability to cope, or to adapt. For the wives, the measure of coping ability was the EDO, used above. With respect to the husbands, adaptability was measured according to

the socioeconomic status (SES) they had achieved at the time of
our studies. We employed the same scale mentioned in Chapter
Four, namely, that devised by McGuire and White, a scale which
had already been successfully applied in the study of powerlessness
and verbal accessibility among adolescents from our area. In view
of the fact that all families were relatively low in income, lived near
each other, and were relatively homogeneous, it may seem strange
we should be scaling them on SES. But even within this group, we
detected a range of scores—let us say from lower-lower to upper-
lower and a few from lower-middle class. Such variations may
seem small when described in writing, but they are impressive in
fact.

Is the woman's premarital social development related to her
husband's current SES? This relation would indicate that her
maturity level was probably influential in her choice of a mate, that
her maturity level might affect her level of child care directly
through her own performance and indirectly through the earning
capacity of the father. The data on this issue were clear. Women
with superior premarital adjustment (as measured on the EDO)
were likely to be married to men scoring high in SES. (P < .01 by
chi-square test).

We already knew that the mother's psychic maturity was
related to her CLL score. The last finding raises an interesting point.
Is the higher score on the CLL due primarily to the father's contribution, economically and otherwise? Having chosen the right
man at the right time, perhaps the question of the mother's maturity becomes irrelevant. One way to study these issues is to analyze the data, taking into account both those constituting exceptions as well as those fitting the rule. This issue was studied by
analysis of variance. We determined the contributions of the
mother's EDO score and the father's SES score to the CLL scaling.
What is the influence of the mother's personality as compared with
her husband's in determining her child's living standard?

The mother's ability, as operationalized on the EDO,
makes a consistent difference. Women married to men above average in SES score higher on the CLL if their own EDO scores are
above average (P < .05 by t-test); but, the same is true among

women married to men below average in socioeconomic status (P < .01 by t-test). The impact of paternal SES, however, is also visible when we look at the mothers high and low on EDO, and both these differences are also statistically significant at beyond the 5 per cent level by t-test. In short, *both* the maternal EDO and the paternal SES independently influence the Childhood Level of Living; furthermore, the effects of the two variables are evidently simply additive. That is, the best scores are those where both mother and father score "high," the worst where both score "low."

We may conclude, therefore, that where marginal child care occurs, both parents are typically inadequate, and the odds are that these inadequacies predated their marriages. Each marital partner has an effect, but since the less competent mothers tend to marry the less competent fathers, it is *not* typical to find a husband in our kind of rural, poverty group who compensates for his wife's incapacity. Rather, it is more common that the child is doubly cheated or doubly blessed. We do not argue that such compensation never occurs, but only that it is not the usual state of affairs statistically, and although we hope for the best, we are mostly indulging in wishful thinking.

From the data presented in this chapter, we may draw the following general inferences.

(1) Even among a group of women as homogeneous as our sample, there is noteworthy variation in the quality of care offered children. This variability is significantly related to the mother's personality structure in respect to her intellectual development, her style of organizing perceptions, and her stance toward moral issues.

(2) Our results further indicate that inadequate child care is more likely than not to be a manifestation of *pervasive* incapacity in the mother. That is, the woman who has had difficulty with such other life tasks as education, employment, and courtship is also likely to be failing in her child-rearing. The evidences of psychic immaturity are widespread. The typical problem in child neglect or marginal child care, then, is chronic and characterological immaturity in the mother.

(3) Those pervasively inadequate women who were offering their children poor care were likely themselves to have come

from families of origin in which living standards left much to be desired. We encountered, in other words, a microcosm of the "cycle of poverty."

(4) Socioeconomic factors introduced by the husbands were also influential in determining the CLL of the focal children in our investigation. The least competent women are more than likely to have married the least-achieving men. This combination results in exascerbating the difficulties of the children involved.

A profile of the mother most at risk of child neglect looks something like this: She is of limited intelligence (IQ below 70), has failed to achieve more than an eighth-grade education, and has never held public employment. She married the first or second man who showed an interest in her, and he proved to be inadequate in his education and vocational skills. She has at best a vague, or extremely limited, idea of what her children need emotionally and physically. She seldom is able to see things from the point of view of others and cannot take their needs into consideration when responding to a conflict they experience. She herself has grown up in a family in which her parents were retarded or showed deviant or criminal behavior.

7

Transmission
of Futility

The results of our exploratory-diagnostic study thus far presented are in accord with a notion that, typically, inadequate mothering is pervasive and ingrained. Speaking psychoanalytically, we can say that it reflects character. Yet, as clinicians, we doubt that any of these mothers asked to grow up childlike. Searching for causal clues in their social histories, we found that the women whose children were living at low standards often, themselves, had parents who betrayed severe psychosocial problems. Speaking broadly, then, we found evidence of the intergenerational treadmill which dooms so many of our poor to continuing deprivation. Thus, we were in a position to take up the next questions: How did the mother become as she was? And, more urgently, what effect was her pattern likely to have on her children? Does the inadequate mother, so often her-

self a victim of the apathy-futility syndrome, produce similar traits in her child?

Questions of this order involve major issues in the study of child development and personality theory.

Irritated in their pocketbooks, the general public has become excited for the past few years about the "cycle of poverty": the phenomenon of families who remain dependent upon public assistance and social agencies for two generations or more. The 19th century explanation for intergenerational transmission of dependency and behavior disorders was heavily rooted in social Darwinism and Mendelian genetics. Volunteer social philosophers, in fact, issued diatribes against the "hereditary pauper." Gradually, evidence has accumulated that environmental influences also play a major role. The emphasis has shifted to the proposition that, "the mother's personality and behavior are among the strongest influences affecting children, and both are affected by her situation" (Herzog and Sudia, 1969, p. 163). Hardly anyone would cavil with this statement; it was a basic assumption in our own work.

Yet, a basic assumption is inadequate theory, especially for practical work. For example, in discussing child neglect, we distinguished between conditions in the home *obviously* and *immediately* dangerous to a child and facets of his care which we believe are *probably* dangerous—now, or in the future—but which we cannot prove. If we are to identify neglect by saying that this type of woman or that type of handling undoubtedly damages the child's personality in the long run, then we need to be able to base our testimony on reasonably definite associations between maternal behavior and consequences in her child. Lewin used to say, "There is nothing so practical as a good theory." This would seem to be the kind of established theory practice requires.

Unfortunately for such simple formulations, research in child development often yields amorphous results. For example, varied consequences in children appear to stem from closely related parental patterns. Studying the aggressive child, Bandura and Walters (1959) found his parents differ systematically from "normal" con-

trols; the nature of the difference reflects their immaturity. Reiner and Kaufman (1959) also call attention to the massive pregenital fixations prevalent in parents of delinquents. As one aspect of their impulsivity, the child's acting out is both condemned and encouraged by parents whose infantile needs are unconsciously gratified by his delinquent exploits. The mechanism proves reminiscent of Bateson's (1956, pp. 251–264) "double-bind" mechanism—but he uses it to explain withdrawal into schizophrenia. Hoffman (1960, pp. 129–143) demonstrated an association between unqualified power assertion by mothers and the child's hostility and resistance to influence in nursery school. Arieti (1955), and Lidz and others (1957, pp. 214–248) report, however, that schizophrenic adults are likely to have experienced excessive domination by their mothers in childhood. In short, the schizophrenogenic parent is described in much the same terms as the delinquogenic. What are practitioners to gather from all these results? Confusion or insight?

Possibly such results lead to an insight, namely, that we cannot insist that for each parental trait there is an identifiable effect on her child. Transmission is never simple and direct; the process is always mediated by the child's personality and his own unique experiences. Nor must we expect each symptom to have its specific cause. Physiologically, we know that generalized stress reactions like shock can accompany heart attacks, broken bones, or emotional upsets. Generalized psychological stress reactions may exist too. Nor, to return to the example given, are schizophrenia and delinquency dynamically disparate. Most of us have seen clients and patients of whom we would say, "If he were not delinquent, he would probably be schizophrenic."

Yet, it is suspicious when results of our researches continue to be diffuse. We cannot believe that all pathology boils down to whether one has had mature parents or infantile ones. One resolution for our dilemma has been to hypothesize that the same parental treatment of the child may have varying effects, depending on the child's age when the damage occurs. Despert (1965), and Peck and Bellsmith (1954) have taken this tack. For example, one might formulate that maternal deprivation in earliest infancy produces schizophrenic withdrawal; if the deprivation occurs at the toddler stage, it results in delinquent behavior. This formulation hypothe-

sizes "critical periods" in ego development analogous to those in
which following response may be imprinted in greylag geese
(Brown, 1965, pp. 32ff).

In short, it would be a great convenience in making professional decisions about child neglect and judicial determinations with
respect to removing children if we had established a series of one-to-
one connections between child-rearing practice and subsequent
pathology in the personality. But thus far, we have established few
such simple and direct associations. Moreover, we can dispute on
theoretical grounds whether we should expect to find them. Nevertheless, we continued to search for specificity between maternal
handling of the child and sequellae in his personality. Our reason
for doing so was simple: If one gives up on the search too soon,
one never knows whether or not it might have succeeded.

MECHANISMS OF TRANSMISSION

The major directions of theory linking maternal personality
and behavior to pathology in the child may be listed as follows.

(1) *The deprivation-detachment hypothesis.* This line of
theory follows the outlines offered in Chapter Three. The infant
desperately requires assurance that the physical care necessary to
survival will be forthcoming. The issue for the infant is whether he
comes to believe that intimacy with his mother will be rewarding or
whether it will be unsatisfying and frightening. The infant given
supplies inconsistently, matures with what Erikson (1950, Chap.
7) calls basic mistrust. To spare himself the pain he anticipates
from reliance on humans, he invokes interconnected defensive maneuvers—refusal to care about other people, withdrawal, and numbing himself. Emotionally, he experiences futility, a feeling that
nothing he does will guarantee affection and security. Behaviorally,
we see lethargy and an unwillingness to act. The deprivation may be
said to lead to detachment.

The deprivation-detachment hypothesis was first advanced
by Spitz (1945, pp. 53–74) and by Bowlby (1962) from observations of infants and young children residing in hospitals and group-
care institutions away from their mothers and without consistent
care by a single person. This formulation has had tremendous im-

pact on arousing opposition to congregate living arrangements for preschool children and in the promotion of foster-family care for those neglected. However, in recent years, much thought is being given to the development of group care for preschool children of working mothers during the day. Thus, the validity of the deprivation-detachment hypothesis is of contemporary relevance to public policy regarding day-care centers and the insistence that mothers receiving public assistance leave young children in order to engage in remunerative employment.

Despite the popularity of the hypothesis that deprivation by the mother leads to defensive detachment in her child, the concept of "maternal deprivation" has never been much better specified than was neglect. Mech (1965) noted that maternal deprivation often has been used synonymously with maternal *separation*. Thus, we are not sure that the detachment of which Bowlby speaks and which Spitz and Wolff (1946, pp. 313–342) observed in hospitalized infants was brought about by reactivation of primal-separation anxiety occasioned by a disruption in maternal relationships that once were satisfying to the child. Another possibility, first noted by Howells (Howells and Layng, 1955, pp. 285–288), is that the psychological consequences for children separated from their mothers is due, not to the separation, but to deprivation of maternal care and affection, either before the separation or following it.

Recent studies testify to the idea that the deprivation syndrome is not invariably associated with separation from the mother. Maas (1963, pp. 57–72), for example, showed that twenty children placed in wartime residential nurseries in England failed to manifest significant personality damage in later follow-up studies as young adults. Other evidence indicates that the same sort of personality damage observed by Spitz and by Bowlby can occur in children who have never been separated from their parents.

Maternal deprivation also has been used synonymously with maternal rejection and punitiveness. That is, passive failure to provide care and affection to the child is often equated with active abuse in which the parent consciously or unconsciously expresses dislike of the child and seeks to wound him psychologically (and perhaps physically) out of anger. The differential consequences of deprivation and rejection for children have been amplified by Gold-

farb (1945, pp. 247–255). According to him, rejection is less likely than deprivation to produce detachment, lack of goal-directed behavior, and lack of capacity for self-insight in the child.

In our formulation of the deprivation-detachment hypothesis, we see maternal deprivation as passive omissions in the care of the child, probably a consequence of the mother's own defensive detachment. We believe that detachment can occur out of this deprivation, regardless of whether the child has been separated from his mother. We do not regard maternal deprivation as consisting of active rejection, although rejection may occur concomitantly with deprivation.

(2) *The stimulus-deficiency hypothesis.* According to this theory, inadequate stimulation of the infant results in a stunting of intellectual development. The hypothesis was given its first strong impetus during the 1930s by Skeels (Skeels and Fillmore, 1937, pp. 427–439) at the Iowa Child Welfare Research Station and was in contradistinction to the view of Terman and others that intelligence was hereditary and unchanging. Skeels demonstrated surprising gains in the IQ scores of a group of orphanage preschoolers who were given more individual attention than was customary while those receiving routine care showed progressive decrements. Spitz (1945), too, was aware of the behavioral and other evidences of emerging retardation among institutionalized infants.

Views differ with respect to why stimulus deficiency leads to lowered cognitive competence. One possibility is that the intellectual stunting is secondary to the emotional withdrawal and other growth-inhibiting states produced by generalized maternal deprivation. The other viewpoint is that the growth of cognitive structures, themselves, requires "stimulus nutriment" in the form of opportunities to interact with and manipulate facets of the external environment. (Experts in progressive education once strongly argued that development requires actual manipulation, but subsequent evidence indicates that even the registering of stimulation passively moves the infant along.)

Much of the current interest in the stimulus-deficiency hypothesis is among those wishing to better the chances of children from socially and culturally deprived circumstances. Although most such investigators have been at work in urban slums, we number

ourselves among them. Deutsch is a good representative of the stimulus-deficiency hypothesis. In interpreting the reasons why children from the slum environment may fail to develop cognitively, he states (1961, p. 361): "The sparsity of objects and lack of diversity of home artifacts . . . in addition to the unavailability of individual training give the child few opportunities to manipulate and organize the visual properties of his environment." Both perceptual-motor and (by a similar reasoning) verbal competencies are deterred since the slum environment lacks a variety of objects and communications systems. Or, if variety exists, the children are not exposed to it in a planful way. This argument is an interesting contrast to the observations by the German sociologist, Simmel (Wolff, 1950, p. 410), who spoke of the emotional shallowness and impersonal relationships which derive from the "intensification of nervous stimulation" experienced by urban dwellers. Plant (1937), more recently, wrote of the urban slum as excessively stimulating, tiring the child. We all seem to agree that cities are bad, but we clearly must rethink some of the classical views of what is bad about them. The most recent view, of course, is that although low-income neighborhoods in the city may be highly stimulating to the very young child, the variety they offer is limited, and, beyond a certain age, they cease to stimulate as compared with a middle-class neighborhood.

The work of Goldfarb (1945), in particular, comes to mind in supporting the point of view that maternal deprivation gives rise to intellectual deficiency which is part of generalized personality damage. He ascribed the difficulty with abstract thinking, which he encountered in children reared in institutions, to two factors: (1) a volitional defect, expressed in a generalized emotional passivity and impoverishment; and (2) an absence of normal maturation and differentiation of the personality. Interestingly, those who regard the intellectual decrement as part of a generalized pathology are not optimistic about its reversibility later in life. Thus, Goldfarb reports little improvement in the intelligence level of institutionally reared youngsters after foster-home placement at ages as young as three. It is, of course, necessary that those involved in the programs for cognitive enrichment of deprived children believe in the reversi-

bility of early damage. But, we recognize a serious question as to how much can be accomplished after the preschool years.

Although much of the research and theory on the effects of low-income living on intelligence relates to urban settings, we have been brought into contact with the same problem in our work, too. We were struck, for example, by the number of homes in which we saw no printed material lying about. We missed not only children's books, but newspapers and even the traditional Bible. Paper and pencil as *toys* to distract a preschooler on a rainy day, if nothing else, were also nonexistent. Especially if the mother were engrossed in the apathy-futility syndrome, the paucity of environmental stimulation was a real issue in many families. For, one can live with nature in a rural cabin, too, and yet learn little about it.

(3) *The deprivation-aggression hypothesis.* The notion that frustration leads to aggression is old in common sense and psychoanalytic psychology. It has traditionally entered into the debate whether aggression should be treated as an instinctual given or is secondary to the failure to meet the infant's nurturance needs. For we expect the inadequate mother to prove frustrating to her infant much of the time.

Levy (1937, p. 643) called attention to the fact that maternal deprivation is associated in children with "various hostile acts designed to punish the one who denies love and to prevent the possibility of its withdrawal." The deprivation-aggression hypothesis was given formal statement and much impetus by the work of Dollard and others (1939). In their formulation, they specifically relocated the source of aggression from an instinctual reservoir to an environmentally elicited drive. Bender also ascribed aggressiveness in children to deprivation. "Since the child is under the impression that adults can satisfy his needs, he considers any deprivation an act of aggression . . . and reacts accordingly. . . . A failure in this regard is a deprivation and leads to frustration and a reactive-aggressive response" (Bender, 1948, p. 360). Bowlby (1946) noted that "an affectionless, psychopathic character given to persistent delinquent conduct" was a possible outcome of early, prolonged inadequacies in mothering.

Widespread acceptance of the common-sense version of the deprivation-aggression hypothesis has been used to explain such

social movements as urban riots. Thus, *Report of the National Advisory Commission on Civil Disorders* (1968) noted: "The handicap imposed on children growing up . . . in an atmosphere of poverty and deprivation is increased as mothers are forced to work to provide support. The culture of poverty that results from unemployment and family breakup generates a system of ruthless exploitative relationships within the ghetto. . . . Children growing up under such conditions are likely participants in civil disorder."

Naturally, this formulation can be oversimplified too. Violence by the parent against the child is much more regularly associated with aggressiveness than is deprivation. Not all hostile feelings by any means are expressed directly—in many people, they take the form of sullen negativism, and the like. But, this remains a plausible and powerful explanatory theory.

(4) *The identification hypothesis.* Broadly speaking, the identification hypothesis refers to the child's modeling his behavior after his parents'. This modelling can occur out of a wide variety of dynamics—learned imitation in accordance with the law of effect; conscious copying; retaliation; or, identification proper in the service of defense.

Freud (1925, pp. 152–170) advanced the notion of identification as a defensive maneuver to counter the anxiety over loss of a love object or to prevent abandonment by a loved person. The child (or adult) incorporates or imitates behavior in order to make that person one with himself, thus maintaining the presence of the other if loss is threatened. This maneuver might be termed identification out of love. Following a suggestion of his, Anna Freud (1946, pp. 117–131) later elaborated the conception of "identification with the aggressor." If one takes the feared object symbolically into oneself, the threatener is less to be feared. For example, Jewish prisoners in German concentration camps took over the manner, and some of the dress, of their guards. This identification resulted from fear.

We have been more interested in modeling that follows on processes of identification than in learned imitation or conscious copying. But, as we have noted, children also take over their parents' behaviors out of simple social learning. When the imitation is based on learning, it follows the general laws relevant to such phe-

nomena. For example, nonreward or punishment extinguishes the behavior. Modeling based on identification does not follow these patterns.

A fair amount of literature now exists regarding ways in which children pick up aggressive behaviors from their parents. For example, several studies (Bandura and Walters, 1959) have shown that the chronically hostile child is likely to have been punished physically by his parents; years later, such a youngster may become an abusive parent. Passivity and withdrawal are also modeled by children, but we came across no studies specifically testing our hypothesis regarding the transmission of the apathy-futility syndrome.

Finally, let us note that we do not equate depriving a child or rejecting him with physical punishment or assaultiveness, although it may have the same ultimate effect. The former has to do with the frustration-aggression hypothesis, the latter, with the identification hypothesis.

(5) *Other mechanisms.* Three other lines of theory are described below briefly. They play lesser roles in our thinking with regard to transmission of parental aberrations. However, they are relevant to research on the process of infantilization reported in Chapter Nine.

The first is the controls-system hypothesis. Adoption and eventual internalization of standards requires loving guidance and consistent patterns of reward and punishment by each parent and by the parents acting in concert. For example, if the mother impulsively punishes the child for lying on one occasion and treats the same action as amusing on another, the child cannot learn. If one parent permits the same behavior the other proscribes, this behavior also creates an ambiguous learning situation. Finally, partial withdrawal of love is the mother's ultimate weapon, and if the child does not feel loved, he has nothing to lose.

The next secondary line of theory is the domination-aggression hypothesis. Presumably, most normally developing children exhibit needs for autonomy and independence as they become mobile. Frustration of these needs is thought to lead to aggression, just as would frustration òf needs for nurturance. Martin Hoffman (1960) demonstrated anger and negativism among nursery-school children handled by their mothers with "unqualified power asser-

tion." The classical experiments by White and Lippitt (1960) showed more hostility within a boys' group handled by an authoritarian adult than in one offered more democratic leadership style. That monumental study of prejudice, *The Authoritarian Personality*, (Adorno and others, 1950) found that people with hostility toward other races and toward persons they perceived as weak or different were likely to have been reared by oppressively rigid parents and to be displacing early resentments outward.

The last secondary line of theory is the domination-passivity hypothesis. The child given inadequate autonomy may develop a self-image of weakness and of having been damaged. Such an image deters him from attempting difficult or unfamiliar tasks and reduces his initiative. Dynamically, the passivity is often thought of as representing a reaction formation against aggression engendered by the domination. Inertness is commonly a spiteful way of foiling the parent. The child exaggerates his weak position into a general ineffectualness, thereby exasperating those responsible for him. Of course, all such discussions of activity-passivity have been rendered more or less obsolete by the recent sophisticated treatment in Rapaport (1967, pp. 530–568), but the clinical implications of his fine integration still have to be worked out.

It has become common, in the behavioral sciences, to place a theory in apposition and opposition to another and then to seek a crucial experiment to determine *which* is true. Although such an exercise may advance a reputation, it does not always advance knowledge. Clearly, in anything as complex as the transmission of traits from one generation to the next, more than one mechanism may be at work in a single mother-child pair at any one time, and a large number of decipherable mechanisms may be involved when we examine a whole sample of mothers and children. Therefore, in listing the genotypes, we do not wish to forward an argument of insidious intent so much as to set the stage for examining the data we shall next present. Every mechanism identified has *a priori* plausibility; each *could* be present at one stage or another in most mother-child pairs. However, it is fair to ask, in a study like this one, which dynamics seem most often applicable to describing the effects of maternal inadequacy on the children in our study. Such a problem is not a matter of theory, but of fact. We return to the results of our empirical work.

8

Impact on the Child

~~~~~~~~~~~~~~~~~~~~~~~~~~~~~~~~~~~~~~~

We have shown that the maternal personality affects the mother's style of child-caring. We now turn to the evidence regarding the manner in which both maternal personality and child-caring seem to affect the child. We had two reasons for studying these relationships: first, the practical and ethical concern of when community intervention into the lives of families who are engaging in marginal child care is justified. In other words, "Does the *child* mind a low standard of living?" Polansky and Polansky (1968) pointed to the reluctance of many agencies to intervene since intervention is usually experienced by the family as an intrusion. Agency reluctance is often rationalized by the belief that below average care is compensated for by an abundance of love or emotional nurturance. But, as we reported in Chapter Two, "poor but well loved" did not usually hold among these low-income families. The correlation between physical care and cognitive/emotional on our CLL scale was +.75. The child provided poor shelter, food, clothing, and medical care was also likely to be disciplined inconsistently, have poor models for parents, and receive little affection and intellectual stimulation.

Our second reason for studying these relationships derived from a theoretical concern. Which of the mechanisms listed in Chapter Seven seem operable among the youngsters in whom we were interested? In this chapter, we attend particularly to hypotheses dealing with deprivation-detachment, deprivation-aggression, identification and stimulus-deficiency.

SEQUELAE IN CHILD

(1) Child Behavior Characteristics Scale (CBC). The reader will recall Fanshel and Borgatta's instrument from Chapter Five. We relabeled their factors with terms that seemed to us more descriptive of their content, for instance, withdrawal, lethargy, sociability, clingingness, and hostility.

(2) Familial Attachment. During psychological evaluation using Weinstein's technique, the youngster was asked to name the person(s) to whom he would turn for satisfaction of various physical and psychological needs. High scores were given to those naming parents or other relatives frequently; those naming no one, or persons outside their families received low scores.

(3) Intellectual Competence. Each child was administered the Stanford-Binet. Procedures were devised to extract assessments of verbal competence and visual-motor skill. Scoring verbal ability drew on the Stanford-Binet and utilized: the vocabulary words for ages five and six; opposite analogies for ages three, four and a half, six, and seven; and the difference question (age six). The correlation (r) of this extracted score with the overall measure of IQ was +.73. Visual-motor development was assessed by asking the child to: draw a square; draw a diamond; draw a human figure; print his name. Each production was scored by the psychologist on a four-point scale according to objective criteria of adequacy. The score for visual-motor skill derived correlated +.55 with IQ.

ASSESSMENTS OF MOTHERS

The level of care being provided the child was judged, as before, by the score on the Childhood Level of Living Scale (the CLL). We also needed to place each mother on each of a series of

psychological dimensions thought relevant to outcomes in her child. To do this, we brought into play our Maternal Characteristics Scale (MCS). (See Appendix B.)

The purpose of the MCS was to encode and quantify observations and impressions of the mother's personality which our research caseworkers were forming. The scale, as finally evolved, included 205 items. Each item involved a specific, observable behavior or trait lending itself to objective appraisal. As with the CLL, items consist of declarative sentences to which the rater indicates yes or no. Our scale was modeled on the admirable Psychiatric Status Schedule developed by Spitzer, Endicott, and Cohen (1963) of Columbia University's Department of Psychiatry. Their instrument, however, is geared to inpatients and involves pathology too severe and usually irrelevant for discriminations in a research population like ours. Therefore, we substituted many items in modifying their idea to our use. Using the ratings made by our social workers, we grouped the items into subscales or indices, which permitted giving each mother a score on a particular dimension. Our grouping was done by a combination of rational and empirical methods, relying heavily on the investigator's judgment of theoretical relevance.

Our selection of major dimensions of maternal personality was heavily influenced by the results of the pilot study of neglectful mothers. The reader will recall that the neglectful women fell largely into two syndromes: the apathetic-futile woman and the impulse-ridden character. The women in the present study were all relatively economically disadvantaged, but hardly any practiced the extremely poor care one could label neglect, even though they varied markedly in the caliber and the style of care they offered their children. We could also scale them on a dimension of *degree* of apathy-futility, but none reached the extreme of several women seen in the pilot study. Thus, we could try to determine whether the presence of many apathetic-futile features in a mother, for example, was associated with qualities in her child which were discernibly different from qualities in a child whose mother showed little evidence of this syndrome. In effect, we converted a syndrome or character-type into a dimension.

Two subscales or indices were combined in order to assess the degree of apathy-futility—a grouping of items labeled detachment and another labelled immobilization. The detachment subscale contained such items as: "daydreams much of the time; gets out of touch with current daily happenings; keeps eyes closed or averted." Items typical of immobilization were: "hair is usually unkempt, tangled, or matted; shows enthusiasm; answers questions by single words or phrases only."

The other maternal dimension studied we called childish impulsivity. This measurement also involved adding the results of two subscales—dependency and impulsivity. Items affirming or discounting dependency included: "whines when she talks; clings to husband in a fearful, dependent way; has at one time shown capacity to hold a job." Relative degree of impulsivity was judged from such things as: "lacks persistence in pursuit of goals; shouts, yells, or screams frequently at something or somebody in interviewer's presence; accumulates savings."

Because our concern was with pathology on each dimension, we gave no attention to the semantics of what the obverse of apathy-futility or childish impulsivity was. Because both represent modes of infantilism, the opposite of either would probably be the same—mature ego-integration. Like the CLL, these scales were so constructed that a high score represents the pathological end of the scale, a low score, the more desirable or "better" end.

Some interrelationships among the measures should be mentioned before we proceed with the results. For example, we assumed that both childish impulsivity and the apathy-futility syndrome would correlate with the mother's relative infantilism. They do. The correlation (r) between the two dimensions was $+.60$.

Judgments about the CLL were made by the same social worker who scored the MCS, so the two are not independent. Still, as noted, a lot of effort went into making these judgments as objective and specific as possible. Both dimensions of the maternal personality examined are indicative of degrees of immaturity, so we should expect them to correlate positively with the CLL (all three instruments give higher scores for the "undesirable" direction). The correlation (r) of childish impulsivity with the CLL was .53; the

apathy-futility dimension correlated higher—$r = .62$. Within the range of the population sampled here, therefore, the hypothesis relating level of care to maternal maturity was further supported.

DEPRIVATION-DETACHMENT HYPOTHESIS

Guntrip (1969, pp. 24f) postulates that the infant most neglected in infancy reacts by becoming "hungrier and hungrier." His desire to possess the object becomes so ravenous he senses it is dangerous, and this feeling leads to his distancing himself from the mother in a syndrome that also includes massive affect inhibition, immobilization, and futility. How do our results accord with his hypothesis?

Attachment to his family, as the child volunteered it, was tested in the interview with the psychologist; the CLL may be taken as a gross index of deprivation. The correlation between the CLL and deprivation offers support to Guntrip's formulation. We found a low but significant relationship between the child's attachment score and his CLL ($r = -.29$; $P < .05$).[1] Does the impact of inadequate care generalize also to the day-care center? The children receiving poor care were adjudged significantly more withdrawn ($r = .42$, $p < .01$) and less sociable ($r = .35$, $p < .01$) by their nursery teachers than those better cared for. Along with the withdrawal, we found evidence of the hunger described by Guntrip in the form of diffuse clinging, which is indiscriminate and unattached to specific personal objects—the sort we all experience with patients fixated at an infantile level. Thus, despite the relationship of withdrawal to poor child care, it also correlates with clingingness ($r = .40$, $p < .01$).

The availability of teachers' ratings on the CBC (from observation of the children) afforded us an opportunity to check the validity of the technique used to measure family attachment. Interestingly, the relationships were as one might expect *among the boys*. The attachment scores correlated $-.37$ with adjudged withdrawal; $+.49$ with sociability; $-.37$ with clingingness and $-.42$ with lethargic behavior. Among girls, these relationships did *not*

[1] Our findings support Leontyne Young's contention that neglected children do not look kindly at the parents who fail them. (See Young, 1964.)

hold. They seemed to compensate for lacks in their families by throwing themselves into school activities. The *less* attached the girl was to her family, the less likely she was to be rated lethargic by her teachers ($r = -.40$). Otherwise, we found no significant relationships between attachment and behavioral traits in the girls. These results will remind the reader of our discussion of the relatively greater infantilization of boys than that of girls in this subculture. Boys seem vulnerable to emotional currents at the ages four and five.

Although it is strange to use a concept like apathy-futility in respect to children as young as four and five, one cannot help but remark the traits which their teachers associated with low Childhood Level of Living scores: withdrawal, lethargy, unsociability, and diffuse clingingness. Theoretically, we have proposed that defensive detachment underlies all of these emotions. Therefore, the sequence of deprivation and then detachment is substantially supported by this diagnostic study.

RESEMBLANCES OF MOTHERS AND CHILDREN

In order to test the identification hypothesis, we had to explore more than one dimension of the maternal personality. We had to show differential effects in children correlating with varying maternal personalities; otherwise, the results would simply imply that children with problems are likely to have mothers who are immature. By examining two modes of maternal immaturity, it was possible to determine, at least, whether a differential association existed between the child's pathology and the mother's.

The correlations between mothers' scores on apathy-futility and childish impulsivity and the teachers' ratings on the CBC are tabulated in Table 8. The traits associated with the CLL are spelled out in the table, plus an additional child characteristic which went unmentioned immediately above, namely, hostile-defiance.

We see that dimensions of the children's personalities associated with the pattern of detachment correlate with the pervasiveness of apathetic-futile elements in the maternal character. However, none of these traits was significantly related to the degree of childish impulsivity in the mother. In other words, detachment in the child

has to do with apathy-futility in the mother but bears no regular relationship to her impulsivity.

Table 8

MATERNAL PERSONALITY CORRELATED WITH THE CHILD'S BEHAVIORAL CHARACTERISTICS

| | Maternal Personality Dimension | |
Child's Trait	Apathy-Futility	Childish Impulsivity
Withdrawal	.33**	.23
Lethargy	.25*	.08
Sociability	−.36**	−.20
Clingingness	.25*	.22
Hostile-Defiance	.17	.42*

* p < .05   ** p < .01

What we find, however, is that the child's degree of hostile-defiance is significantly correlated to maternal impulsivity. Given the errors of measurement probably present, this correlation is noticeable. Thus, even in a sample as homogeneous as this, we detected differential relationships between maternal character and traits in the children, independently assessed.

Do these results demonstrate that the child has been modeling his mother, perhaps identifying with her? This explanation would be plausible, but others are also plausible. For example, we knew that women with high scores on apathy-futility were likely to be implicated in poor child care. Does the detachment in the child result from modeling the mother or from deprivation? We attempted to throw light on this issue by the use of partial correlations. With the CLL held constant, the correlation between the mother's apathy-futility and the child's various evidences of detachment dropped to insignificance. In other words, we only find the reaction in the child via the chain from apathy-futility through poorer child care, not

only what the mother is, but what she fails to do. Hence, we are not pushed to add the identification hypothesis in order to explain our findings. The deprivation-detachment formulation remains the most parsimonious to encompass them.

The findings with respect to hostile-defiance in the child, however, require another type of explanation. We recognize no association between this dimension of child behavior and the CLL ($r = .14$). For our five-year-olds, the deprivation-aggression sequence seemed to play little role. In fact, as one would expect with the CLL held constant, the mother's impulsivity and the child's negativism in the school setting still correlated considerably. These results are consistent with the identification hypothesis; however, they could also be due to the failure of these women to inculcate workable controls in their children, the controls-system formulation. Of the two possibilities, it is our *impression* that identification with the mother's own rebelliousness probably plays the greater role, but this impression is clinical rather than founded in statistical results.

What we have, then, is evidence of differential associations between maternal character and child traits, specifying somewhat the general proposition that infantile women produce children with problems. When various explanations are scrutinized in terms of our data, we again find support for the deprivation-detachment sequence and some evidences of the identification and controls systems mechanisms in explaining negativism in young children. Within the limitations of our studies, we found no support for the deprivation-aggression hypothesis in relation to maternal personality. Rather, aggression in the child regularly accompanies underlying rebelliousness in his mother.

STIMULUS-DEFICIENCY HYPOTHESIS

Not long ago, clinicians, confronted by seeming paradoxes in differential diagnosis of children, came to the realization that many of the same factors in the etiology of a child with emotional problems were also found in a child with a learning disorder. Although different ego functions are at stake, mothers who are unable to ensure emotional certainties are likely to be the same mothers

who do not provide for the growth of intellectual competence. How does the style of mothering contribute to the development of abilities and talents?

The extent to which the general adequacy of mothering (the CLL) correlated with indices of cognitive and perceptual-motor development in the child was surprising. The CLL correlated significantly with overall IQ, verbal skill and visual-motor skill. With CLL partialled out of the other correlations, only that between maternal apathy-futility and the child's IQ remained significant. Apparently, both the mother's freedom from apathy-futility and the caliber of the child's total home situation independently affected his IQ in our sample. Thus far, the results are in accordance with the stimulus-deficiency formulation.

However, the best available evidence continues to argue that IQ is greatly affected by inheritance. We cannot evaluate the meaning of a substantial correlation between the CLL and the child's IQ without taking into account the fact that the intelligent mothers afford the high levels of living. In fact, maternal IQ correlated with *both* the CLL ($r = -.49$) and the child's IQ ($r = +.45$). Again, we attempted, through partial correlation, to assess the relative importance of each factor to the child's development. With maternal IQ partialled out, the child's IQ still correlated significantly with the CLL ($r = -.36$). But, with the CLL partialled out, the relationship to maternal IQ became statistically insignificant. We cannot discount genetic factors in our setting any more than we can do so elsewhere, but such weightings as we have been able to make indicate that the *mother's intelligence influences her child's intelligence only as it is accompanied by a poor level of child care.* Whether this inference is equally valid in a sample of women varying more widely in intelligence than did ours is a problem for future research.

Also of interest was the significant negative correlation between children's visual-motor skills and both the maternal personality dimensions. Of course, these correlations can generally be explained as due to the inadequacies in child care provided by mothers with either type of characterological immaturity. Nevertheless, the correlations are suggestive of some specific psychodynamic speculations.

The correlation between maternal apathy-futility and lowered *visual-motor* competency reflects a general orientation of the deprived child toward immobilization and withdrawal from life. The child's lowered visual-motor skill may represent a general pattern of avoiding participation in nonsocial as well as social activities. But why should maternal childish impulsivity also correlate with greater deficit in the child's visual-motor skills? Perhaps the child reacts anxiously to the maternal impulsivity, and this anxiety interferes with development of his physical skills. Another possibility is that the child adopts his mother's erratic approach to motor tasks, thereby producing clumsiness, confusion, and poorly controlled motoric activity.

The relationship between the CLL and the intellectual factors sampled here is, of course, in line with the results of many other investigators working in urban settings. Our results show that the stimulus-deprivation hypothesis generalizes to our rural mountain culture. The new phenomenon identified is the significant role played by the apathy-futility facet of the maternal personality.

In summary, our data show that the deprivation-detachment sequence is implicated in explaining the transmission of futility from mother to child. Hostile-defiance in the child seemed better explained by a youngster's identification with childish-impulsivity in his mother, rather than by a deprivation-aggression sequence. If deprivation leads to hostility, the child's rage does not seem to find overt expression unless his mother, herself, responds with behavioral manifestations of impulsivity. Finally, our empirical evidence identifies deprivation as a source of deficits in cognitive competency among these low-income, mountain children too.

9

Infantilization

After our pilot study of ten neglectful mothers, our attention was repeatedly caught by the issue of infantilization. Our outstanding impression of those women whose children were receiving the poorest care, was the low level of psychogenetic development at which they were operating. They do not usually present clear-cut symptoms since these presuppose conflict, symbolization, and the ego's capacity to wrap its troubles in a neat package. What we see, rather, is a series of miseries, false expectations, failures to foresee, and lack of skills—less symptoms than manifestations of underlying character problems. We are dealing with an adult who is still, in many respects, a child, and therefore unable to cope with the demands life makes on grownups. It is not useful to think of these mothers in terms of regression, as if they had fallen back from a better level of organization. The fact is that these persons have never advanced.

Subsequently, we have seen that the grossly immature woman may fail to provide her child with experiences by which he

might outgrow her. Thus, we can identify an intergenerational *cycle of infantilization* as another prevalent phenomenon in child neglect. The woman's immaturity invades her mothering, and her own children are prone to emerge as childish people.

This cycle of infantilization is an overall sequence, glimpsed from clinical evidence and correlational studies of distal variables. But, what do we know about the specific transactions out of which infantilism emerges? We indict deprivation; we cite overindulgence. However, statements at so general a level do not advance theory. For counseling parents in a preventative way, they are disastrously smug and nonspecific. In the course of our work, the opportunity presented itself to conduct two interlocking studies focusing on the processes in which we were interested: child-rearing practices by mothers who appear to have those effects on their children that we term infantilizing. The studies, reported more fully in their dissertations by Sharlin (Sharlin, 1971; Sharlin and Polansky, 1972, pp. 92–102) and Borgman (1972), of our group are the substance of this chapter. Let us begin with some conceptual clarifications and definitions.

SELF-REGARDING ATTITUDES

Analysts generally agree about distinguishing marks of the grossly immature personality when encountered among adult patients. In cognitive-intellectual functioning, such a personality reflects an absence of fine distinctions among ideas, a concreteness, an impaired reality-testing, and a limited ability to integrate or solve problems. Emotionally, we remark inability to bind frustration, the raw quality of affect, and the proclivity to all-or-none response. Interpersonal relations are dominated by separation anxiety; lonely clinging substitutes for mature object relations. In his original paper on the infantile personality, Ruesch (1948, pp. 134–144) pointed out that ineptness in resolving tensions realistically through taking action resulted in somatization with consequent disturbances in the gastrointestinal and cardiovascular systems. Infantilism may be said, then, to pervade the whole personality, finding representation in each functional sphere.

The process of infantilization was first given comprehensive

treatment by Levy in 1943. He listed it as one of four forms of maternal overprotection. The others were: excessive contact; prevention of independent behavior; and lack or excess of maternal control. Levy's usage (1943, p. 53) was literal, referring to care given the very young child. "Infantilization consists in the performance of activities in the care of the child beyond the time when such activities usually occur. Infantilization refers also to the continuity of the same type of care ordinarily modified in later years."

We prefer a more generic conception according to the following definition: Infantilization refers to actions and communications by which we encourage another to remain, or to become, less competent and self-sufficient than he might otherwise be—to act as if he were a young child, helpless, fearful, selfish, and at the mercy of his impulses. We do not, however, limit the conception to mother-child interaction. One need not be chronologically young in order to be infantilized. We regard it as appropriate to recognize women who "infantilize their husbands," a pattern not uncommon in mountain families.

The substance of Levy's conception is interpersonal. Fixation describes a vicissitude in the investment of libidinal energies, but by infantilization we have in mind a relationship through which this inappropriate persistence of investment is made more likely. Because the conception is an interpersonal one, motivations in both persons concerned come under scrutiny. Infantile personalities succeed in inducing complementary indulgences from those who remain intimately involved with them. And, of course, the mothers or others articulating with them are having their own needs met. Speaking conceptually, we cannot assume that one partner to the interaction is the victim of the other.

Despite the significance infantilization has to clinicians, few empirical studies on its explication have been done since Levy's germinal writing. Of course, an enormous literature exists dealing with effects of child-rearing practices on limited dimensions of the child's personality, such as dependency (Hartup, 1963; Yarrow, Campbell, and Burton, 1968), self-reliance (Baumrind, 1967, pp. 43–88), aggression (Bandura and Walters, 1959) and the like. Closest to our interest was the study by Baldwin and others, reported in 1949, in which they devised a Babying Scale. Mothers

rated high on this scale were said to "actually underestimate the child's level of ability—or, they may find it more convenient to control his behavior by keeping him in a relatively helpless state" (Baldwin, Kalhorn, and Breese, 1949, p. 8). Not unsurprisingly, these studies contain contradictions; conflicting results testify to the difficulty of finding an optimal balance to foster growth.

We organized the approach to data-collection along another avenue. We noted that gross immaturity in the adult personality finds its reflections in cognitive, affective, interpersonal, and even somatic spheres. It is also expressed in the bizarre blend of arrogance and self-abasement which often accompanies the syndrome. It seemed worthwhile to us to attend seriously to malformations in self-regarding attitudes. In infantilization, the mother communicates to her child her own perception of his worth and abilities. Rightly, and sometimes wrongly, the youngster infers her perceptions from her actions as well as her words. What he thinks she wants of him invades his perception of himself. Therefore, we thought that the process by which mothers and children become pervasively fixated might fruitfully be conceptualized in terms of the crucial intervening role of self-regarding attitudes.

We began by reviewing treatment experiences we and colleagues have had with immature adults, especially with neglectful mothers. We found self-attitudes which seem common to many. Such attitudes usually come across in the way the patient treats himself, and we have to infer them; but, occasionally, they are conscious, formulated, and openly expressed.

Briefly, the patient acts as if he feels: "I am helpless"; "I am weak"; "I must be careful"; but, at the same time, "I am too perfect to fail." Underlying such feelings is an insistent voice within him, experienced as not quite his own, saying: "You are still a part of your mother"; "You are fragile and easily damaged"; but also, "You are—or should be—special." The cost of being special is to be defective and weak; and the price for an illusion of fusion with one's mother is to be an indistinguishable personality.

What are the consequences of these feelings in the evolving person? One effect is bodily incoordination, which is common among infantile characters. The clumsiness may be attributed to generalized difficulty with integration, but a structural explanation

does not allow for the dramatic improvements we see in response to shifts in dynamics. Infantilized persons show lack of confidence in using themselves ("I am weak"). Another effect is the failure of infantalized individuals to acquire skills. Because failure is such an insult, their attitude is, "If at first you don't succeed, the hell with it." ("I must be perfect.") So, they are unable to practice.

Other clinicians will add their observations and their own permutations to those we have sketched here, and we do not urge that other explanations of developmental arrest are irrelevant. We do emphasize, though: (1) that the self-image of the infantile person is distorted in predictable patterns; (2) that these self-regarding attitudes have been influenced by communications from the mother; and (3) that they articulate with other inadequacies that are common, albeit not universal, in persons with such character structures. Briefly, we postulated a deviant maternal role in which a mother infantilizes her child. The child plays into this role with pathological complementation; he obliges his mother by failing to develop to his fullest.

STUDY DESIGN

Subjects were recruited from among children seen at the Developmental Evaluation Clinic of Western North Carolina, in Asheville, through the cooperation of B. H. Hartman and his staff. This service is free for exceptional children under public auspices. The child population served comes from socioeconomic strata similar to those we had been studying. However, those served are likely to be retarded, which of course, introduces an important new variable.

The study was planned as a follow-up of youngsters seen between one and two and a half years previously. So, while cooperating in our research, the family was offered a service in the form of a reevaluation. Of those approached, 85 per cent cooperated fully; most of the others had objective reasons for nonparticipation. Fifty-two mother-child pairs were finally included.

The children were chosen to be between seven and twelve years of age on follow-up. All were being cared for in their own homes. They were also selected to be mildly to moderately retarded,

that is, in the range from one to three standard deviations below the mean (Heber, 1961, Table 3, p. 59), or from 52 to 84 in IQ. At follow-up, median IQ was 64; median mental age, 6.03 years, with a range from 3.8 to 10.0 years. According to Hollingshead's scale (1958), the sample was nearly entirely working or lower class. In fact, over half the families were in class V and forty-four of the fifty-two were in classes IV and V.

Information was obtained from both mother and child. We began with a social work interview in the home, largely covering child-care practices. Subsequently, mother and child came to the clinic, where the child received psychological and other examinations, the mother was further interviewed, and both were seen for a situational test. We were interested in data regarding: the criterion for having been infantilized; communications from mother to child; direct observation of mother-child interactions; and an estimate of the patient's gross motor coordination.

EXECUTIVE FUNCTIONS

We have noted that infantilism tends to pervade the whole personality and to be visible in various aspects of the ego. However, for purposes of study, we examined only a limited number of facets at once. Our first study, by Sharlin, dealt with ego functions most involved in dealing with one's environment, namely, the executive functions. We shall report on this study first.

How shall we decide which parental behaviors are, in fact, infantilizing? We may use two approaches. We may observe the child-caring and label what we see. It will be recalled that Levy labeled infantilization care given the infant beyond when it is age-appropriate. An alternate approach is to look for sequellae in the youngster as evidence that he has been infantilized. Those patterns of child-rearing empirically associated with the criterion are inferred to be infantilizing. We follow the latter logic here.

To operationalize *having been infantilized,* we needed a measure which would be objective and independent of data on the mother. Each subject had, of course, had previous psychological testing. Retesting was done by Borgman, using the Wechsler Intelligence Scale for Children. Test-retest correlation between our

results at follow-up and those of previous testers was +.72, validating the whole testing program.

The IQ reflects development of capacity in proportion to chronological age. A lowering of this quotient indicates failure to continue development at the expectable rate. Of the fifty-two subjects, thirteen gained, four remained the same, and thirty-three dropped. The average decrease was 4.5 points (from 69.8 to 65.3). Hence, we set as our criterion of having been infantilized a relative drop in IQ of five points or more. In other words, the criterion for having been infantilized in intellectual spheres was a decrement in IQ greater than average.

The aim of this pilot study was to learn how the self-regarding attitudes that deter development are communicated. We undertook to see what could be discovered by interviewing the mothers. We designed an interview outline to probe areas of child-rearing—feeding policies, practices at bedtime, supervision—in line with hypotheses about dimensions of maternal behavior which seemed relevant and feasible to study through mothers' reports. Questions were open-ended, and the interviews were coded subsequently, without knowledge of the child's status on the criterion variable, of course.

In order to observe directly mother-child interaction, we used a standardized situation which would appear to the participants a part of the reevaluation procedure and also be likely to induce relevant behaviors. A situational test was devised for the clinic visit in which the child was given a series of four puzzles, graded in difficulty, to be solved in the presence of his mother.[1] Instructions to the mother about whether or not to intervene to help her youngster were deliberately ambiguous. A complete process record was kept, using precategorized data sheets and narrative protocols.

One dimension to observe was suggested, oddly enough, by the fact that many immature adult patients watch the therapist's expression closely. In the test situation, the child was seated at a low table. Nearly all mothers chose a seat behind the child, so we

[1] We are indebted to Rebecca Johnson Stradley, director, Hillcrest Head Start program in Asheville, for assistance in pretesting and for valuable suggestions for format.

could easily count the number of times a child "looked at" his
mother while saying nothing. This visual clinging we termed
mother-relatedness in the study. Children who silently looked at
their mothers four times or more were above the median of the
present sample.

The situational tests were also scored for maternal zealousness. Sixteen mothers remained passive during their children's work
on the puzzles, but the other thirty-six intervened to help in varying degrees. Their actions ranged from offering suggestions verbally
to showing the child the solution by doing the task for him. Levels
of intrusiveness were subjected to scalogram analysis, yielding a
94 per cent coefficient of reproducibility. The probability of chance-
ordering, estimated by Polansky's method (1960), was .001.
Hence, the mothers could be dichotomized between those high
versus those low on zealousness in this setting.

We mentioned our hypothesis that attitudes toward the self
prevalent among infantile personalities are related to physical coordination. We composed a Gross Motor Coordination Test from
a set of indicators which the clinic, following Ozer (1967), was
already employing during neurological examination. The eight items
in this scale range from "throw a ball" to "skipping" and "tandem
walking." The scale adopted proved easy for our youngsters: about
60 per cent passed all items. Still, the scale was independent of
chronological age and did prove to have interesting psychological
correlates.

MANIFESTATIONS OF INFANTILISM

We postulated that infantilism is a single constellation with
reflections in a variety of ego functions. Taking the intelligence
test as a reasonable index of general intellectual development, we
defined *having been infantilized* in terms of relative decrement in
IQ.

Several features of the operational definition should be kept
in mind as we present our data. First, the relative drop in IQ is
a *difference score,* not an index of level of intellectual functioning.
In this study, the size of the decrement was not correlated to absolute mental age. Second, all these youngsters were substantially

below average on their initial test scores. Therefore, one must not confuse IQ decrement with "regression toward the mean"; our decrements signify the opposite. Finally, experienced researchers will be conscious of the constricted range among children in our sample. Typically, the more constricted the range, the harder it is to overcome measurement error and demonstrate substantive relationships. Let us begin by comparing the IQ decrements with two concurrent measures in disparate ego spheres.

(1) IQ Drop and Physical Incoordination. We postulated that one reflection of infantilism is poor physical coordination because of a sense of one's own tenderness and the dread of failure. Although the idea seems reasonable, we do not know that it has ever been shown. Is it true among children, all of whom are intellectually below average?

Large-muscle skills were assessed with the Gross Motor Coordination Test (GMCT). Of those youngsters who held their own in IQ, 70 per cent passed the GMCT; of those whose IQs declined, 46 per cent passed. The difference is significant at .05 by chi square test.[2] These results support the conception of infantilism as pervasive.

(2) IQ Decrement and Visual Clinging. One dimension selected for study out of the situational test of mother-child interaction was the form of visual clinging which we termed mother relatedness. We predicted infantilized children would show more mother relatedness than those without this problem. Of the children whose IQs dropped, 65 per cent were above the median; of the non-infantilized children, 38 per cent were above the median. The difference was significant at beyond .03, confirming the hypothesis. This result further supports the conception of infantilism as typically pervasive. And, just to complete the triangle, we should add that children high on visual clinging were also likely to be poorly coordinated physically (P < .01).

To our knowledge, the associations among these distal variables have not previously been reported. Taken together, they encourage acceptance of the validity of measuring infantilism

[2] Unless otherwise specified, all associations in the predicted direction report one-tailed tests.

through IQ decrement as we have done in analyzing the data presented below. Let us turn next to data regarding the maternal communication of infantilizing self-regarding attitudes.

To begin with a broad overview, we asked whether and to what extent we could predict the IQ decrement from child-rearing attitudes revealed in the totally independent interviews with mothers. We dichotomized our group into the twenty-six who showed a relative drop in IQ and contrasted them with the other half who—relatively speaking—held their own. After having been coded without knowledge of the youngsters' IQ scores, interviews with the mothers were analyzed in search of variables which associated to infantilism.

Even within the constricted range of the sample, our success in identifying relevant variables far exceeded chance expectancy. Of thirty attitudinal variables coded, nine showed differences in the direction predicted at beyond .05; another eight showed "trends" (significant at beyond .10). From these seventeen variables, we derived a composite scale made up of forty-two specific behavioral items. Each item was then assigned a simple + or − weight, depending on whether or not it was positively or negatively associated with infantilism in the child. (We give the Infantilization Scale in full in Appendix C.)

The scale gives us a composite view of the process of infantilization in one particular group and permits us to determine the *extent* to which the IQ decrement was predictable from the maternal interviews. The Infantilization Scale correlated $r = +.59$ to the size of the IQ decrement; this correlation was significant at beyond .01. In other words, the greater the infantilization, the more the IQ declined between initial testing and our follow-up study. As one would expect, the scale also associated significantly to mother-relatedness in the situational test ($P < .05$). We also found a negative relationship between large-muscle coordination and infantilization by the mother ($P < .02$). Obviously, we had considerable success, in an exploratory study, in identifying relevant child-care dimensions.

But, is the mother infantilizing, or is she responding to the youngster's helplessness? We must recall that the correlation was not to the child's absolute mental age but to his relative *change* in ability, which we took as evidence of infantilism. Another conclusion we may draw from the findings relates to the direction of the infantilization. The danger of infantilizing the youngsters in this sample lay *more in maternal overconcern than in overdemandingness*. This result is not always the case.

COMMUNICATING A SELF-IMAGE

We propose that infantilization may be understood as a process in which the child's self-regarding attitudes are shaped by his mother. From reviewing immature adult patients, we formulated four "messages" from their mothers which they seem to have partially incorporated into their self-concepts. These are: (1) You are part of your mother. (2) You are fragile. (3) You are special. (4) You are unlovable. Although these attitudes are not semantically consistent with each other, they are not psychologically discordant. We commonly find them compresent in immature patients. Let us now go beneath the overall Infantilization Scale, therefore, to examine how each of these messages is communicated to the young child through his mother's behavior and attitudes.

(1) You are part of your mother. A number of responses in the interview may be taken as indicative of the mother's own resistance to separating herself. One way in which this resistance came through was in discussing the father's role. More infantilizing mothers reported that their husbands took no part in caring for the infant than noninfantilizing mothers; more also described the father as inconsistent in discipline. Of the fifty-two women, ten reported never having left their handicapped children, with a babysitter or otherwise; eight of these paragons had youngsters whose IQs declined.

We also inquired whether another adult, other than the child's parents, was significant in the child's life—a teacher, a neighbor, or a relative. According to their mothers, 58 per cent of the noninfantilized children had such contacts in contrast to 19 per cent of the infantilized children ($P < .01$). We constructed a pic-

ture of a mother unable to share her child. The reasons for this timorousness must lie within her own personality, of course (Polansky, Boone, De Saix, and Sharlin, 1971, pp. 643–650). It is consistent with an inference of maternal separation anxiety that whereas 77 per cent of the noninfantilizing mothers had had employment outside the home for over a year at some point in their lives, less than half the infantilizing mothers had such jobs.

(2) You are fragile. Three concerns among the infantilizing mothers appeared to communicate to the child a sense of his own vulnerability; close supervision (keeping the child always in the yard); the conviction that the child often hurts himself; and—oddly enough—a reluctance to spank, which was occasionally attributed to fear of harming him. Of eighteen sets of parents who did not spank the child at the time of the interview, thirteen had youngsters whose IQs declined; ten of the twelve who had never been spanked showed decrements. It seems to us doubtful that intelligence can be raised by repeated pressure on the bottom, so we infer that it is the attitude expressed by nonspanking that warrants scrutiny.

(3) You are special. The sense that he has been chosen is a mixed blessing to the infantile person. Does it mean he is atypically bad? Or uniquely good? This issue is particularly poignant for the person with a defect.

Very few youngsters in our sample were only children, so we were able to ask most mothers to compare rearing their handicapped child with caring for his siblings. An interesting pattern of response came through. The infantilizing mothers showed a mixture of indulgence, denial, and some complaining.

In describing their children, the noninfantilizing mothers made more openly unfavorable remarks about the handicapped youngster. They were also more openly critical, for instance, of the child's annoying behavior at mealtimes. Infantilizing women, however, were more likely to give in to the child's demandingness and to be more permissive toward misbehavior. No wonder significantly more infantilizing women report the damaged child harder to rear than his siblings than noninfantilizing mothers. One might broadly characterize the noninfantilizing mother as both more realistic and more even-handed. Infantilizing women deny their irritation; they treat the retarded child as "special"—and burdensome.

However, we found no clear evidence of a blatant statement to the child that, "you are unlovable." Nearly all these children are loved. Based on the present research, we can only conclude that the sense of worthlessness which accompanies infantilism can be based on the *reintrojection of hostile impulses* as much as on response to reading the mother's unconscious message.

STIMULATION

Finally, we picked up some leads in this exploratory work which may involve maternal attitudes but can be interpreted parsimoniously in terms of the theory of cognitive stimulation. One finding, for instance, confirmed findings of other investigators. Youngsters placed in regular classes in the schools were *less* likely to show an IQ decrement than were those in special classes. This difference was significant at beyond .05, using a two-tailed test, since it was not predicted.

We also queried the mothers on whether they had played much with their child when he was an infant. Half the infantilizing mothers report *never* playing with the infant, as compared with less than a fifth of the noninfantilizing. Again, we see the pattern of an anxious, unstimulating relationship.

The data regarding stimulation are fragmentary since they were peripheral to the study. But, we were intrigued to discover discernible effects of cognitive stimulation in a sample of children of whom all are borderline or mildly retarded and in their later childhoods.

Let us summarize our findings thus far. Infantilization is defined as a process in which a person is encouraged by another to become, or to remain, less competent and self-sufficient than he might otherwise be. The resulting infantilism is, typically, pervasive of the personality; it has manifestations in a variety of perceptual and executive ego functions. We explored some dynamics of the process from the point of view of how self-regarding attitudes are shaped in the course of mother-child communications. We investigated these dynamics within a group of borderline and mildly retarded children. However, the conception of infantilization is intended to be broadly applicable.

The operational definition of "having been infantilized" was a drop in the intelligence quotient greater than average between two testings. Two concurrent measures were found significantly related to IQ decrement: poor large-muscle coordination and visual clinging to the mother in a task situation. These relationships among distal variables support the postulate that infantilism is usually pervasive. An extremely childish person can, conceivably, be highly gifted in one or more areas, but that case is exceptional.

Through interviewing mothers about their child-rearing practices, the mechanisms by which limiting self-attitudes are incorporated were studied. We showed that a drop in IQ was predictable from a composite scale of child-rearing practices, demonstrating the existence of such a relationship in principle. We posited self-regarding attitudes which appear to be taken over from the mother. The children who were objectively identified as having been infantilized had mothers who often transmitted three messages: "You are part of mother"; "You are fragile"; "You are special." We did not find evidence, in this sample, of transmission of the other attitude also common among grossly immature patients, namely, the sense of being worthless and unlovable.

We have long been aware, clinically, that environments which are undernourishing as well as those which are overindulgent both deter psychological growth. Among these mothers of handicapped children, we found a tendency to err toward solicitousness rather than demandingness. One should remember in counseling parents of the retarded that the mother unable to separate herself from her child may well exacerbate an existing handicap. The study strongly suggests concrete guidelines for work with such mothers. Those children did better whose mothers were even-handed and realistic in assessing their limitations, who shared the child with others, and who could be firm and even use spanking when indicated.

MORAL REASONING

Sharlin's study dealt with infantilization from the viewpoint of the *content* of the mother's child-rearing behavior as it affected the child's self-attitudes and thereby certain aspects of his executive

functions. Borgman undertook to examine a related problem, the development of moral reasoning in the child from a *structural* point of view. Take, as an example, the mother's spanking or not spanking the child. The issue in Borgman's approach was not whether spanking is an effective or desirable way of disciplining a child. Instead, he focused on the fact that spanking is to be seen as a relatively primitive mode of disciplining because of its concreteness, as a motoric form of expression and its evidence of failure to find an integration of the mother's needs and her child's. Reasoning with one's child would appear more mature than spanking, from a structural standpoint, because it embodies abstractness and ideational expression.

Borgman's study investigated the relationship between the maturity of the child's moral reasoning and the (structural) maturity of the mother's conception of child-rearing. Maturity was described according to the principles of Werner (1957) and Piaget (1948), mentioned earlier in this book. For present purposes, primitivity is characterized by vagueness, concreteness, motoric expression, and egocentricity. Relatively mature thought and behavior manifests greater differentiation, integration, abstractness, ideational expression, and allocentrism.

There are three approaches to forecasting the relationship expected between the maturity of the mother's conceptualization of child-rearing, and development of the process of ethical reasoning in her child. Each of the three has *a priori* plausibility and a history of theory and research to support it. The approaches are not mutually exclusive since each contributes to understanding the child's developmental process.

(1) One approach predicts no substantial relationship between maternal child-rearing conceptualization and the child's maturity of moral reasoning. This position we term the *internal-maturational* model. This stance is taken by Terman, who wrote (1916, p. 11), "Moral judgment or any other kind of higher thought process is a function of intelligence. Morality cannot flourish if the intelligence remains infantile." A similar position was taken by Kohlberg (1964) as the result of his research on moral reasoning in children. He concluded that maturity of moral reasoning was largely a function of advancing age and intellectual level in the normal child.

(2) Another approach predicts that a direct relationship exists between maturity of the maternal child-rearing conceptualization and the maturity of the child's moral reasoning, provided that the general intellectual competence of the child is held constant. This viewpoint we term the *sociological-learning-theory* model. Sociologists, such as Davis and Havighurst (1947) and Hollingshead (1949) were among the first to note that certain kinds of values are class-linked. The notion was that the child acquired parental moral values through social learning and the identification process. In Chapter Eight, we presented evidence that this identification mechanism was operable in regard to a child's defiant behavior. Possibly, the parental conception of child-rearing sets a model for the child's conception of all social relationships, which then manifests itself in his moral reasoning.

(3) The third approach predicts an interaction between maturity of maternal child-rearing conceptualization and the level of the child's moral reasoning, depending upon the general cognitive level at which the child is functioning. That is, no simple relationship between maturity of the parent's child-rearing conceptualization and the child's ethical judgment may exist, but, a significant interactional effect may be present. This view appeals to common sense. We all know of books and professors who talk over the heads of their audiences; likewise, we know of those who mistakenly talk down to their listeners. Optimal communication depends on a match between what is presented the individual and his capability to comprehend. This view was supported by Turiel's experimental study (1966, pp. 611–618) of the acquisition of moral concepts.

Perhaps a four-year-old child is likely to develop a more mature view of the meaning of stealing than he hithertofore held if crisp rear-end pressure is applied, rather than an attempt at a reasoned discourse on honesty. But, does this hypothesis hold true for a seven-year-old? The interactional hypothesis implies that parents need to shift the maturity of their child-rearing conceptualization as the child grows in order that he may develop optimal maturity about ethical choices. Can parents do this? *Do* they do it?

Before we move to a description of the empirical study of these propositions, we should clarify what we mean by "maturity of moral conceptualization." Specifically, we mean the maturity of the

reasons or *concepts* the child uses in making a choice about some ethical issue. Maturity is again defined by the systems of Werner and Piaget, which regard egocentricity, vagueness, concreteness, and so forth, as more primitive than allocentrism, abstractness, and social integration in one's moral ideology. For example, giving "fear of the police" as a reason for not stealing is more primitive than the idea that "it is not fair to the victim," because of the greater concreteness and egocentricity embodied in the former. Thus, we are concerned with the reasons or concepts used in justifying moral choice rather than with the conduct of the child.

Whether maturity of the child's moral conceptualization is, in fact, related to the conduct he exhibits is an empirical question beyond the scope of this study. Those interested in this issue are referred to the admirable review by Kohlberg (1964). Suffice it to say that the evidence shows that children with the mature moral concepts behave in conventional ways regarding simple moral choices such as cheating in the classroom.

The research reported here utilized data from the same mother-child pairs who participated in Sharlin's study. However, two mother-child pairs were eliminated in this study because the child was unable or unwilling to respond to the instrument for assessing his moral maturity. Hence, the total sample was reduced to fifty children between the ages of seven and twelve at the time of the research.

ASSESSING MATURITY

The subjects were presented with seven short vignettes involving issues of moral conduct in the areas of stealing, destructiveness, lying, bearing false witness, and assaultiveness. The stories were written by Borgman, following a Piagetian format. They were intended to capture the child's interest by using situations familiar to him. The sentences were deliberately short, the wording concrete.

After each story, the subject was asked to tell why the story's hero (or villain) was good or bad, what should be done about him, and why. These three questions were intended to tap the child's ideas of right and wrong, his notion of sanctions, and his concept of justification for sanctions. One such story was as follows:

Mary asked her mother for ten cents to buy some candy. Mother said no, but when mother wasn't looking, Mary went into her purse and took out ten cents. She went outside and dropped the money in the dirt and couldn't find it. Was Mary bad? Why? What should mother do to Mary? Why should she do this?

The child's responses to these questions were scored for degree of egocentrism, concreteness, and impulse domination, on a four point scale. The scores for each were summed across all questions to yield a grand total, reflecting the general degree of maturity in moral conceptualization for each child. The higher the score, the greater the maturity in moral reasoning. Intercoder reliability was r = +.87 for total scores.[3]

To assess the maturity of the mother's child-rearing conceptualization, we used twenty-five of the same open-ended questions used in Sharlin's study, but with a different kind of scoring system. The twenty-five questions dealt with the mothers' conception of social experience for the child, her differentiation of her child, parent-child relationships, and the mother's concept of the maternal role. Responses were scored on a four-point scale, according to the degree of egocentrism-allocentrism, concreteness-abstractness, and vagueness-differentiation/integration embodied in each.

Generally speaking, the most primitive replies were those in which the mother evaded the issue presented or indicated that she ignored completely the behavior or feelings of both herself and the child. The next level was characterized by concrete, "mother-centered" responses. The third level consisted generally of abstract and "child-centered" ideas. At the most mature level, the mother indicated that she tried to handle the issue by some integration or compromise between the needs of the child, herself, and other parties involved.

For example, one question was: What kind of things do you praise Johnny for? Answers such as "nothing" or "everything" were deemed most primitive. Praising the child for things that were convenient for the mother, such as making his bed or dressing quickly, were considered to be at the next level of maturity. Approval for

---

[3] We wish to thank Donald Boone for assisting in the check of inter-coder reliability.

a skill the child had developed, such as reading well, was considered at the third level. Credited for the greatest maturity were responses involving integration with other people, such as being kind to a neighbor, or being brave in the doctor's office. Interrater reliability for this scoring system was only r = +.75. Therefore, the scores used in this analysis represented consensual judgments by the two raters. (High scores meant great maturity.)

CHILD-REARING CONCEPTUALIZATION RELATED TO MATERNAL
MATURITY

The first step in validating our measurements was to determine whether the mother's child-rearing concepts were correlated with other independent evidences of psychic maturity in her character. One reason for this step was to rule out the possibility that her answers might simply reflect her response to the general maturity of her child. Only after establishing the construct validity of the measurement of their level of conceptualization could we move on to test our main hypothesis.

In Chapter Six, while studying a group of low-income mothers in a rural county, we found the mother's psychic maturity reflected in her previous achievements in school and at work. Would related measurements of our new sample of women replicate the earlier findings? The mothers were given Education-Employment scores based on history information acquired while interviewing them. A low score, for example, indicated a woman who had less than a seventh-grade education and who had never worked outside the home.

A median test of the educational-vocational score was then run against total score on maturity of child-rearing concepts. Striking differences emerged. Of the eighteen women in the lowest third on education-employment, only two were above the group median on level of conceptualization. Of the sixteen mothers with the best education-employment histories, thirteen were above the median in conceptualization. The association was significant beyond .01 by chi-square test (2 d. f.).

We have also commented on the relationship between a woman's maturity and the socioeconomic status of the man she married, from which we inferred that the women in our rural

county married men similar in development to themselves. Was there a relationship between husband's social class and the present index of maternal maturity? The median test shows a striking difference between women in Class V and in the other classes in our study. Of mothers rated Class IV or higher, 74 per cent scored above the median; however, only 30 per cent of those in Class V scored above the median (P < .01 by chi-square test).

Of course, all these results are reminiscent of the relationship between social class and intelligence. Does class reflect intelligence in an open society, or does class membership give one the values and vocabulary to score well on standardized tests? One could say that the beliefs and attitudes about child-rearing rated here are class-linked, rather than indicative of maternal personality. We doubt the former explanation if only because it is not what we had in mind in making our predictions. We recognize, however, that it cannot be ruled out here or in analogous findings.

Our previous research had also shown that many indices of intrapsychic maturity are associated with readiness to verbalize important feelings—verbal accessibility. Therefore, we would predict a relationship between VA and the mother's level of conceptualization. Again, the relationship was strong in the predicted direction and significant at beyond .01 by chi-square test.

However, the evidence is against the notion that the level of conceptualization found in a given mother's answers is a response to her child's developmental level, rather than an expression of her own character. The correlation (rho) between the child's mental age and his mother's level of conceptualization was an insignificant +.08; similarly, we found no relationship to the child's chronological age (rho = −0.08). From the data available, therefore, we concluded that the mother's conceptualization was determined more by the sort of person she is than by her reaction to her child's condition.

MATURATION OF MORAL REASONING IN CHILD

As expected, increasing mental age and chronological age (regardless of IQ) are accompanied by an advancing maturity of ethical judgment in these retarded children. Rank-order correlation between mental age and maturity of moral reasoning was +.46

(p < .01); between chronological age and ethical maturity, as we assessed it, the correlation was +.29 (p < .05).

Nevertheless, children of primitive overall mental development are occasionally capable of abstract, allocentric moral reasoning, but they do not seem to choose to use it as frequently as children with greater cognitive competence. For example, eight children with mental ages below 6 gave at least one response indicative of abstraction and allocentrism, including a child with a mental age of only 4.14 years!

In order to control for these maturational effects in the development of the child's moral reasoning, we divided our sample of fifty children in half at the median of mental age. Because the median of mental age was 6.03 years, one group represented retarded children of *school-age* mentality. This group contained the generally mildly retarded youngsters as well (mean IQ = 72). The other group consisted of children of *preschool* mentality, who also happened to be more severely handicapped mentally than the first group (mean IQ = 57).

Our findings suggest that the general maturity of the mother's child-rearing concepts is connected to the maturity of her child's moral conceptualizations, but in an interesting fashion.

For the twenty-five children of school-age mentality, the more the mother used differentiated, abstract, and socially integrated concepts of the parenting function, the more likely was her child to use allocentric, abstract concepts in his moral reasoning. Eighty-three per cent of these children with mothers above the median in maturity of child-rearing concepts showed moral reasoning above the median for their group. In contrast, only 23 per cent of children with mothers more primitive in child-rearing concepts were above the median in maturity of their ethical conceptualization (p < .02 by Fisher's Exact Test, two tailed). The relationship is *direct*.

What about the twenty-five children of preschool-age mentality? In this group we found an *inverse* relationship between the maturity of the child's moral reasoning and maturity of his mother's child-rearing conceptualization. The more primitive the mother's ideas about rearing the child of preschool mentality, the more sophisticated the child's ideas about moral choice relative to his men-

tal-age group. In this group, only 25 per cent of children with mothers above the median in sophistication of child-rearing concepts were above the median in maturity of moral conceptualization. But 77 per cent of children with mothers below the median in maturity of child-rearing ideation were above the median in maturity of moral concepts (p < .05 by Fisher's Exact Test, two tailed).

In short, we found need for a match between the level of thinking about child-rearing the mother finds most comfortable and the mental age of the child in order that the child will develop in moral reasoning. Apparently, children whose mentality is at school age and beyond profit from a model of thinking about human relations that is differentiated and abstract. But, the child of preschool mentality whose mother is sophisticated does not find her an effective model. More primitive children seem to do better, relative to their own group, with mothers whose own ideas are unsophisticated, according to our operational definitions.

The idea of appropriateness of match received further support from a final set of data, to which we turn next.

MATERNAL ZEALOUSNESS AND DEVELOPMENT OF MORAL
REASONING

Part of the procedure in the clinic, it will be recalled, was to put mother and child together into a kind of situational test. The child was given puzzles to solve; his mother usually sat behind him while he worked. The child was observed for mother relatedness, operationalized as visual clinging. His mother was also being observed and rated on what we termed maternal zealousness. This rating was based on a scaling of the amount of help she proffered her child while he was working on the puzzles. Sharlin found no clear relationship between the index of maternal zealousness and the child's infantilization as measured by decrement in IQ.

Borgman used the same scaling in studying the relationship between maternal child-rearing attitudes and the child's moral reasoning. Among the children in the lower half of the group, those with preschool mental ages, he found no relationship between the variables. However, among the children with mental ages of six and

beyond, he found a relationship. Mothers who were below the median on maternal zealousness had children scoring higher on moral maturity. That is, 77 per cent of those mothers who intruded little into the child's problem-solving had youngsters above the median in maturity of moral conceptualization; only 25 per cent of those *above* the median on zealousness had children above the median on moral maturity (P < .05 by Fisher's Exact Test, two-tailed). These results imply that the mother who permits freedom encourages sophisticated moral concepts in her child, provided the child's mentality is capable of making use of such handling.

CONCLUSIONS

While studying marginal child care and child neglect, our attention was drawn repeatedly to the phenomena of infantilism. Markedly infantile features are ubiquitous among parents involved in neglect. In fact, we discerned an intergenerational cycle of infantilization, underlying the cycle of neglect, in which a woman's immaturity pervades her mothering, and her children are prone to emerge as childish people. The concept of infantilism and the processes of infantilization acquired increasing theoretical and practical significance for the problems with which we had begun.

Surprisingly, we discovered that, despite the familiarity of these conceptions among dynamically oriented clinicians, hardly any quantitative studies bearing directly on them existed in the literature. As part of our overall research program, therefore, we conducted a study of fifty-two preadolescent children and their mothers, recruited through an agency serving the mentally handicapped in our area. That these children are retarded introduced new issues into our work, of course. The advantages of the sampling, however, lay in the possibility of joining a clinical service to the research effort and thereby securing optimal cooperation from families: The families were to a large extent comparable to the population of working-class mountaineers with whom we were already so familiar.

The research entailed a variety of measurements and incorporated two phases. One, spearheaded by Sharlin, dealt generally with effects of child-rearing attitudes and practices on the de-

velopment of certain executive functions of the ego. The other, by Borgman, was focused specifically on the child's development of moral reasoning, according to the tradition exemplified by Piaget.

We have referred to the child's level of living as an expression of his mother's overall level of functioning. Implicit was the conception of infantilism as typically pervasive in the maternal personality. This conception was supported here in findings which not only deal with a new sample, but with children rather than adults. Such relatively distal variables as clinging to the mother, gross physical coordination, and relative decrement in IQ were found significantly associated with each other.

We hypothesized that maternal attitudes and practices influence the child's pace of development. Even in this sample of mildly and moderately retarded children, a substantial proportion of child-rearing variables examined related significantly to the criterion of having been infantilized, and these variables were summarized in the form of an Infantilization Scale. Of course, we did not expect the same items to prove predictive for all children under all circumstances. However, the scale illustrates that, in principle, a discernible relationship exists between child-rearing practices and infantilization. We made an advancement toward analyzing and specifying some of the processes of infantilization and the intervening self-attitudes the mother encourages.

We studied, of course, handicapped youngsters. For them, the infantilizing mother appeared to err on the side of overconcern and overindulgence. We do not believe this behavior is the only way infantilism is produced. Among the grossly immature, neglectful mothers we studied, the predominant danger appeared to have derived from *lack* of caring and attentiveness in their own poverty-stricken families.

The second phase of the study, albeit in a limited sphere, offers a potentially exciting advance beyond the first phase. Borgman turned up evidence indicating that, as far as moral reasoning is concerned, the child's development is facilitated by an appropriate *match* between his mother's style of approach to child-rearing and his own general level. A mother's style may be too sophisticated for her child if he is still primitive. But, beliefs about child-caring that foster structural growth at one stage may be infantilizing at another.

Hence, in order to foster optimal growth in ethical reasoning, parents need to move in tandem with the child from primitive to mature notions. Such movement requires perceptiveness and flexibility in the parents. We are reminded of an earlier finding, again reported in Chapter Six, that mothers offering adequate cognitive/ emotional stimulation showed *primitivity*, as well as integration, in their responses on the Rorschach. It is as if the adequate mother can deliberately primitivize her thought processes to deal with a younger child—in the service of the ego. Based on that theory, the mother with good ability to conceptualize should have done well, regardless of the mental age of her child. Unfortunately, the current study does not show her as so responsive when she is "doing what comes naturally." Especially if she has the added puzzlement of dealing with a youngster who is handicapped, to whom the folklore about normal children does not apply, the mother needs help and guidance in her child-rearing.

Of course, the pattern of many women is so fixed that intellectual help is of little use. A truly infantilizing mother cannot change herself by a simple act of will, so we need to understand the dynamics of her overconcern (Polansky, Boone, De Saix, and Sharlin, 1971). Levy regarded maternal overprotection primarily as a reaction formation against unconscious rejection of one's child. In our work, we are more impressed with the role of the mother's own unresolved separation anxiety. She clings to her child in direct expression of her own horror of loneliness. Of course, the two mechanisms are not mutually exclusive; it is simplistic to attribute the need to infantilize solely to one ego mechanism or the other.

We see, then, that the best way to interrupt the cycle of infantilization is to help the mother grow up so she may become less needful of having a helpless child, more perceptive, and more flexible. Ideas about how to help such mothers will be given in Chapter Twelve.

10

Verbal Accessibility
in Diagnosis

Considerable evidence exists that the roots of futility lie predominantly in experiences of early childhood. Related attitudes may be further reinforced by one's subculture. But the suggestion is strong that the feeling of futility, like many other pathologies, is part of an intergenerational cycle. Mothers with markedly apathetic-futile elements in their personalities rear youngsters who, already by ages four and five, show stigmata of a profound detachment. How can this cycle be interrupted? In the last chapters, our emphasis is increasingly on clinical issues.

At the time we write this work, the chief protection of rural mountain children who are at risk of neglect or marginal care is the corps of child welfare workers and caseworkers attached to their county social service (formerly welfare) departments. Research is not action; at its best, research yields guides to action which improve effectiveness. What can we tell these caseworkers?

Practical help does not call for an effervescence of creative new ideas or radically new approaches. As the farmer said, explaining why he never sought out his county agent, "Shoot, I *already* know better how to farm than I'm doing now!" The immediate need in welfare departments is for concepts and techniques that are suited to work with a poverty clientele spread out in a rural area by available personnel. The principal method of changing standards of child-caring will probably continue to be protracted contact, mostly in one-to-one relationships and mostly with the mothers. Such contact will exist whatever the service program comes to be known as in the future.

As of now, there is a chronic scarcity of fully trained staff in the front-line positions of public welfare in our mountains. The workers who are there are frequently shrewd and dedicated; as a group, they are noticeably less job mobile than those in comparable roles in the cities. What they need are techniques that are sufficiently precise and describable to be meaningful to practitioners who have talent but limited academic training. At the same time, technique must be based in knowledge and theory that are also credible to sophisticated workers. Reducing casework to specific behavior does not mean watering it down. There is no advantage to a method that is readily teachable if it does no good. We hoped that the concept of verbal accessibility, which had occupied the senior author over a period of years, might integrate the kind of knowledge needed.

VA IN PERSONALITY

Verbal accessibility (VA) is defined as the readiness of the client to communicate verbally and to permit others to communicate with him about his most important attitudes. This dimension of personality has been mentioned twice earlier in this book. Inaccessibility is a noteworthy feature of the apathy-futility syndrome described in Chapter Three. And, in examining subcultural influences within the mountain area, we found that girls tend to be more accessible than boys; VA was also related to class status and perhaps to geographic isolation. Despite differences among social strata, however, strong individual differences remained. We now discuss the relationship of VA to other facets of the character.

A client's VA can be observed incidentally, without any special effort, in the regular course of casework contact. One would have to be obtuse not to notice it. Most of us would regard the dimension as diagnostically significant if it seemed a reasonably stable facet of the person being interviewed, that is, if it did not fluctuate wildly from one interview to the next or depend too much on who was doing the interviewing. Polansky (1971, especially Chaps. 8 and 9) has previously summarized a series of researches demonstrating the stability of VA as an attribute of personality. In one study, the subjects were emotionally disturbed boys in a treatment institution. By scrutinizing histories submitted at the time of admission, it proved possible to predict how accessible the boys were going to prove in casework treatment fifteen months later. Other children were seen in groups in a guidance clinic as part of the intake process. Observations of how they organized their play and of their capacity for self-observation proved predictive of their VA in *individual* treatment, months later. So sometimes, the variable *is* stable and central enough to be predicted over time.

Results of Rorschach testing indicated that, among the boys in the treatment institution, a youngster's VA was linked to his general level of ego integration or personal maturity. A study was also done of preadolescent boys out in the community. It was anticipated that those who were delinquent, or delinquency prone, would be lower in VA than nondelinquent youngsters, and in fact they were. Even among paranoid schizophrenics studied in a state hospital, those whose pathology was rigid and widespread proved lower on VA than other paranoid schizophrenics who retained some flexibility.

There has also been some success in making predictions from knowing the client's VA. Hollis (1966, p. 66), for example, found that the client's readiness to discuss feelings in his first interview was predictive of whether or not he would continue for five interviews or more. VA had also shown promise for predicting the success of student social workers in subsequent field placements; and openness of communication has been shown to be a positive prognostic sign for screening potential student nurses.

So, the client's VA is a facet of his character stable enough to *be* predicted and to serve as a basis *for* prediction. At least this

is what we had learned in previous research. The question was whether such generalizations would hold in the new population being studied here.

Any concept used in a varied series of studies has, or usually ought to have, more than one operational definition. In Chapter Four, for example, several alternative paper-and-pencil methods for estimating VA were described. Each mother in our major diagnostic study was well known to her research social worker. Therefore, the estimate of VA that seemed most appropriate was derived from ratings by the worker. These ratings were made in two ways because of our interest in the concept. We rated mothers first in the form of a composite index and then in a simple, Global Rating.

The Composite Index of the mother's VA was extracted from the pool of items judged on the Maternal Characteristics Scale. (See Chapter Eight.) Forty-eight items were thought relevant to measuring VA, including: "Evidences a (verbal) negative or discouraged attitude toward her future accomplishments or attainments. Speaks in a faint voice, or voice becomes weak and fades away at end of sentences. Verbalizes shame. Shares problems with husband." The research caseworker recorded either an affirmation or a negation on each statement.

The Global Rating of VA was made on a six-point scale for spontaneity and depth of communication. This scale was devised originally by Polansky and Weiss (Polansky, 1971) for scoring the VA of emotionally disturbed boys in casework. It proved valid in subsequent research applications.

Two issues were involved in ratings on the Global Scale. The first issue was the subject's spontaneity/responsiveness versus reticence. The second issue was the significance of the attitudes she was willing to discuss. The aim was not simply to rate verbosity or to give a high rating for circumstantiality. Bearing in mind, then, the "depth" of the content, the scale points were: (1) spontaneous verbalization; (2) spontaneous with caseworker's explicit encouragement; (3) responsive, equal give and take with the caseworker; (4) receptive, little give, lots of take; (5) unresponsive, complete

lack of response despite explicit encouragement; (6) avoids or evades verbal expression.

Using the same scale as the caseworker used, a Global Rating was also made by the psychologist, Borgman, on the basis of his contact with the mother during the psychological examination. The examination took place in an office, away from her familiar surroundings, in what many mothers experienced as a stress situation. Nevertheless, the correlation between the psychologist's ratings and those of the caseworkers was significant ($P < .01$), albeit moderate in strength—$r = +.42$. The interobserver reliability of the Global Scale was also studied in the research on infantilization reported in Chapter Nine. Each mother was seen in the home for an interview and was subsequently also seen in the clinic by Sharlin while her child was being tested. In thirty-one cases, the home interview was done by a different worker than the clinic interview, which was usually done by De Saix. The correlation between these two sets of ratings was $r = +.69$ ($P < .01$), which is as high as one might expect. In short, the interobserver reliability of the Global Scale has been encouraging when used by those familiar with it. Concurrently, these results indicate that the mother's VA remained stable, even with two different interviewers.

A comparison was also made between ratings on the Global Scale and the mother's score on the Composite Index, which was from the same caseworker. The correlation between these two ways of recording the judgment of VA was $r = +.77$ ($P < .001$). This result indicates good correspondence, but some variance is unaccounted for. For a variety of reasons, our most valid measure on the mother in the present study appeared to be the Composite Index. Unless otherwise specified, this measure was employed in the associations reported below.

Finally, we would like to have had some check on the extent to which the Composite Index was influenced by the mother's willingness to talk. Women who simply will not say anything inevitably score low on VA; yet, we did not want the rating to be based entirely, or even primarily, on volubility. The best independent measure we had of a mother's verbosity was the tape recorded interview. We simply counted the number of lines in the typed transcript of her participation. In this study, there was no correlation to the Com-

posite Index. If nothing else, therefore, we have reassurance that the worker's were not unduly influenced by verbosity alone. The child's VA was also of interest to us. Their VA scores were based on the Global Scale.

MATERNAL VA AND PSYCHIC MATURITY

Previous studies of VA had strongly suggested that it reflects the overall level of maturity of the personality. However, none of the previous research had been done with a sample of adults chosen from the normal population of the community. What did the present research show?

(1) Cognitive/intellectual development. Intellectual competence is not the same as maturity. Still, one expects that level of ego functioning is also reflected in IQ. The correlation between VA and IQ was +.32 among these women. As one might have expected, verbal adeptness played the greater role of the two. The correlation between Verbal IQ and VA was +.40, between performance IQ and VA, +.22, which was not statistically significant (P < .10). We hypothesize that the relationship between IQ and VA is one of interdependence. Those who lack adeptness with words are undoubtedly inhibited from trying to express their feelings; but, the failure to verbalize unquestionably deters development of thought processes through the internalization of language (Vygotsky, 1962).

In the present connection, we pursued some of the other indicators of cognitive maturation considered also in our discussion of the personality correlates of adequacy as a mother. The differentiation of feelings expressed on the tape recorded interview with regard to school was compared with ratings of VA. (It will be recalled that the interview was coded independently of the worker who conducted the interview.) The correlation was r = +.33, significant at beyond the 1 per cent level of confidence.

Differentiation of role relationships was estimated by examining the TAT protocols. The score was simple and direct: How many times had the mother used kinship terms in talking about the pictures administered? Mothers scoring high on VA (scored by the Global Rating) were likely to use kinship terms, especially the words "mother" and "husband and wife" (P < .02 by chi-square). We

had also devised a way of scoring differentiation of conception of the maternal role, which is described in Chapter Six. Scored on a scale in which replies containing specific actions, coordinated through use of abstractions, were weighted higher, maternal role conception correlated with her VA at $r = +.36$ ($P < .01$). Obviously, many of the personality measures found to be associated with the Childhood Level of Living Scale also relate to the mother's VA.

(2) Other evidences of ego-strength. We had also adapted from Phillips (Phillips, Kaden, and Waldman, 1959, pp. 267–285) a way of rating the woman's achievements by the time of her late adolescence. This rating involved coding her educational, occupational, and dating patterns, as she gave them in her history, into the EDO score. The women who reported schooling, public employment, and dating experience prior to marriage were higher on VA ($P < .02$ by chi-square test) than those who reported none of these. Synthetic functions also entered in, according to our data. Thus, the functional integration responses on the Rorschach, scored according to Phillips' procedure, were associated at beyond the 5 per cent level of confidence to the mother's VA as judged by her social work researcher.

A number of these measures seemed mutually contaminated. That is, one would anticipate that the person who is verbally accessible would also obtain superior scores on various scales in which the data are all based on verbal behaviors. For this reason, one index was particularly interesting—the "loneliness score." Loneliness was introduced as an issue into our investigations because of the clinical and theoretical considerations detailed in the chapter on desolation.

The psychologist scored TAT stories for: (1) expressions of loneliness; and (2) the primitivity of these feelings. A tale in which the woman described the protagonist as lonely, forlorn, forsaken or rejected, *with no explanation of why the person felt that way,* was scored as primitive loneliness. Other stories rated lonely had a character who was disliked, rejected, or left out. Degree of primitivity was assigned on the basis of accepting responsibility for being alone, as contrasted with blaming those outside oneself. Seventeen of the fifty-five mothers did not mention loneliness feelings at all. Results show that the mothers who expressed more primitive loneliness and

more loneliness feelings on the TAT were otherwise scored by their caseworkers as *less* accessible verbally (P < .01 by chi-square test). Since, in this instance, the expressions of loneliness came from women who were otherwise regarded as verbally inaccessible, they cannot be regarded as artifacts of simple openness. Substantively, of course, the presence of such feelings among mothers unwilling to describe their feelings reminds us that the wellsprings of inhibited speech have much in common with the roots of futility!

(3) Competence as a mother. In view of the other relationships, a further question comes to mind: Did the verbally accessible mothers appear to be providing a more adequate level of child care than the verbally inaccessible mothers? Both ratings were, of course, derived from judgments made by the same caseworker, so they are not independent. However, as we have shown already, each dimension (namely VA and the CLL scale) has given evidence of validity when checked against independent observations.

The correlation of VA with the overall standard of care being offered the child, (the total CLL score) was r = +.47 (P < .01). As one might have suspected, the correlation was higher with the cognitive/emotional facets of the scale (r = +.58) than with the Physical Care sections (r = +.38), but the latter was also statistically significant at beyond the 1 per cent level.

Because both maternal intelligence and VA correlate with the CLL, one might wonder whether the latter relationship derived simply from the woman's higher intelligence. However, with the mother's verbal IQ partialed out, the correlation between the CLL and VA was still +.33 and highly significant. Something about maternal competence that goes beyond her intelligence score, as such, is picked up by observing her readiness to communicate feelings in interviewing her.

INFLUENCES OF HOME ON CHILD

What does the mother's VA tell us about what to expect of her child? Is it encouraging to know the child has a mother who is open in discussing feelings? During previous research, we had speculated that, for each individual, verbal accessibility is probably determined to a noticeable extent by identifications with parents. Both in clinical practice and from observations during these investi-

gations we observed many instances of strong family patterns with respect to VA—whole families that seemed unusually open and others in which no one seemed able to discuss important attitudes at all. Yet, as always, we also observed exceptions to the rule; one person in a silent family might prove surprisingly communicative. Haring (1965), in a study of adolescents entering casework in a youth-serving agency in Cleveland showed a correlation between the adolescent's VA and the mother's VA; the association was stronger for daughters than for sons. Prior to the present research, however, we had no opportunity to get comparable data on family patterns from any "normal" group.

In our study, the child's VA was rated by the day-school teacher on the Global Scale. This rating was compared with the caseworker's judgment of maternal VA on the composite index, made independently, of course. The association was significant by chi-square test at beyond the 5 per cent level of confidence.

We believe this effect is produced partly by processes of identification with the mother and partly reflects outcomes, in these four- and five-year-olds, of other aspects of the home atmosphere, including the total security of his family life. Ratings of the *child's* VA by the nursery-school teacher and, again independently, the psychologist were both significantly associated with the CLL score given the home by the caseworker (P < .02 and < .05 respectively by chi-square test).

We may infer that there are discernible effects in children as young as four and five of the home atmosphere associated with a verbally inaccessible (or accessible) mother. Under the conditions of this field study, the effects were statistically significant, but not very strong, and their meaning remains unclear. However, they are compatible with the idea that her VA is a surprisingly sensitive and efficient indicator of the mother's general maturity and effectiveness.

IMPLICATIONS FOR PRACTICE

As we have done in western North Carolina and north Georgia, Looff identified nonverbalism as almost a cultural trait in the area of eastern Kentucky where he did his work. But he, too, noted that many individuals were more open than were others. Not

only do our observations accord with his, but we have been able to identify some of the sources of individual differences and their possible meanings with respect to the total level of maternal functioning.

Looff cites a theory of Ford which may link familial reticence to pathology. Ford postulates that, in this subculture, the family system is held together by bonds of obligation, not necessarily by affection. Children are taught to maintain closeness and to avoid confrontations that might disrupt family unity. Therefore, when strain develops and affectional ties are lessened, the pressure is great not to discuss grievances. Looff concludes (1971, p. 86), "Presumably, then, the most severely strained families would show the greatest lack of verbal communication." Ford's theory (Polansky, 1971) is reminiscent of our own explanation of restraints against communication in the service of the fusion fantasy. More important, since Ford's theory was arrived at independently of our work, it is compatible with the observations we have made regarding the relationship between the CLL and the child's VA as observed in the school setting; it will also be recalled that the verbally inhibited women reported a deep sense of alienation and loneliness.

According to our statistics, the woman at greatest risk of marginal child care is also likely to be least verbally accessible. Can such clients be reached by a "talking treatment"—meaning casework? For reasons to be set forth in detail in Chapter Twelve, we think so. Many inadequate mothers can be helped to become open as a step toward their treatment.

The attitude that "talking treatment cannot be applied" has even been extended to apply to all contacts with the poor. We middle-class professionals are said to be "unable to communicate" with the poor. Although we encountered a number of difficulties in our studies and field work, almost none of them had to do with "inability to communicate." Because, once again, we were spitting into the wind of conventional wisdom, this fact troubled us somewhat. Were we being obtuse? What were we missing? But then, we came across unexpected corroboration in a report by Jeffers of her own experiences as a participant observer in a public-housing project in the heart of Washington, D.C. Like us, she had felt no great problem of being unable to talk with those about her, nor did she feel

the need to pretend a special language adopted from her surroundings. "Poverty, more often than not, does not foster niceties of language any more than it fosters the development of social graces. The problem is not one of having to speak a different language but of being willing to listen to what is said and to respond with respect and sincerity" (1967, p. 121). Amen! And, who among us has been middle class all his life? For how many generations back? There is more than a little snobbishness in the idea that we cannot "communicate" with the poor.

11

Exercises in Futility

Having examined some of the legal, theoretical, and clinical issues surrounding marginal child care, the obvious next step was to study its treatment. We saw two ways to go about such a study. One way, probably the better way, was to establish our own treatment program and see what we could do toward bringing about change in mothers at risk. However, we did not have the resources to mount such a program, nor were we in position to make the major life commitments involved. The other alternative was to study the treatment efforts of others already engaged in child-welfare work and see what could be learned from their successes and failures.

We shall now report, therefore, on another study in our series. In this study, we set out to investigate a sample of reasonably representative cases carried by reasonably representative workers from reasonably representative counties in western North Carolina. We assumed that either planfully or intuitively these workers had tried a variety of approaches in working with the people who interested us. We hoped that by a systematic scrutiny of their efforts, some generalizations would filter out, which could be used in help-

ing others. Of course, we brought to the study a background of previous research, built up over several years, and a theoretical system, which might hasten the process of finding guides to treatment.

In most of the rural counties, the person directly in contact with the typical neglect situation is a welfare worker, more often than not, female. She usually has had little or no formal training in the practice of social casework, and the supervision she receives varies from shrewd and supportive to nonexistent. If the case is beyond her, she often has no other resources. For better or worse, our worker *is* the county's child-welfare resource.

We chose six counties in Appalachian western North Carolina. Because the counties vary in their economies, we made an effort to make the selection representative with respect to this variable. We constructed an index of economic status, ranking the counties according to the sums of their ranks on the following criteria: per capita income; per capita sales-tax collections; percentage of the population receiving public assistance; and per capita expenditure for public assistance. The six counties selected represented all levels of prosperity, from relative poverty to relative affluence.

Cases were selected in each county from among those currently under care under Aid to Families of Dependent Children. In order to ensure that the current worker was familiar with the case, we limited the selection to families known to the agency at least a year and to the worker at least six months. Through this procedure, ninety-one cases with seventeen workers were chosen.

Much has been written about the effects of mobility on AFDC families. Our families were very stable. Eighty-nine per cent of the mothers were born either in the county of current residence or in one immediately adjoining. Our need to have families who were fairly well known to the agency may have biased the sample to include families with long histories of dependence on AFDC. The median length of time was nearly five and a half years; one quarter had been receiving this assistance for ten years or more. Otherwise, the characteristics of the sample are comparable to those reported by Burgess and Price (1963) from a nationwide study of AFDC.

Information about each case came from two sources: the

record and the worker. From experience, we have learned it is essential to supplement record review with conferences because much more is known than is recorded in many instances. Furthermore, many caseworkers are chary of making explicit their own thinking and the details of treatment they have tried. Our workers were no exception to this rule, and, in order to get these data, we had to interview them. Finally, we had a number of scales for describing the mothers involved. We wanted these filled out by persons who knew the mothers personally. The CLL Scale, for example, was completed by the worker in an interview with us, but our participation was limited to clarifying for him the meanings of the terms in the scale. These interviews operated like training sessions. A worker who had four or five cases in our study was likely to complete the instruments on the latter ones independently.

For this study, new instruments had to be invented, particularly for the survey of casework practices and the worker's conception and formulation of the case situation. Other instruments were adapted from previous work. Thus, we used the Maternal Characteristics Scale (MCS) again but reduced it in length for two reasons. By now, we knew which dimensions of the maternal personality interested us. Also, especially on the CLL, there were a number of factual items which the average staff worker usually did not know about the mother's child-rearing practices and which, therefore, had to be deleted for this study. The scales as modified interested a number of the workers, and we discovered, months after data-collection ceased, that our instruments were being employed as guides to relevance of facts about new cases in which our friends had become involved. This incidental benefit to the agency one hopes will occur when staff gives of its time to participate in research.

The data fell into three areas: (1) the nature of the client (mother); (2) the casework practices and approaches tried, including the caseworker's assessment of the client's dynamics and his feelings toward her; (3) the client's reactions to the casework efforts, including changes, if any, in the level of child-caring in those families in which we would hope to find it.

We had hoped to see changes, then, over the years, in the child-caring practices of the families whose records we read. We

hoped to relate these changes to the casework treatment attempted. This endeavour proved futile. Information about previous functioning in child care was often not present in the record; moreover, we were unable to determine from the record the reasons for such changes as were in evidence. Social work researchers know that agency records seldom support study of a refined hypothesis unless the workers have the issue of the research in mind when they are carrying the cases. So, the present study was a gamble that some broad hypotheses about effects of treatment, at least, could be checked against available material. In this respect, we lost the gamble.

Of course, improving the family's child-care functioning is only one of several possible missions for the AFDC worker. We were struck, in fact, by how often protective services to the children were virtually ignored in many of the records we read. For some workers, the primary foci seemed to be motivating and assisting recipients to obtain employment, or the pursuit of financial assistance from absent fathers, or determining eligibility for AFDC.[1] Although we were unable to pursue the worker-client interaction very far with quantitative data and statistics, we did come away with a series of clinical insights about their relations, which forms much of the substance of this chapter and from which it takes its title. But, first, some coincidental learnings from the study.

CHILDHOOD POVERTY AND AFDC

An obsession with marginal child care led us to an elaborated view of the many faces poverty wears for the children of the rural poor.[2] Genteel poverty is a rarity, but shabby poverty is all too familiar. We may also enumerate listless poverty, drunken poverty, empty-gut poverty, and gap-windowed poverty. The very young child, if he survives, does not seem to "mind" poverty—but we have shown by earlier statistics that he responds to privation with with-

[1] Since completion of this research, state regulations require that in each county casework services be separated from determination of eligibility. The latter, in principle, has become the task of another individual.

[2] For a fuller treatment of this topic, see Polansky, De Saix, and Sharlin, 1971.

drawal and other sequelae. Some wealthy men even romanticize their hard beginnings, denying their own discomfort so violently they have no empathy for the current generation of the poor. Many would like to say that having been poor was good for their characters, but this view is just another form of smugness.

Work with the various levels of child care sensitized us to small distinctions in children's lives which might not seem noteworthy if viewed from a middle-class standpoint. The Childhood Level of Living Scale was available to quantify such differences and had shown validity in previous studies. With our research into AFDC cases, we had a chance to contrast the lives of a group of youngsters on public assistance with those of a comparable group, also low in socioeconomic status, who were from self-supporting families.

Some previous research has contrasted the care of the AFDC youngster with that of an "average" American child, but this gap is too large. For the terribly poor, the discrepancy in income is enormous. A family of four lives for a year on less than an upper middle-class family spends annually to replace and maintain its cars. A difference in life style also goes with social class, which further confuses the picture. Bonem and Reno, for example, surveyed thirty-three New Mexican families (1968, p. 11) and concluded: "Practically the entire income of the AFDC families is spent on the bare essentials of life. AFDC children are excluded from many aspects of life that are the normal lot of children in our society." The same statement, alas, can be made about all the children of the poor. What is different for those on AFDC?

Of the sixty-five youngsters included in our main, diagnostic study, no more than four were receiving public assistance. At the same time, their family incomes were nearly all $3,000 per year or less, so the group might fairly be called the self-supporting poor. The Childhood Level of Living Scale was applied, in this new study, by the AFDC worker to his own case. However, he frequently did not have all the information we had obtained in our research, so we had to shorten the CLL Scale somewhat to make it feasible under these new conditions. All AFDC cases contained at least one youngster roughly in the age range of our original study. We then went back to the original data and rescored the CLL, deleting items

which had to be dropped from the AFDC application of the instrument. We were then ready to compare the two samples; the comparison is summarized in Table 9.

Table 9 shows that the children on AFDC had a higher (less desirable) score on the total Childhood Level of Living Scale than did the nonrecipient group, but individual variations were large enough so that the difference between means was not statistically significant. The data document that the nonrecipient children were living at a standard no different from those on AFDC on such factors (or subscales) as food, shelter, safety, and medical care.

When life is reduced to such basics, the advantage of the self-supporting poor appears to lie only in a few amenities. According to the results, they have more changes of clothing and clothing that fits than the AFDC families; they sleep with bed linens; the family has more eating utensils; and the furnishings of the house are less barren. The AFDC children are also at a disadvantage on the subscale, promoting curiosity. They were even less likely than

Table 9

LEVELS OF LIVING OF AFDC AND NONRECIPIENT CHILDREN

	AFDC Families	Self-Supporting Families	t
Total CLL	29.9	25.2	1.91*
Housing	6.23	6.17	n.s.
Feeding	2.65	2.18	n.s.
Safety	2.64	2.52	n.s.
Medical Care	1.55	1.57	n.s.
Grooming	2.41	2.55	n.s.
Clothing	2.43	1.37	2.70**
Home Comforts	5.60	3.46	3.32**
Promoting Curiosity	3.95	3.08	2.73**
Maturity of Discipline	1.85	2.32	2.58***

* $p < .10$ ** $p < .01$ *** $p < .05$ (opposite to prediction)

the other poor youngsters to be taken on trips or exposed to what we have come to call "enrichment" experiences. Only on one sub-scale were AFDC youngsters adjudged to have superior care, namely, parental discipline. We frankly find the difference incredible and are inclined to attribute it to laxer standards on the part of the AFDC workers than were those used by our researchers with the original sample.

What we have documented, therefore, is what we suspected. Life is hard for any poor child in our mountains; it is even bleaker for those on AFDC than those who are not. With the standard of living of all the children of the poor so close to the standard of those on welfare, we get an impression of what a massive undertaking it is to raise the standard for all. The costs far exceed sums of money yet talked about, of course.

We had not fully anticipated the traumas to which AFDC children have commonly been exposed in their familial living. Much has been written about the "lower-class" life style, but, in this in-stance, we were able to compare a group of youngsters from low-income families with those who had been on AFDC for some time. Here is a list of family catastrophes which were more prevalent among the AFDC families than our others to a statistically signifi-cant degree (Polansky, De Saix, and Sharlin, 1971, Table 2, p. 40): maternal pregnancy out of wedlock; extramarital affair of one or both parents; incapacitating use of alcohol by one or both parents; physical violence between parents or against relatives or neighbors; severe psychosomatic complaint in one or both parents; eviction; frequent moving; overcrowding due to families' moving in on each other; complaint of neglect filed with welfare department. Some of these differences were expectable; they contribute to the need for AFDC in the first place; but we were unprepared for the amount of instability prevalent in these homes. The amount of pathology in AFDC families has been totally overlooked by those who have planned the separation of social services from the determination of financial eligibility.

The public often indulges in fantasies of getting substantial numbers of these women off public assistance and into public em-ployment. A high percentage of mothers of poor youngsters in our section are already at work if they are competent. Otherwise, *their*

families would also be on AFDC. A working mother who is successful at both tasks is an admirably well organized person. Of our
original study group, 60 per cent had a work history lasting over a
year; of the ninety-one welfare mothers, only 25 per cent had
equivalent employment histories during their lifetimes (P < .001).

The Maternal Characteristics Scale utilized in the original
study was adapted for this study and applied by the AFDC workers
to their clients. With suitable rescoring of the original data for comparability, we were able to see how the two groups of women were
judged on several subscales of maternal personality which interested us most. In general, as the evidences of familial instability
indicate, the AFDC mothers were assessed as less mature than the
self-supporting mothers. The AFDC mothers were rated more apathetic-futile, more impulsive, and less verbally accessible. Those
who propose putting them to work plan to recruit from among
women already less competent than average women and ask them
to double their work loads. Obviously, something has to be added to
the picture before this scheme can be carried out without irreversible
harm to the children.

EFFECTS OF MATERNAL PERSONALITY

Thus far, we have talked about the AFDC group in an undifferentiated way. But, even at this relatively desperate level of
living, the maternal personality continues to make a perceptible
difference to how her children live. We discovered that a number
of correlations found among judgments by our workers in the original study were verified in this later study. In the original study, we
correlated the Composite Index of Verbal Accessibility against the
Childhood Level of Living Scale and found a relationship of $r = +.47$. In this replication with seventeen workers rating ninety-one
AFDC cases, the correlation was $r = +.43$ (P < .01). Circum-
stances alter cases, but so do personalities!

Of course, both CLL and VA scores are based on judgments
by the same worker. Probing for other predictors of how well children on AFDC live, we hit on the relatively simple-minded criterion
of the reason precipitating the need for AFDC in the first place.
The AFDC cases were simply sorted in terms of the initial reason

for being on relief, and then we noted the proportions falling above or below the group median on the CLL scale. The results of this little analysis are given in Table 10.

A whole literature exists dealing with one-parent versus intact families, and a popular superstition has it that intact families are likely to be better off. In this AFDC sample, the children living better are those whose mothers have formalized the breakup of their marriages. Worst off are members of intact families whose fathers are in prison, but those with fathers in the home are nearly

Table 10

CHILDHOOD LEVEL OF LIVING RELATED TO
REASON PRECIPITATING AFDC

	Mother Widowed, Divorced, Separated	*Father Deserted*	*Unmarried Mother*	*Father Disabled*	*Father Incarcerated*
Good Care	90%	58%	50%	36%	30%
Poor Care	10	42	50	64	70

as badly off. For the husband to be in the home and the family still be eligible for AFDC, he must never have attained social security coverage. We found many men who were mentally and emotionally limited; also, quite a few were elderly, with relatively young wives, and with a reproductive ability that far outlived their earning power. We found, as a matter of fact, a statistically significant association between discrepancy in parents' ages and CLL scores: the closer the parents were in age, the better the CLL! So much for the folklore about aging lechers and their nubile sweethearts.

We encountered some other interesting facts, but, of course, they divert us from our main discussion. For example, we found an interaction between economics and personality affecting AFDC which seems most understandable once located, but which we would not have predicted in advance. In counties with fair econ-

omies, length of time on AFDC tended to be short, since women who were able did find jobs and leave the rolls. By the same token, the caseloads in these counties had a *greater* loading of pathology and maternal infantilism than did the poor counties. This *residuum effect* warrants research in its own right. However, the main conclusion to be drawn was this: even among families, all living on AFDC, we found marked variations in the Childhood Level of Living and these were, as before, related to the personality of the mother. As had happened so often before in our work, the evidence pointed to the need to try to help the child through helping his mother become more effective.

CASEWORK PRACTICES AND VERBAL ACCESSIBILITY

Let us revert to the issue with which this chapter began. We set out to try to learn useful methods of treatment through analyzing the successes and failures of a group of colleagues already involved with the rural poor. We have indicated our belief that an important avenue in helping the immature mother is through making it possible for her to "open up" to us in casework, or, more technically, through fostering her verbal accessibility. Accordingly, we tried to determine which casework techniques seemed to increase the client's VA.

An instrument labelled the Casework Practices Inventory was developed for coding casework. It consisted, once again, of a set of descriptive statements to be judged true or false of the casework under scrutiny. Field work for this study was done by De Saix, Borgman, and Sharlin. After reading the record on the case and talking with the worker, the researcher completed the CPI form on that case. The agency worker completed the Maternal Characteristics Scale, and from his judgments the composite index was assembled for assigning the mother a score on Verbal Accessibility. These scores were the basis for dividing the mothers into those "high" versus "low" on VA so that appropriate chi-square tests could be run against items in the inventory of casework practices. We shall report some of those scores which proved to be significantly associated to VA.

The results support the notion that when the mother is open,

greater accessibility occurs on both sides. One is not surprised to find that where the VA is high, "caseworker allows or encourages mother to express feelings" about her current life situation, about the caseworker herself, about her past life, and about other family members. In a number of instances, we were impressed by the worker's courage in facing the mother's anxieties and hostilities. Certainly, receptivity to such feelings is important to their expression. So is concern. Associated with heightened VA were the worker's interest in discussing other adults important to the client as well as her hobbies, skills, and other activities. What was not so predictable was that the *worker* would be significantly more open about her own feelings with the accessible mother than with the inaccessible ones. This phenomenon was demonstrated in spontaneous verbalization of feelings about the mother's situation. The worker also shared her feelings and experiences with the client. So, the data support the idea that with verbally accessible mothers, openness is mutual.

The increased involvement with the client is apparent in other facets of the interaction. A strong difference was found between the high and low VA mothers with respect to their workers' verbalized emotional reactions to them. High VA mothers earn comments which are primarily positive and significantly less frequently negative; their workers "show warmth in discussing the mother." The closeness begets empathy. When the mother is accessible, her worker describes her situation from the point of view of how she sees and feels about it rather than as a third person might view her plight. The positive affect in the relationship may go beyond the point where it is helpful. The judgment that the worker was "overly sanguine in view of the personality of the mother" was significantly more often made about communicative women than about uncommunicative women. Their workers were also more frequently adjudged gullible.

Toward inaccessible women, workers expressed feelings of being rejected and frustrated in their inability to influence the mother. We have commented that futility is highly contagious, and we observed that phenomenon in these workers. With low VA women, the caseworker sees contact as a duty and admits pessimism about achieving anything. Such reactions contrast to the evidences

of planfulness often in evidence among those dealing with the relating client.

Clearly, then, we identified a number of differences in casework thinking and approaches associated with maternal verbal accessibility—with whether or not the mother was being "reached." But, do these associations imply cause and effect? And, if so, in which direction? Based on what we otherwise knew of the workers and the difficulties presented by inaccessible women, it was hard to believe that specific worker actions of the kinds described had made the women more accessible. We assumed, rather a pattern of *responses by the workers* to what they encountered among their clientele. Given that VA correlates with general emotional maturity and relatedness, we are not surprised that the open women engender affection and enthusiasm among their workers. This reaction probably leads to a circular process, a spiraling upward or downward of the relationship, the worker's feelings about it, and his effectiveness with the case. A typical sequence with the noncommunicative mother is a growing impatience in the worker, followed by a flurry of activity to try to reach the mother verbally or with concrete services, and ending with infrequent visiting and concentration on questions of eligibility. Initial eagerness gives way to frustration, the frustration resolves into detachment, and finally the worker throws in the towel. One way in which the worker's detachment shows itself is in uncertainty about how many children there are in the household. The passive aggressiveness pandemic among inadequate mothers seduces unwary workers into acting the same way—which is, perhaps, just what the client intended.

In short, rather than having made discoveries about successful or unsuccessful casework tactics, about workers' effects on clients, we learned more about clients' effects on workers. Or, a better way to put it is that we began to discern the outlines of *mutual* effects between the mothers and their workers. Their transactions strained toward a stable congruency in which the worker's interaction only served to preserve the major behavioral characteristics the mother brought to the relationship.

The reality of client-worker interaction contrasts with the mission proclaimed by most agencies and the community which supports them. Why does the reality fall so far short of the ideal? It

does not fail for lack of good intention in the worker; neither does it usually reflect total obliviousness. By way of serious fun, we now set forth some of what we observed when worker-client operations were looked at more clinically than sober statistical analyses permit.

GAMES WELFARE WORKERS PLAY

Stabilized transactions between worker and client come to resemble the games which Eric Berne (1964) has so amusingly and incisively identified from his practice of group psychotherapy.[3] An advantage of Berne's mode of analysis is that it offers clues to the dynamics of all parties involved, for Berne assumes that when the patient or client is succeeding in playing her game, there is something in it for all who participate with her. Victims and bystanders may be presumed to have the same motivations she does, or motives to complement hers; otherwise the game would not go on. Analysis of each transaction hopefully provides crucial clues to the important motives involved and so suggests ways pathological complementations can be interrupted.

Most welfare transactions fall under the general heading Berne (1964, p. 48) identifies as *social games*. He defines a social game as "an ongoing series of complementary ulterior transactions progressing to a well defined, predictable outcome. Descriptively, it is a recurring set of transactions, often repetitious, superficially plausible, with concealed motivations. Every game is basically dishonest and the outcome has a dramatic quality." The aim of the social game, namely, to achieve the *semblance of intimacy* without undertaking the hazards of reaching for it, sets it apart from others. The dilemma to be resolved is the same as that detailed in Chapter Three on desolation. How may one get close without hurting or being hurt?

We have emphasized throughout this book that many clients have trouble with true closeness. The problem is acute among those

---

[3] Of course, dynamically oriented clinicians talked half-seriously about their patients' "games" long before Berne's book. In social work, such writers as Fritz Redl and David Wineman, Alfred Kadushin, and Polansky have engaged in the same kind of search for clinical nuggets in interviews and in supervision.

with many infantile elements in their personalities, for they achieve clinging in place of closeness. But, let us look also at the barriers the worker must overcome to reach toward true intimacy from his side of the relationship. Some of these barriers are part of the human condition, but others are characteristic of the work and agency situation.

The worker is constrained by a maze of bureaucratic regulations which, if not consciously designed to hamper efforts toward direct communication with her clients, have that effect. Misguided or misinterpreted injunctions to "professionalism" operate to discourage development of worker-client intimacy. Workers are told, for example, to avoid fostering dependency, to treat all clients uniformly and to be objective. Workers are also often mobile people. Young female workers get pregnant, young male workers impregnate them and seek more prestigious positions inside or outside their agency. Administrative requirements of "good business management" dictate endless reshufflings of caseloads with little regard for ongoing relationships or their possible effectiveness. Last, but perhaps foremost, is the cumulative impact on the worker of dealing constantly with so many clients who resist intimacy out of their own limitations; often, they do not even offer the minimal superficialities of good manners or other hypocrisies that help us survive the day. They wear on one. It is no wonder, therefore, that the constraints from both sides of the desk create a situation in which the worker relies on semblance rather than reality, games of seeming to be, rather than being close.

What follows, therefore, is not a critique of workers, but an attempt to understand what goes on in their lives in these relationships. Similar transactions are constantly being played out in the business and academic worlds.

APATHETIC-FUTILE GAMES

We have identified four games which are played frequently by the predominantly apathetic-futile client and seem to result in an apathetic-futile response from the caseworker. The games are: (1) look how hard I'm trying; (2) why don't you . . . ? yes, but . . . ; (3) stupid; and (4) schlemiel. We do not have a com-

plete thesaurus of games played by apathetic-futile clients, but these four impressed us as common and serve well to illustrate the process of transmitting futility from client to worker, and back again.

(1) Look how hard I'm trying. The maneuvers of the passive resister are, of course, classic exemplars of what analysts have labeled "anal-retentive," "passive-aggressive," or "passive-resistant" character. Less well studied have been the dynamics and encouragement given to passive resistance by the authority figure, the alleged victim.

The prototype is the parent who demands something from the child. The child complies, but covertly resists. He does what is requested but fails to accomplish what the parent wants (hostile-compliance). In this situation, the parent is saying: "I'm going to make you do it." But the child is responding: "See, it doesn't work." Because the child has complied, he escapes blame by saying: "Look how hard I'm trying." The advantages of this game, for the child, or passive resister, are expressions of defiance without blame and hostility without risk of retaliation from the authority being resisted. However, the advantages to the authority figure are crucial for understanding how and why a situation is created that stimulates passive resistance.

Apparently, the authority figure, too, is playing the look-how-hard-I'm-trying game with a third party. That is, the worker is covertly resisting the making of the demand or request and does so only because he feels that some authority over him wants him to do so. He can then say to *his* authority figure: "Look How Hard I'm Trying."

Apparently, the victim collaborates with the following maneuvers: (a) The request or demand is unrealistic or inappropriate so that the potential resister could not successfully comply with it even if he wanted to; (b) The request is given in a provocative way, as if to say that resistance is expected; (c) The authority figure neglects the motivation of the potential resister or fails to involve him to the extent that good sense would require; (d) Despite repeated sabotage by the passive resister, the authority figure never seems to profit from experience.

The welfare-department versions of the game are: (1) employment office; (2) nonsupport warrant; (3) health department

and (4) dirty house. In the employment-office version, the welfare worker suggests or demands that the client register at the employment office and get a job. The client dutifully complies, even to the extent of going for job interviews (for which she dresses inappropriately and at which she is vague). The client may even accept employment, which she quits or from which she is fired in a few days. The caseworker's covert resistance to helping the client obtain suitable employment is manifested by the following maneuvers. (a) The client is advised to obtain work where regular transportation is hard. For example, one caseworker verbally supported a client's efforts to obtain employment at a factory forty-five miles from her home. (b) The client is advised to seek employment for which she is obviously unqualified or which might get her into trouble. (c) The client is not asked how she feels about working or what kind of work she would like to do.

In nonsupport warrant, the caseworker demands that the client go to the police station and take out a warrant for the deserting father. The client tells the caseworker that the husband's parents know where he is. The caseworker ignores this information but tries to have the father traced through social security records. The client dutifully goes to the police station, takes out a warrant, but advises the police that she has no idea where her husband is. The warrant sits in the police station, and, nine months later, social security furnishes an address for the deserting father. The client is advised to tell this address to the police. If the information is pursued, the father "cannot be located at the address furnished," or the client advises the police she will not prosecute, and thus the warrant is withdrawn. If the client does this several times, the police may not allow her to take out any more nonsupport warrants; hence, she is exempted from this requirement.

Both caseworker and client have tried hard to go through the motions leading to apprehension. But *neither* of them wants the father apprehended. Sometimes, one or both do not even wish him located. Both may fear that if the father is caught, he may bring back to the family not only the problems in evidence when he deserted but even more belligerence at being apprehended. Moreover, if the court orders him to pay support, he is not likely to do so regularly, creating an uncertainty of income. The police are often

confederates in this game. They hesitate to bring a known trouble-maker back to the county. When played by the impulsive client, nonsupport warrant fades into a game of cops and robbers.

In health department, the caseworker persuades the mother to go to the health department or to a doctor for immunizations or medical treatment for her children. The mother goes but then fails to follow the prescribed treatment. In this game, the caseworker tries hard to get the client to go but then fails to follow up in seeing that the treatment is followed, perhaps failing to communicate with the doctor at all.

In dirty house, the caseworker herself observes or receives a report from a community source that a certain AFDC mother keeps "a filthy, dirty house," that her children are unfed, unwashed, and unclothed. The caseworker reacts by overly vague advice to the mother, for example, suggesting that she ought to be "a better mother." The advice may also be overly limited, such as: "You should clean up this dirty floor." The mother tells the caseworker that she will do so "right away." Three months later the caseworker returns to find the house and children as slovenly as ever and the mother busily scrubbing a tiny spot on the floor with a dilapidated mop. The mother says she has not had time to clean the rest of the house, she has been ill with a cold. The caseworker then compliments the mother for the effort she is making and offers to have the homemaker come to bring the mother some curtains or "cleaning supplies."

Sometimes, the caseworker is angry with the person or agency who made a child-neglect report. She is resentful because she feels the complainant is invading her field of expertise or because she interprets the complaint as a criticism of her effort—which it often is. Consequently, the caseworker wants to "show them" they cannot control her while simultaneously averting criticism for "doing nothing about it." For childish-impulsive clients, this situation enables them to convert their dirty house into a game of Let's you and him fight.

Of course, the caseworker may also feel inadequate to the task of dealing effectively with such clients. Admittedly, not a great deal is known about how to motivate clients to offer a good standard of care to their children in spite of the limitations of an AFDC

grant. One outcome of this state of affairs is for the caseworker to prove that the problem lies in the client or in some external factor like no cleaning facilities. To prevent a client from playing the look-how-hard-I'm-trying game, the caseworker must free herself of her own need to play it. She must come to terms with her own authority figures and with regulations governing AFDC eligibility.

Passive resistance is unlikely to occur in demands the client is capable of fulfilling. The worker must make a judgment on the basis of what the client has achieved in the past. The request needs to appeal to the client's own motivation, or at least some attempt should be made to elicit the client's open verbal expression of negative feelings about the request. For example, a caseworker was successful in inducing a retarded mother to provide a nutritious low-cost diet for her child by telling her that certain foods would taste good to her and to the child. The request also needs to be made in a way conveying expectation that the client will voluntarily want to comply. Finally, the worker must follow through and modify goals and plans on the basis of experience.

(2) Why don't you . . . ? yes, but. . . . This game is closely related to the look-how-hard-I'm-trying game and may be played to satisfy the same motivations. The prototype is the child who complains: "I have nothing to do." The parent who plays the game responds by offering suggestions, all of which are rejected with the comment: "Yes, but . . . ." Sometimes, the parent initiates a request to which the child replies: "Yes, but . . . ." The parent then tries to answer the objection, but again receives a "Yes, but . . ." reply from the child.

In adult situations, the game is often played between friends and colleagues or between a client and a helping professional. The Yes, but . . . person presents a problem to which a solution (or the lack of one) is obvious. The helping person gets satisfaction from acting the sage. The Yes, but . . . player gets his satisfaction from proving that the helping person is not all that wise. Both parties are then able to say: "Look how hard we're trying."

In the child-guidance version, the mother complains to the welfare worker that her child will not mind or do his school work. The welfare worker suggests that the mother "whip him hard." The client then says: "Yes, but I've tried that and it doesn't work." The

welfare worker then suggests sending the child to his room, to which the mother replies that there are not enough rooms in the house. The game continues until the welfare worker runs out of suggestions—or becomes physically exhausted.

In the vocational-rehabilitation version, the caseworker advises the mother to look for a job. The client responds by saying she would like to obtain regular employment, but there is no one to look after her children. Pleased by the woman's willingness to work, the caseworker suggests a day-care center. The mother replies: "Yes, but there is no way for me to get the children there." The worker then suggests that the grandmother keep the children. The client replies that she had thought of this, but grandmother is "too sick" or "doesn't want to."

One of the reasons this game is relished by caseworker and client is that it avoids any real discussion of the client's feelings, in this instance her feelings about working, separating herself from her children, or her relationship to her own mother. Of course, the client would not want to face such feelings and the worker would feel helpless if they should come out. However, both try hard to find a solution to a realistic problem.

(3) Stupid. The prototype of this game was perhaps first formulated in Kipling's notion of the white-man's burden, and in America it was enshrined in the relationship between Southern servants and their Caucasian masters. Stupid is one of the most efficient ways of transmitting apathy-futility from client to helping person.

In this game, the client grins broadly, answers questions vaguely, fails to meet responsibilities, and acts as if she has no sense. She responds, "Yes, ma'am" to every suggestion and promises to do better. The critical transaction is for the client to seduce the caseworker into ascribing the behavior and noncommunicativeness to low intelligence or mental incompetence and then to react accordingly. The client seems to be saying: "I'm stupid, so do me something."

If the caseworker is playing the game, she begins dealing with the client through other people and plans without consulting the client whom she regards as "too limited to understand." The client then frustrates the caseworker by failing to make the hoped-

for changes, again pleading lack of understanding. The caseworker becomes exasperated, perhaps suggesting a sterilization. The exasperation turns into "What can you do for someone so low in IQ?" which becomes the justification for giving up and leaving the client alone.

Stupid enjoyed considerable popularity in welfare departments a quarter century ago. White welfare ladies and black clients were well schooled in this transaction, which governed the relationship of the races in the larger society. With the advent of the civil rights movement, racial pride, and social-action organizations, stupid is becoming gauche in welfare circles.

The aim of the game for the client is to make the caseworker feel helpless, with the hope that the worker will give up and leave her alone. The client escapes the threat of closeness to the caseworker; she is also able to escape retaliation for failing to make an effort. For the caseworker, stupid may justify her need to keep her distance from someone whose squalid life is upsetting, offensive, overwhelming, or threatens her innocence. The game also helps the worker externalize responsibility for outcome.

Nevertheless, some clients' life situations reflect real, rather than pretended, incompetence. Moreover, we suspect that some deterioration in adequacy accompanies chronically playing stupid. Therefore, assessment of mental incompetency should not be based solely on overt actions. The best antidote is expectation of conduct that is realistic to the client's level of mental competence.

(4) Schlemiel. The name of this game is taken from a Yiddish word implying incompetence. The prototype is the child who "accidentally on purpose" spills ice cream on the carpet in the home of a neighbor and then begs forgiveness on the ground that it was "an accident, but what do you expect from a child as clumsy as I?" The schlemiel's motivation seems to be a desire for absolution as well as pleasure at another's discomfort. The victim, or schlemazel, appears motivated by a desire to grant forgiveness in order to bolster his own moral superiority and to cover his resentment against the schlemiel. The victim may also participate out of a desire to discomfit some third party. In this game, the schlemazel's forgiveness is used as license for the schlemiel to continue his havoc.

One welfare ploy is broken appointment. The caseworker,

at the request of the client, makes an appointment with an expensive medical specialist in a distant city and agrees to provide transportation. The caseworker plans her day for this trip, and the client promises to be ready. The caseworker arrives at the client's home to find her still in bed, with four children underfoot, and without breakfast. By the time it would take the client to dress, care for the children, and arrange baby-sitting, it would be too late to make the trip. The client apologizes, saying she meant to call the caseworker, but forgot. She explains that she decided not to make the trip because it is raining, one of the children is upset, and the medical complaint no longer exists. The client then adds: "I'm awfully sorry to inconvenience you after you went to so much trouble." This statement is often the most irritating part of the scene to caseworker. One counterploy is to set the time of departure an hour earlier than necessary. Or, the caseworker might insist that the client go anyway and explain to the doctor why she is late. Another ploy is for the caseworker to withhold *both* forgiveness and pique.

CHILDISH-IMPULSIVE GAMES

Other games are typical of the childish-impulsive client and her caseworker. These games appear to be favorites of the client with a hysterical character who meets an obsessive-compulsive caseworker. Childish-impulsive games described below are: (1) peasant; (2) Let's you and him fight; (3) I'm only trying to help you; (4) cops and robbers; followed by (5) courtroom; and ending with (6) gentlemen's agreement. The latter three games seem most enjoyed by clients and caseworkers who have litigious, somewhat paranoid, traits. Nearly all of these transactions are noteworthy for the manipulativeness they express.

(1) Peasant. The paradigm for this game is the child who flatters his parent for privileges or favors the parent would not ordinarily grant. In a more vicious adult game, a woman presents herself as an unsophisticated peasant to a somewhat naive, gullible, professional man of scholarly demeanor. The shrewd "peasant" proceeds to flatter the man about his educational credentials, the astuteness of his observations, and the magnificence of his achievements. Beguiled by the woman's flattery, the man becomes blind to

creeping sarcasm and sly digs; he gladly surrenders whatever she may be wanting from him. If the woman's aim is primarily to cut him down, she may be heard saying to her friends or his friends: "Dr. So-and-So thinks he's great, but let me tell you . . . ."

The welfare version of this game is usually played out between a female client and her male caseworker. The woman flatters him for the sharpness of his advice, the high-mindedness of his service, and the impressiveness of his education. She promises to do whatever the caseworker advises. Of course, she does exactly what she wants. If the caseworker has been sufficiently seduced, he fails to notice whether the client has done what she promised. He also avoids insisting that the client face realities that are unpleasant. The client then is heard bragging about how she fooled Mr. Caseworker. In the more vicious form, the client is set to justify her position that welfare workers (and male authorities in general) are suckers and that her contempt for them is reasonable. Such a client may have been disappointed by the failure of her father to rescue her. The caseworker enters the game because flattery counters insecurity about his inexperience or perhaps because it bolsters his masculinity. The peasant also supports defensive *rescue fantasies* in the worker. The caseworker can satisfy himself with the illusion that this client, at least, is better off as a result of his services.

(2) Let's you and him fight. The paradigm of this game is the child who entices his parents into an argument about his discipline. While the parents are arguing, they lose sight of the issue and the child escapes punishment. Another outcome is for the one parent to countermand the discipline of the other out of spite so that the child has his way in the end. Everyone enjoys the fight. The child strengthens his idea that parents are contemptible, although this also makes him anxious. The gain to the parents is that each can blame the other for the child's problems.[4]

The welfare versions of this game might be called: (a) interagency roundtable; (b) mental-health clinic; and (c) coordination of services. In interagency roundtable, the client exploits conflicts within the welfare department, among other community

---

[4] This transaction is familiar also to staffs of mental hospitals. See Stanton and Schwartz, 1954 (especially Chap. 15).

agencies, and between professional persons. Schools, health departments, antipoverty groups, churches and physicians are favorites.

For example, the school complains to Mrs. Jones about the truancy of her twelve-year-old son. Mrs. Jones states that she cannot send her son to school as the welfare department will not allow her enough funds for his lunches, books, shoes, or decent clothing. Mrs. Jones then goes to the welfare department saying that the school is angry with her because her son has no books, lunch money, decent clothes, and so on. Her angry welfare worker telephones the school about discrimination against the poor. An angry, defensive school principal retorts that the welfare department is being niggardly toward a deserving mother and son while otherwise promoting and subsidizing illegitimacy. The uproar sometimes ends in a squeeze play. That is, school and welfare department resolve their conflict by squeezing out Mrs. Jones, agreeing that she is a bitch, a bad manager, or a conniving liar. In the uproar and squeeze play, the issue of how to deal with the Jones boy's truancy is forgotten.

Mrs. Jones wins because she escapes facing responsibility for doing something about her son's truancy, which she can now blame upon an unsympathetic school and caseworker. Her resentment and contempt for these agencies is now justified by their quarreling. She can then say: "If only the school and welfare department would get together, my boy wouldn't be truant." The welfare worker enters the game partly out of her own ambivalence toward school officials and partly out of guilt concerning inadequate public assistance payments. However, she wins by avoiding the more difficult task of motivating a negativistic teen-aged boy to attend school.

In another variant, the welfare worker and the other agency restrain themselves from fighting. To avoid it, they do not communicate; instead they act unilaterally. The school furnishes books and lunches, and the welfare department secures funds which are also given to the mother. In their smugness, both school principal and welfare worker fail to note whether the child actually resumes regular school attendance.

In mental-health clinic, the client seeks conflicting advice from the welfare department and some other agency or professional.

The issue often is child guidance, and the other agency is frequently a mental-health clinic. For example, Mrs. Smith complains to her caseworker about the unruliness of her children. The welfare worker suggests that Mrs. Smith go to the mental-health clinic for help with this problem. Mrs. Smith goes to the mental-health clinic and when asked why she has come replies only: "The welfare department sent me." With growing bafflement, clinic personnel inquire further, only to be told that the Smith boy is "sassy" and bites his fingernails. The clinic reassures Mrs. Smith that these are not serious problems and that no treatment is necessary. Mrs. Smith then reports to her welfare worker that the mental-health clinic does not think her child's problem is serious and would not give her another appointment. Later, the welfare worker and the clinic worker meet. The clinic worker refers to "inappropriate referrals" by the welfare department, and the welfare worker refers to the clinic's refusal to deal with "the hard-core problems of the poor."

In the coordination-of-services version, the client obtains something from another agency or another caseworker which has been denied her by her own welfare worker. A variant of this game is for the client to seduce her caseworker into giving her what she wants by reporting that the other agency has granted, or is going to grant, her request. Here, the worker is being trapped into competing with the other agency for the client's gratitude. The antidote to Let's you and him fight is usually communication among the agencies the client tries to manipulate. However, communication alone is not enough. The communication needs to be focused upon the personality problem the client presents, not upon the rivalry between agencies.

(3) I'm only trying to help you. This sport is a close relative of Look how hard I'm trying. Whereas Look how hard I'm trying is marked by dramatic ineffectuality, I'm only trying to help you requires bad judgment by both caseworker and client, and the outcome is destructive to the client, further enmeshing her in difficulty. The prototype of this game is the situation in which a child or adult asks for, or is offered, tangible help or advice. The advice or help appears useful, but both the helper and the person receiving help foresee unfortunate consequences. When things turn

out badly, the recipient of the help says: "Look what you made me do." The helper responds with: "But I was only trying to help you."

In this game, the recipient seems to accept the help or to follow the advice against her better judgment, out of a need to externalize responsibility. The recipient may also want to make the helping person feel inadequate or to lock him into a position of remorse. The recipient can thereafter manipulate the helper through playing on his guilt. The helper or adviser may proffer unwise advice out of frustration with the client while maintaining a semblance of kindness. An occasional motive in the worker is to prove that the suggestions of his supervisor or consultant do not work or that certain professional principles, social welfare programs, or bureaucratic regulations are unrealistic and ineffective.

Two familiar versions of this game are baby sitter and assault on a female. In baby sitter, the mother on AFDC resists paid employment, saying that she cannot find a baby sitter she can trust with her children. The welfare worker suggests that the mother employ a disabled welfare recipient for this purpose, even though the potential baby sitter cannot hold public employment because of a physical or mental handicap. Or, the welfare worker suggests that the mother use another nonworking AFDC mother with three preschool children of her own. Or, the worker wonders why the mother cannot use her own teen-age daughter to tend the younger siblings, since her job could be on the night shift. The mother gets a sitter and, predictably, some major or minor tragedy befalls a small child, which can be ascribed to the inattentiveness of the baby sitter. Or, the teen-age child, in the mother's absence, slips out to meet members of the opposite sex.

The AFDC mother has now shown that outside employment is not feasible. In addition, she is now in a position of moral superiority which she can use to manipulate the caseworker into allowing her to have her way on other issues. The welfare worker has proved that agency policy about employment for recipients is "bad."

In assault on a female, the client complains dramatically to the caseworker that someone with whom the client is feuding has

assaulted, trespassed against, or severely annoyed her. The offending party is often her husband, in-laws, or neighbors. The client asks the worker for advice. The caseworker, suitably indignant, urges the client to swear out a warrant for the arrest of the offending party. The client may or may not protest but does follow advice which she probably had toyed with all along.

The issue goes to court, but the case is promptly dismissed with the client fined for "prosecution declared frivolous." Or, countercharges are brought by the defendant, and both client and defendant are found guilty and fined. If the husband was the offender, he may be fined or jailed for thirty days. In any of these outcomes, the family's meager AFDC allotment is needlessly drained, and if the spouse is jailed, he may lose his job.

In this welfare game, the caseworker is enabled to justify her position that "the court does not understand our clients," which she believed in the first place, and can blame the court for the outcome of the casework. The client is in a position to blame her family or neighborhood conflicts on the court—or even her caseworker!

(4) Cops and robbers. The game of cops and robbers is the first in a well loved sequence of three games played in welfare departments. This game is often followed by courtroom, and ends with gentlemen's agreement. The prototype of cops and robbers is the childhood game of hide and seek. The seeker deliberately looks the other way while the other player runs and hides. The hider then leaves clues as to where he might be. The seeker follows these clues but makes deliberately false moves. The hider keeps getting bolder, but at the last minute scampers off. Finally, the hider allows himself to be caught, and the seeker allows himself to catch the hider, but not too soon and only after surmounting phoney obstacles. This game is the stuff of which good detective movies and television programs are made.

The enjoyment of the game for both cop and robber comes from the thrill of the chase. Therefore, the game must be started with the robber's leaving clues and prolonged by the cop missing them. The aim of the game for the robber is satisfaction for outwitting the cop, followed by redemption by being punished. The aim of

the cop is the thrill of overcoming the cleverness of the robber and redemption by catching the robber. In the welfare department, a common version is man in the house.

In man in the house, an unmarried client (or one whose husband has deserted) confides to a neighbor (often a fellow AFDC recipient) that she may be pregnant. The neighbor then reveals this to the caseworker. The worker confronts the client, who responds by saying it is a malicious rumor, that she absolutely has no boy-friends. The client may next make a more provocative move. She may come to the welfare office asking for maternity clothes from the clothing closet, or she comments to the worker that a car in front of her home belongs to a male friend. The worker continues to question her about pregnancy, which the client denies each time. The caseworker continues to ignore the obvious until she is "shocked" to receive a form from the local hospital requesting pay-ment of the client's obstetrics bill.

Why was she so obtuse? A woman's having an extramarital relationship is regarded as sinful. The worker who identifies with traditional morality fears she is being "unprofessionally judgmental" for even discussing such a relationship with a client, unless she has absolute proof of its existence. Many workers told us that they ignored evidence of such extramarital liaisons because they "did not like to think anything unseemly." For them, cops and robbers was played in order to obtain the proof that would legitimatize such a discussion.

To the extent that the caseworker identifies with traditional morality, she feels that it is her job to break up such liaisons. Yet, she recognizes that such a relationship may be helpful for her client, that a liaison is the only heterosexual outlet possible, since her marriage prospects are poor in view of the number of children she has. Or, the worker may rightly feel she has insufficient leverage to control the client's relationship to the paramour anyway. Thus, the worker acts out her ambivalence in a cops-and-robbers game. Other variants of cops and robbers include welfare fraud and deserting father.

(5) Courtroom. Courtroom is based upon a childlike need for parental sanction of one's actions. The dynamic forces needed to play this game stem from feelings of being in the wrong, coupled

with desires to obtain reassurance from the authorities. Those who regularly play courtroom often start from the premise that their actions and views will be challenged. Litigious clients and caseworkers are, of course, fond of this game, which is enshrined in our legal system. The prototype is two siblings or playmates quarreling about some toy. One, or both, appeal to the parent, each clamoring for justification of his position and control of the other one. The roles in the game are plaintiff, defendant, and judge(s).

In the family-guidance version, the client casts herself in the role of plaintiff and the caseworker in the role of judge or parent. Defendants are the client's children, spouse, neighbors, or some community agency like the school. In synopsis form, the client complains to her welfare worker and asks that he intervene to control the other party. The client tells her worker something she has done that displeased someone else and asks: "Wouldn't you have done the same thing?" The unwary caseworker is seduced into siding with and justifying the position of the client (or sometimes that of the other party). At times, he will even take action to try to control the one deemed at fault. One party uses the opinion of the caseworker against the other. The party deemed at fault then reacts in defiance. In any event, the caseworker, by taking a stand, loses the goodwill of at least one of the parties to the dispute.

Being cast in the role of judge is initially flattering to the caseworker. The role of judge also gives the caseworker an opportunity to act out rescue fantasies or omniscience needs. The client receives reassurance against self-disparaging feelings of being always in the wrong. By focusing upon such disputes, the complainant is able to distract the caseworker from exploration of other issues which might threaten the client's defenses. The technical problem in coping with this ploy is how to decline alignment without feeding the client's need to feel rejected. All experienced caseworkers and therapists know more than one way to handle this problem, but the best of us may be entrapped.

In the appeal-hearing version, the client becomes the plaintiff, the caseworker the defendant, and the supervisor, the state office, or the welfare board the judge. One caseworker whose records we read was prone to bring clients before the supervisor or the agency director when the client protested termination of public

assistance or the caseworker's intervention in child-neglect complaints made against the client. The supervisor and agency director always supported the caseworker's decision, but then the caseworker would turn about and reinstate the welfare payment or go along with what the client wanted!

(6) Gentlemen's agreement. The courtroom game often eventuates in a gentlemen's agreement between caseworker and client. The agreement allows both to win while each saves face. In this way, both parties to the dispute receive reassurance that they were right while, at the same time, they can act as if they were wrong. This happy state of affairs comes about through a gross hypocrisy, that is, avoidance of standing behind one's words. The caseworker says: "I'll do what you ask . . ." and implies "and I won't look to see if you've kept your word." The client says: "I'll promise to do what you ask . . ." and implies: provided you don't hold me to it."

Over and over again, we saw the following transactional pattern in client-worker relationships. The worker demands that the client do something. The client refuses, or performs some defiant or provocative act. The worker takes action—usually denying or terminating public-assistance payments, sometimes initiating or encouraging someone else to bring court action against the client. The client appeals to a higher authority—the agency director, the state department, or the welfare board. The caseworker's decision is upheld. The client seeks the caseworker's favor and requests rescinding of his action. Caseworker reiterates the original demand and the client promises to comply. The client does not keep the promise, and the caseworker avoids another confrontation.

For example, Mrs. Carmichael, mother of seven children, was receiving AFDC based upon her husband's desertion. She revealed that she was working as a domestic servant one day a week. (This assertion proved to be a provocative statement.) In checking the client's wages with her employer, the caseworker was told that Mrs. Carmichael was also working a day a week for other friends and neighbors of this employer. The caseworker therefore terminated Mrs. Carmichael's AFDC payment because she failed to furnish complete information about resources. Mrs. Carmichael induced one of her employers to complain about the caseworker to

a local welfare-board member. The matter was discussed at the welfare-board meeting, and the caseworker's action was upheld. A month later, Mrs. Carmichael reapplied for AFDC, telling the caseworker what a nice person he was, and promising to be truthful in all that she told him. The caseworker reinstated Mrs. Carmichael's public assistance, but never again did he check out the earning reports she claimed.

CONCLUSIONS

According to Berne, games are played hardest by sulks and squares. A sulk is defined as a child who is perpetually mad at his mother or at his father, or at both. Much of this book has been devoted to the psychological characteristics of sulks. In general, the sulk is more interested in collecting reasons for not doing something than he is in finding ways to do what needs to be done. In most of the games discussed here, the welfare client's behavior might be summarized as being that of a sulk. The conditions under which an adult decides to stop sulking are much the same as those under which the child relinquishes sulkiness. She must be able to save face, and she must be offered something as gratifying as sulking in exchange for not sulking.

However, in this chapter, we have been more interested in the forces motivating the welfare worker's behavior in relation to the client than in further descriptions of client's sulkiness. In most of the games described here, the welfare worker best fits the description of a square. That is, much of her activity seems motivated by a hypersensitivity to censure from parental, supervisory, or other authority. The welfare worker conforms to the demands of bureaucratic authority and tries to protect herself from criticism. Yet, at the same time, she is often rebelling covertly against that authority, often without awareness that she does not accept the legitimacy of what she is being asked to do.

When asked why they do what they do, the standard welfare-worker reply is: "Because we have to." The crucial question is then voiced, "But what would happen if you did something else?" If the welfare worker is a chronic square, she will reply: "But we have to do the other." Or, she may respond with some form of:

"If it weren't for them . . ." ("them" being supervisors, agency policy, federal or state requirements, or public opinion). She may also reply: "They'll take our money away."

If the welfare worker is truly interested in obtaining more genuine, honest relationships with people, she might reply: "Probably it would be better." Or, more honestly: "I'd be afraid to try." The welfare worker's task is, then, to develop awareness of the individual needs and characteristics of her clients and to respond to them accordingly, rather than in terms of cliches and stereotyped rituals designed to satisfy the establishment or motivated by desires to defy it.

One need only review some of the statistics at the beginning of this long chapter to recognize that AFDC clients vary like the rest of us; enormous individual differences exist among them. Only a minority of AFDC mothers are sulks. Any worker, from time to time, will be seduced into acting the square, but he or she usually recovers spontaneously, permitting herself to recognize what has been going on.

Why, then, did we include these analyses in the book? We included them for two reasons. First, at a time when the movement is strong to dismantle "social work" from administration of welfare, we wanted to demonstrate that some of us, at least, have been acutely aware of transactions that have been going on at a level that will be missed by the squares and administrative types who will succeed us. Second, it must now be obvious that still another root of futility grows out of the success of the mother who entraps the one whose task it is to help her. What can be worse than for the patient to take over the treatment and defeat it?

12

Breaking the Chain

We have sketched some rituals in which welfare workers participate with their clients. A few are Dionysian and orgiastic; most resemble stately minuets. All have at least one aspect in common: They are designed for passing through the motions without the client's undergoing change. A message implicit in these analyses is that an otherwise inadequate mother may have surprising strengths. To avoid penetration of her defensive detachment, she can maneuver in ways that are unexpectedly adroit. No wonder the worker finds herself enticed, enthralled, and eventually entrapped.

If the approach to treatment presently under way is so often ineffectual, what do we recommend to replace it? This book is primarily dedicated to analysis of a problem rather than its cure, but it would be truncated if we offered no pragmatic guides. We offer these guides with suitable reluctance, cognizant of our limitations as preachers of treatment technique. The state of our art is not advanced to the point at which one can strictly derive prescription for treatment, even from precise diagnoses. Also, the personality problems of the women most in need of change baffle the wisest

and most expert therapists. Anybody who is humble about the treatment of infantile personalities has—to quote the quipster—much to be humble about.

In a socioeconomically homogeneous, stable, rural population, all with incomes near and below the poverty line, we found a noteworthy association between maternal personality and the level of care children were receiving. Mothers of children scoring poorly on the Childhood Level of Living Scale showed deficits and relative immaturity in a variety of areas. They had achieved little by late adolescence; were likely to come from families which were inadequate; showed few signs of maturity on Rorschach and TAT testing; had low IQs; and were verbally inaccessible. Inferior childcaring is not typically an encapsulated problem, a delimited neurotic conflict. Instead, it usually reflects a pervasive, characterological trend in the mother. Varying degrees of infantilism appear in most of those implicated. In extreme cases, it seems appropriate to label them *infantile personalities.*

We have emphasized that our studies were on child neglect rather than on child abuse. At about the same time we were at work, David Gil was engaged in a nationwide study of child abuse. He does not report the clinical detail our work permitted, but an overview of his results is instructive. Contrary to many published reports, the two groups of abusive and neglectful parents appear to have much in common. The typical abusive parent also seems to be inadequate, having many infantile features (Gil, 1970, pp. 108ff). We are also reminded of the tendency of neglectful adults to treat children as peers, as fellow adults, and of the more or less unconscious tendency to fuse and confuse them with their own parents. These patterns are common in both abusive and neglectful families. In Gil's study, a third of all abusive parents were also regarded as neglectful (p. 128). Abusive parents are said to have been, themselves, subjected to violence in their own childhoods, but this treatment is reported for only a relatively small minority. The field of child welfare is left with a continuing puzzle, therefore, about what critically determines whether a grossly immature parent will also prove abusive.

Children receiving poor levels of care reflect it in their per-

sonalities. For instance, the child's intelligence is low in households offering poor care; even with maternal IQ partialled out, the correlation remains significant. Effects on other facets of the child's personality are also visible in the school.

Beyond the generalized impact of deprivation, we sought to elucidate *specific* sequellae of maternal character. Previous research has shown, for example, that the mothers of aggressive or delinquent children are, in effect, immature women. The same may be said of the mothers of withdrawn children. In our work, we separated out two modes of maternal immaturity: the apathetic-futile form, and the impulsive. Children whose mothers are marked by extreme degrees of the apathy-futility syndrome are likely to be lethargic, withdrawn, and to relate in an undifferentiated, clinging fashion; those whose mothers show impulsivity express hostile defiance. In many programs of delinquency prevention, the major assumption is that "deprivation leads to aggression." Our results are in line with the hypothesis that severe deprivation leads to withdrawal and apathy, a deprivation-detachment sequence. An aggressive reaction seems to depend on identification with maternal patterns. These results have far-reaching implications for programatic planning for prevention, much of which is now based on a sympathetic, but naive, view of human anger and its expressions. But, the main meaning for present purposes is that apathy-futility in the mother projects an intergenerational cycle of deprivation and withdrawal.

The roots of futility lie in earliest childhood. In an adult woman, however, such feelings may be further consolidated, or "hardened," by interaction with external reality (if such a clearcut distinction between the inner and the outer is made). Sometimes, among patients, one encounters an intelligent, healthy woman in comfortable circumstances who nevertheless is convinced nothing she can do will make her happy. It is sensible, usually, to devote effort to helping her recognize how she is distorting her position. But, what can disconfirm the belief that "nothing will do any good" among some of the women we met? Although their appraisal of their chances might have been rooted, in the first place, in infantile defenses, it is now being fixed, rather than disconfirmed, by bleak reality.

Added to this are certain themes in her subculture which exacerbate matters. To the extent we all depend on the consensus of our neighbors to help us decide whether or not we are crazy, attitudes and opinions prevalent among the mother's family and friends are part of her reality. A cultural theme which may consolidate feelings of futility is the emphasis on fatalism, with its associated powerlessness. Whereas this theme may be, as we have suggested, part of a *group defense,* it will further undermine an already susceptible group member. Our data also support the hypothesis that people are likely to choose mates at a psychogenetic stage of development similar to their own. It is atypical for the low-income inadequate woman to choose or attract a husband whose maturity compensates for her own deficiencies.

As if further to illustrate the presence of a spiral of deterioration, we found another of our initial impressions to be valid. The woman who concerns us has an uncanny ability to transmit feelings of futility to those charged with helping her. She sets up a pattern of role complementation with her welfare worker in which, at best, her defensive detachment remains immune to intervention. But, if she succeeds in defeating her worker, she may ultimately be more hopeless than ever, since once again she has proven "nothing will do any good."

The mother with the apathy-futility syndrome shuts the worker out by her verbal inaccessibility. Unfortunately for her, this expression of her character neurosis means more than barring the door to the helping person. As we have elsewhere reasoned, verbal inaccessibility bespeaks a deficiency in one's own capacity for *self-healing* of psychic wounds; it is a psychological version of low white-cell count (Polansky, 1971).

The result of all this is, for many women, a downward spiral of effects. From the standpoint of systems theory, we see a morbid "funnel of causality," a sequence in which individual pathology reverberates with steadily constricting environmental possibilities in a mutual, interdependent, morphogenetic process (Buckley, 1967, pp. 72 ff). The mother who begins with pervasive feelings of futility is prone to participate in life-situations which justify and consolidate her position. One is reminded of an idea that often occurs in

therapy: Most people deserve what they get, but that doesn't make it any easier to bear!

TREATMENT OF CHILD NEGLECT

Our suggestions for treating the rural poor are limited to issues touched on in our studies. General discussions of protective services for children are to be found in Kadushin (1967) and Costin (1972). We have also just published a small volume on the treatment of neglectful parents, geared especially to the needs of those doing the front-line work (Polansky, DeSaix, and Sharlin, 1972).

It would help our fame if we could now project a panacea. There is a shared fantasy in the field that just because a near-miracle of change occasionally occurs miracles can be made routine and listed as standard agency service. This is nonsense. We are a long way from having a standardized, efficient method for "curing" neglect, as if it were appendicitis or gonorrhea.

An outstanding reason child neglect as a condition cannot be handled in routine fashion is the variation among the parents involved in it. We have focused on mothers as the fulcral persons in these families. From our own observations and reports of others, we would list the types of mothers found most frequently in neglect situations as follows: the apathetic-futile mother; the impulse-ridden mother; the mentally retarded mother; the mother in a reactive depression; the psychotic and borderline mother. Our attention was directed to the apathy-futility syndrome because it constitutes a peculiarly difficult treatment puzzle. But we do not imply that it is the only diagnostic category among the mothers at risk. The woman in a reactive depression bears a number of surface resemblances to her apathetic sister and may be confused with her. However, the treatment of depression in reasonably intact personalities is well understood; their prognosis is usually far more promising.

All the mothers listed as types prevalent in neglect share certain regressive, infantile features, if only temporarily. Therefore, two things are true. It is possible to make some recommendations which

hold, in a general way, for a wide spectrum of cases of neglect. It is also necessary to treat specifically, depending on the diagnosis. Here, then, are some remarks on the treatment of marginal child care and neglect which have general applicability.

The often lonely rural social worker faced with a neglect complaint has to begin by making a decision. (1) The worker can go away, concluding there is not enough evidence of inferior child care to justify serious concern. (2) She can decide the mother is probably treatable, but the only way to determine treatability is to make a trial of it. Meanwhile, to avoid complications, she allows the children to remain with their parents. (3) She may feel the mother has a chance of functioning better than she is, but, at best, her changing will be a long, drawn out affair. For the children's protection, they are removed, with the hope that this step will also mobilize the parent to work toward their return. (4) She may judge that the mother is untreatable or—an equivalent—that she *might* be salvageable, but, realistically, there is no one in the area with the skill she needs to whom she will go. Therefore, there is no recourse but to remove the children, possibly forever.

We have seen variations on these themes, but basically these are the main alternatives. It frequently happens that what one regards as an ideal course cannot be pursued because of lack of money, lack of personnel, or lack of community support. Nevertheless, the professional has a responsibility to clarify his own judgment. It is fascinating, therefore, to watch the ways in which officials manage to decide and not decide, at once, keeping the issues obfuscated because of political, economic, moral, and psychological considerations. Policy statements which hold forth unrealistic objectives for achieving change and "services" doomed to be another procrastination tactic do not help clarify the worker's role or support him in a painful, lonely duty.

Commenting on the fact that many social variables are asymmetrical, Herzog (1970, p. 115) recalled an old Jewish saying: "Money is not as good as the lack of money is bad." Often, in a situation of *marginal* child caring, one encounters a woman on the borderline of competence. One is easily led to believe that if she were less beset by money worries, she would give her children more individual attention. The average American, whose home includes

inside plumbing, floors of tongue-in-groove lumber, automatic washers, and vacuum cleaners overlooks how much such conveniences, taken for granted in any middle-class household, ease cleanliness. By whatever program it is brought in, more money would help at least some of these marginal families. Thus far, however, it seems to us that the Appalachian redevelopment program has done more to combat poverty among road contractors and owners of rights of way than among the poor of the region. Nevertheless, although money usually does not hurt, and probably helps, it is not a solution for the severe cases. Grossly inadequate parents are very likely to have their money milked away from them. The real bases of their problems are not economic.

Any mother with several young children underfoot is likely to look harried and bedraggled much of the time, even if she has a competent husband and household help. How is it to live in a mountain cabin, with four children under five years of age, and a husband who is employed part-time? Some very dilapidated women are densely populated, and this fruitfulness only adds to their feeling of being overwhelmed. It is not hard to infer the effect on the child, pushed aside by a new baby before he has gotten his share of loving.

Experience in these investigations has moved the senior author, at least, from "no opinion" to strong support for abortion on demand, preferably free. Life is hard enough for some children anyhow; none ought to be born who is unwanted. Voluntary sterilization has been more welcomed among low-income women in the mountains than we had been initially led to expect. They have proven equally interested in reliable and convenient methods of contraception.

Programs like these help; there is no doubt. Again, however, such mass solutions, like income maintenance, reduce the incidence of neglect, but do not eliminate or resolve it. The family amenable to rational mass solutions is more likely to be on the margin than truly neglectful.

At the present time, a good deal of impatience, indeed contempt, for social casework exists. Some "don't believe in it," as if it were a religion, a philosophy of the universe, or a piece of fakery. We are cognizant of the need to regard each client as a subsystem,

part of another subsystem within a larger whole. Yet, one need not always engage the whole in order to be effective, for social interdependence is seldom total. If it were, *all* the mothers in a given community would be equally neglectful, and if that were true, we could not have had the variations we found. In short, both autonomy *and* interdependence exist in a typical social system. Therefore, individual casework can, at times, be the most efficient approach.

Take the mother in a mild-to-moderate reactive depression, whose child neglect, as our colleague John Patton remarked, is secondary to self-neglect. We have found it disappointing to discover how many bereft and deserted women on AFDC have been handled as if their problems were solely economic. What does it do to a woman, past her chance of attracting a first-rate man, to lose her lover, playmate, and buffer against loneliness? Might not ventilation and offering her at least a temporary substitute object—rather standard techniques in treating depression—be partially curative? Here one would have to be willing to share her anguish and to take her emotions as seriously as one does her finances.

Other cases cry out for minimal marital counseling. We recall one "agonized martyr," more pitied than understood, whose husband deserted her repeatedly. Finally, a shrewd and mature worker asked her: "Now, just what might you be doing that drives him out of the house?" Only when her incessant nagging was scrutinized could restoration of a family begin. An immobilized housewife, unable to perform any of her chores, may be expressing spite against her husband or—in infantile women—against her own mother.

To be sure, neglect out of delimited dynamics in a more or less intact personality is the exception rather than the rule, and programs based on treating it solely through insight are probably as fatuous as those relying on indiscriminate feeding from the public breast. Therefore, the diagnostic acuity we associate with first-rate casework is an essential ingredient in any program for dealing with child neglect. We must find means to sustain the good workers in rural public agencies. Too often, their superiors neither appreciate nor grasp what they are trying to do (Wasserman, 1970).

Home demonstration agents, like agricultural extension

specialists, are found throughout our countryside. We hear they are now making more of an effort to reach our client group than they did at the time we began our work, when the marginal or neglectful mother typically fell beneath the notice of the county home economist. Instead, the agent's time was preempted for teaching middle-class farm wives how to practice the household arts in which they were already superb. This action, by the way, is no reflection on home economists. Most local ministers also give up on such families. Few have parlors anyone outside is willing to enter, except on pressing business, for reasons documented in our case illustrations. Isolation and alienation are compounded by such homely factors.

Marginal and neglectful mothers need homemakers, mature and even somewhat bossy women, who will come to their homes and work alongside them. Like children, they require steady encouragement to continue tasks they have started, models to emulate, and teaching by example. In discussing the various relationships between powerlessness and depressiveness, we mentioned the theory that helplessness itself may cause depression. The acquisition of minimal household skills and the increasing ability to make things happen is thus important not only for the welfare of the children; it is one possible (albeit not certain) antidote for the mother's infantile depressiveness.

Although the reader will find it almost inconceivable, we encountered women with literally no cooking skills at all. Beyond putting sliced boloney and bread where her children could reach them, such a mother was nearly at a loss. Either she had never been taught, or the character problems she carries with her were already burgeoning in childhood, and she could or would not learn from her own mother.

These patterns may continue, and homemaker service offers no miraculous solutions for them. Some women will require help for months or over a year before it can be gradually withdrawn. Others will require a homemaker indefinitely, a permanent prosthesis for crippled motherhood. Of course, we use day care in the same way —as a form of supplemental emotional feeding for deprived children. The point we want to emphasize, however, is that homemakers ought to be valued not only in terms of their concrete services, but for their potential role in bringing about change within the mother.

The word *dependency* provokes a phobic response in most well-ordered bureaucracies. Officials are afraid of it for two reasons: it bespeaks a hard-core clientele who have brought the wrath of legislators and the public at large down on their cozy operation; and it reminds them of their own passive longings—which, to be sure, they share with the rest of us. It may be a little more complicated to understand than some would like, but, in working with markedly immature people, one of the few chances one has for preventing long-term *economic* dependency is by permitting a hopefully shorter-term *emotional* dependency. It is time we recovered from the nonsense that all dependency is, of itself, bad.

We have more to say on this topic below. But, for the moment, we want to stress that one's leverage for entering the neglectful family and starting to work toward diagnosis and change is going to depend on the use of authority (with some associated fear) or the mother's transferring dependent strivings onto the worker—usually both. Therefore, it behooves us to bring out what we know about techniques—not for making a mother dependent, she is already that—but for encouraging her to attach her dependency to the worker. These techniques include such tactics as frequent contacts; concrete giving; feeding the mother's need to be special; a warm and welcoming demeanor; tact; readiness to discuss feelings; minimal demandingness (at least at first); and the form of moral insulation described as a "nonjudgmental attitude." (For a fuller statement on fostering dependency, see Polansky, DeSaix, and Sharlin, 1972.)

An old casework cliche recommends that one begin where the client is. The natural bent of an immature mother is to relate in a clinging, dependent fashion if she relates at all. Of course, some neglectful mothers are so damaged they refuse even this level of relating, and their treatability is even more greatly lowered thereby —which brings us to the treatment of futility.

TREATMENT OF FUTILITY

We have theorized that futility emerges as the affective aspect of a process of early detachment or splitting in the ego. The affect, as it happens, is bleak rather than acutely miserable; it is

akin to death, and no one welcomes it. But, from a treatment stand-point, its most ominous facet is the depth of pathology we can anticipate if futility pervades the personality. Clinically, one might describe mothers with strong evidences of the apathy-futility syndrome as inadequate, infantile personalities with marked schizoid trends. Nothing in our experience makes us think such persons are easy or promising candidates for therapy. If, by treatment, one means, as we do, bringing about an improvement in the mother's level of functioning and in her intrapsychic balances—an improvement that is reliable enough to withstand most fluctuations in her life-situation—then we are confronting one of the most difficult groups of clients.

Systems theory does not suggest many social psychological hypotheses, but it does clarify those one has. Let us borrow from its language here. Our initial impression of the apathetic-futile mother was the difficulty of getting her moving or "off the dime." Her behavior then seemed to represent *morphostatic* processes, resistant to changes in form or organization, dominated by forces of equilibrium maintenance (Buckley, 1967, p. 58f). In retrospect, the morphostatic model does not fit the most difficult clients. What we have is a person system involved in a vicious vortex, rather than a vicious circle. Given some "initial kick" which put her off the desired path, developmentally, she became entrapped in a process of deviation amplification, isolating her progressively from less crippled fellow humans. It is typical, for example, that following an initial trauma, the potential schizoid cannot accept from her mother such supplies as are forthcoming.

We see, then, that not only is the woman who concerns us not spontaneously improving; she interacts with her surroundings in such fashion that she is slowly getting worse. Hence, treatment requires more than what Lewin (1951) termed "unfreezing" a fixed situation. Treatment requires rowing upstream. Again, using the terminology of systems theory, treatment is an attempt to inject an initial kick, rationally introduced to begin deliberately what is, in effect, *a process of deviation amplification from the patient's normal way of operating.* The new factor introduced must be strong enough to reverse what has thus far been the natural flow of events in her life.

If this logic is valid, as it certainly is for character neuroses, then certain consequences flow from it. We now see why half measures may be worse than nothing. It also follows that a number of social workers' shibboleths have to be abandoned. Let us take, for instance, the client's right of self-determination. If this principle is followed, in the present instance, the odds are great that she will make those choices and mischoices which sustain the pathological process in which she is presently engaged. Someone has to act the parent and choose for her to change things.

We are also grateful to our colleague Donald Boone for pointing out a danger in relating to such women. We have operated as if maintaining the relationship were more important than the quality of the relationship. Client and worker become, at best, locked in a process of equilibrium-maintenance. Given the imperviousness of infantile people to self-observation and insight, we are not hopeful about the results of sending in a caseworker to many of these households, armed, like Arthur Miller's salesman, with nothing but "a shoeshine and a smile." By this statement, we do not wish to imply that we believe no caseworker has ever entered such a family with no backing greater than her own wits and succeeded in bringing about change. Special personalities do this often, but even they cannot bring it off every time—even among them, successes are somewhat "accidental." The question remains whether they are dealing with the extremely apathetic-futile woman we have in mind or with a healthier one. We have not been able to reduce work with these difficult ladies to a system, one that can be taught and followed. Among average caseworkers, more hearts than records are broken in work with neglectful families, and it is time to admit we have been following a wrong tack.

How about some of the new techniques, such as client advocacy? Would not membership, say, in a welfare rights organization or experience of success in a tenants' organization help to disconfirm the attitude that "nothing will do any good"? How about involvement in an action group as a beginning experience, however superficial, in relating to others and in breaking through the mother's isolation? Leaving out the larger social implications of such movements, the ideas involved are appealing. High group morale can certainly counter low individual morale, as we have seen in

nations at war, and a social movement can afford individual healing.

We have several reservations about such programs. First, this type of mass solution seems unlikely to reach the woman who is most withdrawn and inadequate, even in the cities, where it is more practicable than in the mountains. Like other such programs, it will work better for those healthier to begin with. Second, one must never underestimate the capacity of a person with a severe character neurosis to bend the social process in which he is involved to support his major defensive maneuvers. (Patient self-governments in hospitals are regularly taken over by those with paranoid trends.) Finally, we are at a loss as to how such programs might be fit into our mountain area, since so many similar efforts have failed over the years, even when they sought out more outgoing and competent members of the community.

For some time, there has been a movement to do away with the large institution. This trend has been true in psychiatry, in child welfare, and, latterly, in geriatrics. Many state hospitals are unsightly blemishes on the corpus of the mental-health movement. Yet, as always, we must ask whether we have not been throwing the baby out with the bath. Are there not patients for whom institutionalization is the treatment of choice?

The rationale for considering institutional help for the apathy-futility syndrome is both negative and positive. The negative side can be readily summarized. Less heroic measures on an outpatient basis do not do the job in most cases. Although the idea of institutionalizing many of these mothers is undoubtedly startling to colleagues, it is not all that innovative. Maxwell Jones is known, in this country, in connection with treating the severely mentally ill. But many of those seen in his original therapeutic community in England (Jones, 1964) had character problems much like those we encountered in our mountains.

As things now stand, only two groups of women with the syndrome are likely to receive institutional care: wives and daughters of the well to do; and those poor mothers who have the foresight to go all the way and have a schizophrenic break. Even then, the latter are usually superficially treated in state hospitals. Once the acute phase has passed, they are sent home on maintenance

medication with their infantilism and serious character problems untouched.

What are some advantages of the inpatient setting? We wish to change a life style that includes immobilization in the service of detachment. Change requires breaching major defenses. As the patient becomes active, deep feelings of anger and depression, which were split off, emerge to consciousness as does anxiety. Childish people usually will not stand still for this process as outpatients. They break off treatment or they stir up enough trouble in their lives to distract both themselves and their therapists. Treatment is not so easily broken off in an inpatient setting, especially if the patient has attached herself to the institution as well as to her therapist. We can also better guard against serious life consequences of acting out than we can with a person in the community. It is not so easy to get sexually involved extramaritally, to wreck one's car, or to stir up a fight in the family.

The patient's family always contains a complement of folks accustomed to going along with her patterns. It may seem incredible that anyone would have a "need" for a helpless blob as a spouse, but our clients are mothers, mostly legitimately. People married them in full unconscious knowledge. The institution should be a place where others will refuse to go along with the client's procrastinations, her immobilization, and her sullen sulking. So, two functions of the institution are to protect the patient during upsets coincidental to treatment and to challenge her favored patterns by refusing to go along with her symptoms. Even the demand for prompt attendance at meals and obligatory minimal participation in activities will do this much. Finally, a residential setting can, of course, offer treatment modalities nearly impossible to set up in concentrated dosage in the home setting, especially in thinly populated rural communities.

Hardly any intervention occurs without side effects, and residential treatment is no exception. It disrupts the family, and it is expensive for the community. Certain dangers exist in exposing poorly formed, clinging personalities to something as potentially regressive as a well-run treatment center. (See Polansky, Miller, and White, 1955.) So, institutionalization ought not be done except with a clear idea of what one wants to do. It often happens, in

clinical work, that even though the worker may lose, there is only one correct move he can make with his case, and he has to take that stance. What, then, are correct moves beyond those indicated above? Our thinking about this problem is Freudian in theoretical orientation, but not Freudian in tactics—at least not in the sense popularly understood.

Stripped to the core, the woman we are trying to help is childish, sullen because her unspoken demands are not magically met, superficially complaisant, but actually negativistic and rebellious. She has tried to skip a stage of development, so she has not experienced normal dependency until it is no longer necessary. We have to penetrate her detachment, live with her needfulness, and work toward bringing her up. Hence, her residential program has to be psychoeducational, *active and intrusive*. Any fascination with nondirective techniques has to be discarded. For, we are dealing with a woman who, if she is to ever become fully alive, must be stopped dead in her tracks and helped to turn around. Her sullenness cannot be permitted to coerce the staff. Instead, she has to face a situation in which it is made clear: "If you do so and so, this will happen; if you don't, that will."

Along with refusing to be bullied by her sulkiness has to go a readiness to help her and teach her. She feels inadequate because she is incompetent. The residential setting can be a place in which she learns cooking, baking, cleaning, beauty care and personal hygiene. A high percentage of such women are afraid to think concretely about money for it is "something grownups deal with." They have a combination of phobia and ignorance which leaves them incompetent in managing funds. They have to be taught, therefore, to equate money realistically with work and goods purchasable, but they have to be taught as if they were much younger than they are, and money is but one example.

An extremely important aspect of an inpatient environment is the opportunity and pressure to interact with other adults who are, initially, strangers. The nature of the group technique to be employed has to depend on the intelligence, insight, and other characteristics of the futility-laden woman with whom we are working. However, one aim of the group situation would be the same for each woman: to move against her isolation by following her

into her retreat and by offering her the wonderful, new experience that others can care about her and she has something to offer in return through opening up and talking. The group may be a ward-management group, an activity group, a couples group, or openly labeled a therapeutic group. The point is to give her something to which it has been impossible to expose her at home—other adults.

In all these efforts, one area on which to focus is the patient's *verbal accessibility*. Polansky has previously written about the rationale for doing this (Polansky, 1971), and we will not repeat it here. But the client's growing ability to relate on a verbal level will serve both as an index of how far she has matured and as a means to further maturation and integration.

There is, of course, much more that might be said about treatment tactics borrowing, really, from approaches that have proven most effective with middle-class women in private hospitals. These women have surprisingly similar problems to our mountain women. But we have given enough of a taste of the inpatient approach we envisage.

We should also mention some approaches less clinically oriented that have struck as having great promise if they could be implemented with our rural women. Several years ago, faced with similar puzzles, the welfare department in Washington, D.C. (1965) set up a congregate building into which mothers might move, taking along their children. By concentrating a group of mothers into one delimited setting, more could be done for each. Skills were taught, ranging from child care and homemaking to personal hygiene and organizing one's work day. Since this treatment model includes her children, we regard it as better in many respects than the hospital model described above. For one thing, the continued presence of children should provide concrete challenges for the psychoeducational process. For another, it is a chance to try to change not only the fulcral person, the mother, but the whole family relationship system as it has grown up.

There is also a device dating back into the earlier settlement movement in social work—family camping. We have spent the past decade recovering much that was good about the early settlements, and family camping is another example. For, under the guise of an extended vacation, a family could spend several weeks in the com-

pany of others needing similar reeducation. Many of the techniques mentioned as part of institutional treatment could be adapted to this model, and it has the advantage of imposing a *time-limited* demand for change. Practically, such family camps for selected families of the rural poor would have to be centrally financed and operated on a multicounty basis. But, among the group of women not too fixed in their regressive pattern, it would be well worth trying.

No experienced clinician would expect that the sorts of innovations we are recommending will be easy, inexpensive, or initially effective. But the evidence indicates that something new must be tried, whether or not it is consistent with current national priorities. When people-saving becomes a true growth industry, what we are suggesting will not seem radical at all.

A

Childhood Level of Living Scale

The Childhood Level of Living Scale (CLL) was developed by the University of Georgia Child Research Field Station staff[1] to be used as one indicator of the conditions of care under which children are reared—to measure the child's level of living. The scale follows the approach used by Sears, Maccoby, and Levin (1957) but, based on the experience of a pilot study conducted by the Child Research Field Office Staff, was focused to get at conditions at a lower level than the Sears material. Whereas Sears was concerned about three hot meals a day, we were concerned about whether the mother offered any food at all. A second and equally important reason for

[1] Norman A. Polansky, director, and staff members Betty Jane Smith, Mary Lou Wing, Christine De Saix, and Robert Borgman were responsible for the development of the scale.

227

pitching the scale at this level was to give the respondent a chance to be above the lowest level, therefore, a feeling of: "Well, at least things aren't *that* bad around here." The 136 items now in the scale are those actually used in analysis of data and in reports stemming from the study. We believe these items can be used fairly reliably with appropriate training of raters. At least in our study, they proved to be discriminating.

UTILIZATION

Persons using the CLL scale should be thoroughly familiar with the entire content and overall purpose of the scale prior to attempting to use it. To decrease the possible loss of items due to differences in interpretation or application, it is imperative that adequate training be made available to the persons who are to complete the schedule. If at all possible, it should be utilized in pilot studies; when this is not feasible, selected simulated situations should be used to give the user ample opportunity to discover for himself any items which seem ambiguous or otherwise unclear.

Although designed for yes-no answers, this form is basically not of the question and answer variety. Many of the questions are best answered through the observation of the researcher, whereas other questions ask for information best obtained from collateral sources such as teachers, welfare workers, public health workers, and so on. In the same manner, it is not necessary to begin with item one and continue consecutively through the remaining items. There are, however, certain groupings of items that lend themselves to completion during one interview.

The instrument is designed to be flexible. Items can be rephrased or expanded for clarity, if necessary, as long as the meaning remains unchanged. When probes are necessary, appropriate recording of both probes and answers should be done in the margin or on the back of the page. This also applies when some special circumstance alters the meaning of a yes-no answer.

SCORING

The scale is so scored that a high score indicates problematic or low level of living. Conversely, the lower the score the better the level of living. Wherever a plus mark (+) appears, it is counted as

one point. For scoring purposes, items were grouped to make composite scores or indices. Composite or index scores are unweighted in this scale. Our policy was simply to count total plus signs in any score or subscale with the few exceptions indicated.

The following definitions were used by us in completing the schedules. However, should questions arise regarding other words, phrases or items, written clarification should be reached prior to extended use of the schedule. General: appears—is readily apparent from observation; complains—expresses discontent with the situation; expresses—reveals in any manner, as in words, gestures, or actions; mentions—spontaneous reference to; plans—intentional ordering or arranging to achieve purpose or goal; routine—conforming to a habitual course of procedure; seems—apparent from observation. Relative to a specific item: item 3—"naked dropcord" —no fixture, receptacle for bulb only; item 5—"potbellied stove" —if standard is lower, please note; item 11—"stovepipes to flue"— as contrasted with going directly through wall or roof, the latter being considered fire hazard; item 16—"dilapidated"—a house that does not provide safe and adequate shelter and its condition endangers the health, safety, or well-being of its occupants; items 24 and 25—"meal courses"—either meat and one vegetable or two vegetables; item 26—"special occasions"—birthdays, Thanksgiving, Christmas, and so on; item 39—"insufficiently older sibling"— child less than twelve years old or any person who could not reasonably be expected to provide adequate care; item 49—"other than doctors or nurses"—faith healer, voodoo, and so on; item 90—"educational toys"—puzzles, building blocks, modeling clay, and so on; item 126—"takes pride in"—expresses pleasure in, enjoyment from, or feeling of accomplishment concerning.

Table 11 below shows a quintile distribution of Childhood Level of Living scores based upon our sample consisting of sixty-five mother-child pairs living in a rural county of western North Carolina. All families had reported incomes of less than $3,000 annually. Both of the child's parents were at least nominally in the

home. These families included all those in the county who met our
sample criteria, except perhaps a few who were either so geographically isolated or mobile that their children could not attend the
Head Start program.

Table 11

	Total Score	Physical Care	Emotional/ Cognitive Care
Upper Quintile	65–99	38–63	27–38
Second Quintile	49–64	27–37	21–26
Median	41	21	19
Third Quintile	35–48	17–26	16–20
Fourth Quintile	21–34	7–16	11–15
Lower Quintile	7–20	1– 6	3–10

SHORT FORM

Based upon results of a cluster analysis, it appears that
eighty-nine items will sample most of the content universe covered
by the full scale of 136, although with some loss in precision. These
eighty-nine items are contained in the housing composite scale and
eight others. These scales are identified by asterisks and were the
items used by workers in the study of AFDC mothers.

PART A—PHYSICAL CARE

*Key to
Scoring*

Yes   No

                        I. COMFORT*
          +   1. Water is piped into the house
          +   2. Hot water is piped to a faucet
     +   3. Light bulbs are from naked drop-
                                cords
                             4. The mother complains of diffi-
     +   culty in heating house

Yes   No

+
                       5. One potbellied stove is only means of heating house other than cook stove

         +   6. The house is heated by coal or oil

+
                       7. Family lives mostly in one room in winter because of difficulty in heating entire house

        II.   SAFETY*

         +   8. There are at least two exits to the house

         +   9. The exits are easily opened

+
                      10. Electrical wiring appears to be frayed or overloaded

         +   11. Stovepipes go directly to chimney or flue

+
                      12. Fires are sometimes started with kerosene or other flammable agent

       III.   STATE OF REPAIR*

+
                      13. Repairs one usually makes oneself are left undone

+
                      14. The roof of the house leaks

+
                      15. Windows have been cracked or broken over a month without repair

+
                      16. House is dilapidated

+
                      17. House is neither papered nor painted inside

       IV.   HYGIENIC CONDITIONS*

         +   18. There is an inside toilet

+
                      19. There is an outside toilet

         +   20. There are window screens in good repair in most windows

         +   21. There are screen doors properly mounted

        X.   HOUSING COMPOSITE* (combined scores of above four scales)

        V.   FEEDING PATTERNS*

+
                      22. Child frequently arrives at day-care center without breakfast and complains of being hungry

VI.   SAFETY PRECAUTIONS*

VII. DISEASE PREVENTION

Yes	No	
	+	41. Mother has encouraged child to wash hands before meals
	+	42. The floors of the house appear to be swept each day
+		43. There are food scraps on the floor and furniture
	VIII.	USE OF MEDICAL FACILITIES*
+		44. Mother has evidenced lack of awareness of child's possible dental needs
+		45. There has been neglect of obvious medical needs
	+	46. Mother has taken child for shots and immunizations on own initiative
	+	47. Child is taken to medical doctor or clinic after accident
	+	48. Medical care is readily sought if child is ill
+		49. Family uses other than doctors or nurses in case of accident or illness
	IX.	Clothing*
	+	50. Child has both play clothes and good clothes
+		51. Clothing usually appears to be hand me downs
+		52. Buttons and snaps of child's clothing are frequently missing and not replaced
	+	53. Shoes are in reasonably good repair
	+	54. Child is usually dressed appropriately for weather conditions
	+	55. Child is usually dressed appropriately for activity
	+	56. Clothing is clean when child is picked up for day-care center
	+	57. Evidence that underwear is changed as needed
	+	58. Items requiring ironing have been ironed
	+	59. Child sleeps in pajamas or gown

Yes	No		
		XI.	SLEEPING ARRANGEMENTS
	+		60. Child has a place for sleeping at bedtime away from family-living and recreation space
+			61. Child five years old or older sleeps in room with parents
+			62. Some members of the family sleep more than two to a bed
+			63. At least one of the children sleeps in the same bed as parents
		XII.	REGULARITY OF PROVISION FOR REST
	+		64. Bedtime for the child is set by the parents for about the same time each night
	+		65. The child receives at least nine hours of sleep most nights
	+		66. The child has a routine time for arising
		XIII.	GROOMING*
	+		67. There is routine washing of the child before going to bed
	+		68. It is obvious that mother has given attention to child's grooming at home
	+		69. Ears are usually clean
	+		70. Fingernails are clean
	+		71. Head and hair is clean
	+		72. Hair is combed
	+		73. Hair is cut
	+		74. There is a bathtub or washtub for immersed bathing in home
+ (for either)			75. The child is immersed weekly: never
	+		76. Toilet tissue is usually available
	+		77. Each family member has a toothbrush
		XIV.	HOME COMFORTS*
	+		78. There is an operating electric washing machine available
+			79. Mother complains of inadequate covering for warmth

Yes   No

+   80. Mattresses are in obviously poor
                             condition
+   81. Living room doubles as a bed-
                             room
+   82. Furniture is obviously in need of
                             repair
        +   83. Home has a telephone
        +   84. Family owns a car which runs
        +   85. Family owns a freezer
        +   86. Family owns a sewing machine
        +   87. There is an operating electric
                             sweeper

PART B—EMOTIONAL/COGNITIVE CARE

XV.   CULTURAL ARTIFACTS

        +   88. Family has in operating condi-
                             tion (maximum total three
                             points) :
        +   Record player
        +   TV
        +   Piano or musical in-
                                    strument
                        89. Following are available to child
                             for play (maximum total of
                             three points) :
        +   Football
        +   Baseball bat
        +   Baseball glove
        +   Play shovel
        +   Dolls
        +   Toys, trucks, tricycle
        +   90. There are educational toys avail-
                             able to the child in home
        +   91. Child owns a book of his own
        +   92. There are adult books in the
                             home
        +   93. Newspaper is delivered regularly
        +   94. Crayons are made available to
                             the child
        +   95. There is a dictionary in the home

XVI. PARENTAL PLAY WITH CHILD

                        96. Mother mentions that in past
                             year she has:

Key to
Scoring
Yes   No

+	Taught child something about nature
+	Told the child a story
+	Read a story to the child
+	97. Mother mentions that she has played game with the children
+	98. Child is taken fishing
+	99. Child has been taught how to use scissors

XVII.   PROMOTING CURIOSITY*

+	100. Family has been to a town outside the county
+	101. Planned vacation trip has been taken by the family
+	102. Child has been taken by parents to see different animals
+	103. Child has been taken by parents to a county fair
+	104. Child has been taken by parents to a carnival
+	105. Child has been taken by parents to watch construction
+	106. Child has been taken by parents to see some well-known natural attraction
+	107. Mother mentions child asks questions showing curiosity about how things work
+	108. Mother mentions that she answers child's questions about how things work

XVIII. CONSISTENCY IN ENCOURAGING SUPER-EGO DEVELOPMENT

+	109. A prayer is said before some meals
+	110. The child says prayers at bedtime
+	111. The child is spontaneously disciplined for stealing and lying
+ (Yes column)	112. Mother mentions spontaneously that she cannot get child to mind

Yes   No
        +   113. Child is spontaneously punished
                    for the use of what the mother
                    considers profanity
+   114. Mother seems not to follow
                    through on rewards
+   115. Mother seems not to follow
                    through on threatened punish-
                    ments
        +   116. Mother indicates that she pro-
                    tects child from outside influ-
                    ences she considers bad: rela-
                    tives or other people because
                    of language or reputation
        XIX. LEVEL OF DISCIPLINARY TECHNIQUES*
              117. Discipline usually takes the form
                    of:
+   Spanking with a switch
+   Very frequently no action is
                        taken
        +   118. Child is sometimes rewarded for
                    good behavior
+   119. Mother expresses feeling that
                    child should cooperate with-
                    out reward
+   120. Mother threatens punishment
                    by imagined or real fright ob-
                    ject
        XX.   PROVIDING RELIABLE ROLE IMAGE
        +   121. Mother mentions that child, if
                    son, prefers to be with father;
                    if daughter, prefers to stay
                    with mother
        +   122. Mother depends upon father for
                    masculine tasks
        +   123. Mother expresses feeling that her
                    job is the housework
+   124. Mother complains that her work
                    is harder than father's
        +   125. Mother expresses pride in daugh-
                    ter's femininity or son's mascu-
                    linity
              126. Mother takes pride in her (maxi-
                    mum total two points):
        +   Cooking

Key to
Scoring
Yes   No

	+	Sewing
	+	Laundry
	+	Decorating
	+	Flower garden
	+	Mothering
	+	Talents
	+	Other

127. Mother mentions father's skills and hobbies (maximum total two points):

	+	Hunting
	+	Fishing
	+	Building things with hands
	+	Working on cars
	+	128. Father works regularly

XXI. PROVIDING RELIABLE EVIDENCES OF AFFECTION

+   129. Child is often ignored when he tries to tell mother something

+   130. Mother is able to show physical affection to child comfortably

+   131. The mother taunts the child when he has had a mishap, is afraid, or worried

+   132. The mother goes to the child if he cries in the night

+   133. The child receives special attention when he is sick

+   134. The child is often pushed aside when he shows need for love

+   135. The mother expresses to the child her concern for his safety if there is real danger

+   136. Mother is made uncomfortable by child's demonstrations of affection

B

Maternal Characteristics Scale

ᔐᔐᔐᔐᔐᔐᔐᔐᔐᔐᔐᔐᔐᔐᔐ

The Maternal Characteristics Scale, or MCS, was designed by Norman Polansky, Christine DeSaix, Elizabeth Harkins, and Betty Jane Smith. This multidimensional instrument was intended to provide a means whereby judgments regarding characteristics of the maternal personality can be summarized. Rather than have a third person, or "judge," read the narrative recordings of the research social worker who had become well acquainted with the mother, the plan was to provide an instrument on which the worker might directly record her own assessments. Throughout the MCS, the intent was to use items which were as directly descriptive and noninferential as possible to maximize objectivity of the judgments.

UTILIZATION

The MCS is designed for use by trained and knowledgeable personnel. This is by no means a self-administering battery. Information from which the worker makes her ratings is to be obtained

239

from direct observation, skilled interviewing, weighing of collateral reports, and opinions of other professionals. Hence, the MCS is simply a device to facilitate quantification and ranking of the mothers along certain parameters of personality.

Because of the circumstances of the study for which it was designed, items included in the MCS assume the person rated is a female, living with her husband, and with a child (the "focal child") enrolled in a day-care center or nursery school. The basic form used was *presence-absence* coding. Each item involves a simple declarative statement which might or might not be true of the woman being described. The worker then checks whether the statement is true, or simply yes or no.

Despite the effort to provide an objective format, potential problems of interpretation of items survive. Should "verbalizes guilt" be checked if the woman mentions it once, or is such a rating reserved to those who are obsessively self-recriminatory? In general, we regarded a behavior as present, and marked it yes, if there seemed clear evidence that it did, in fact, recur. We did not require extreme instances of the behavior in question. But, as with any new research instrument, interworker unreliability can be minimized in any future study only by a period of training, pilot work, and discussion of ambiguities to arrive at consensus.

COMPOSITE INDICES

It is conceivable that, in a study contrasting two groups of women, item-by-item analysis of differences might be warranted. In our work, however, we were interested in ordering our subjects along major psychological dimensions. Items were combined into indices, or *scales,* to permit such orderings.

In composing such indices, it was not felt that the sample in our first study was large enough to warrant sophisticated statistical treatment of the data. Hence, we used a combination of rational and empirical techniques. Items were grouped under appropriate rubrics on the basis of theoretical considerations and common sense. Occasionally, there was question whether a particular item did, in fact, "fit in" with an emerging cluster; such an issue could be resolved empirically by testing whether the item was associated significantly with the sum of the others already located.

Originally, a total of eight "scales" was composed out of the MCS pool of items. These indices reflect the parameters of personality we thought were both pertinent to maternal competence, as we were conceiving it, and measurable under our research conditions. Subsequently, each of these tentative scales was correlated against other data regarding the mothers in our sample for evidences of validity, fruitfulness, and the like. Our theoretical ideas were simultaneously clarifying. We ended with a set of indices concentrating on three aspects of the personality, only. These were: (1) the apathy-futility dimension, combining (a) behavioral immobilization and (b) interpersonal detachment; (2) the childlike impulsivity dimension, combining (a) impulsivity, and (b) dependency; (3) verbal accessibility—composite scale.

APATHY-FUTILITY DIMENSION

In setting up the present scale, acknowledgement is made of the fact that while there probably is, indeed, an "apathy-futility syndrome" in her personality, a person with a low score on this dimension would fall into the general group of persons we regard as essentially normal—or at least not deviant in *this* direction!

The two subscales making up the A-F dimension are behavioral immobilization and interpersonal detachment. Attempts were made, incidentally, to augment the A-F scale by including also another group of items referring to blunting of affect. The evidence was that this did not improve the validity of the overall index. Below, therefore, we give the items subsumed under each rubric.

The scoring scheme is also indicated. For each scale, the total score is simply the algebraic sum of plus and minus scores. To facilitate statistical work, it is helpful to transform the resulting scores so that all are zero or more. This can be done by adding a constant to each score, of course. The constants added in *our* first study indicated in Table 12 below (for example $K = 12$ for the immobilization scores).

In general, we indicate the direction of credit to be given for a yes answer since, as noted, this is analogous to presence-absence coding. However, there are a few instances in which the no answer is scored; these are also shown. In effect, each item is equally weighted with all others in deriving a given scale score, but there

are a few instances in which an item recurs in the two subscales summed to form the larger one so that it was counted double. One item (number 3) on the immobilization scale was also given double credit *a priori*.

Many of the items used in constructing the other indices are also in this one, since it deals with an issue which "cuts across" the other parameters. Because of these common elements, correlation of the other scales with this one is artifactual, of course.

Table 12

NORMATIVE DATA FOR MATERNAL CHARACTERISTICS SCALE

	Immobilization (K = 12)	Detachment (K = 17)	Impulsivity (K = 6)	Dependency (K = 2)	Verbal Access (K = 0)
Upper Quintile	20–11	28–16	15–10	13– 8	31–26
Second Quintile	10–8	15–12	9–7	7–6	25–23
Median	6.5	9.5	5.5	5	21.5
Third Quintile	7–6	11–8	6–5	5	21–18
Fourth Quintile	5	7–5	4	4	17–10
Lowest Quintile	4–1	4–1	3–1	3–1	9–1

IMMOBILIZATION SCALE ITEMS

Sequence Numbering	Item	Direction for Scoring Yes	No
1.	Claims that she is unable to perform at job or housework or get anything done	+	
2.	Speaks of herself as healthy, strong, and energetic	—	
3.	Has volunteered for extra work in day-care center (double credit)	— —	
4.	Face is sometimes dirty or make-up is smeared despite availability of washing facilities	+	
5.	Hair is usually unkempt, tangled, or matted	+	
6.	Clothes are usually dirty or in disarray	+	
7.	Usually stands or sits erect with concern for posture	—	
8.	Speech is full of long pauses	+	
9.	Speaks in a faint voice or voice fades away at end of sentences	+	
10.	Sometimes expresses hostility through physical aggression	—	
11.	Answers questions with single words or phrases only	+	
12.	Has a sad expression or holds her body in a dejected or despondent posture	+	
13.	Shows warmth in gestures with interviewer	—	
14.	Shows enthusiasm	—	
15.	Is usually aggressive	—	
16.	When frustrated, flies into rages	—	
17.	When frustrated creates a turmoil	—	
18.	Visits with neighbors	—	

Sequence Numbering	Item	Direction for Scoring Yes	No
19.	Has at one time shown capacity to hold a job	—	
20.	Manages family finances	—	
21.	Keeps virtually the same posture throughout the interview	+	
22.	Keeps eyes closed or averted	+	
23.	Has decorated house in some unexpected way	—	

INTERPERSONAL DETACHMENT SCALE

1.	Daydreams much of time; gets out of touch with current daily happenings	+	
2.	Face is sometimes dirty or make-up is smeared despite availability of washing facilities	+	
3.	Hair is usually unkempt, tangled or matted	+	
4.	Clothes are usually dirty or in disarray	+	
5.	Clothing is appropriate to season	—	
6.	Clothing is appropriate to occasion	—	
7.	From time to time becomes preoccupied or shows lapses of attention during conversation	+	
8.	Speaks in faint voice or voice fades away at end of sentences	+	
9.	Talks comfortably with interviewer by the second contact	—	
10.	In discussing children, frequently adverts to self	+	
11.	Talks in ambiguous, obscure, vague, or cryptic manner	+	

Sequence Numbering		Direction for Scoring	
		Yes	No
12.	Shows warmth in tone in discussing her children		—
13.	Shows warmth in tone when talking with her children		—
14.	Evidences fearfulness of shyness about meeting new people or strange social situations	+	
15.	Seems incurious about the inner feelings of others	+	
16.	Expects companionship from husband		—
17.	Appears indifferent to husband's behavior	+	
18.	Appears surprisingly accepting of husband's irresponsible behavior	+	
19.	Shares problems with husband		—
20.	Clings to husband in a fearful, dependent way	+	
21.	Visits with husband's family		—
22.	Shares family decision-making with husband		—
23.	Discusses her children freely		—
24.	Individualizes children noticeably		—
25.	Discusses her children's behavior as if "from the outside"	+	
26.	Belongs to PTA		—
27.	Belongs to church		—
28.	Belongs to other community group		—
29.	Visits with neighbors		—
30.	Keeps eyes closed or averted	+	
31.	Shows interest in and knowledge of larger world scene		—

IMPULSIVITY SCALE

Sequence Numbering	Items	Direction for Scoring Yes	No
1.	Lacks persistence in pursuit of goals	+	
2.	Plans realistically for herself, children, family	−	
3.	Follows through on plans that have been made for herself, children, family	−	
4.	Shouts, yells, or screams frequently at something or somebody in interviewer's presence	+	
5.	Sometimes expresses hostility through physical aggression	+	
6.	Expresses warmth in exaggerated form	+	
7.	Evidences gullibility	+	
8.	Has shown defiance toward authorities in word and deed	+	
9.	When frustrated, flies into rages	+	
10.	When frustrated, creates a turmoil	+	
11.	Shows tolerance of routine	−	
12.	Apparently married to escape an unpleasant home situation	+	
13.	Sets and maintains control on her own behavior		+
14.	Has engaged in behavior not acceptable in her community	+	
15.	Often buys things impulsively	+	
16.	Accumulates savings	−	
17.	Shows belligerence toward interviewer from time to time	+	

DEPENDENCY SCALE

Sequence Numbering	Items	Direction for Scoring Yes	No
1.	Talks of ambitions for self or family which, though not impossible, are extremely unlikely	+	
2.	Has definite, realistic goals for self, children, family	—	
3.	Whines when she talks	+	
4.	Dwells on her problems with her children	+	
5.	Evidences gullibility	+	
6.	Clings to her husband in fearful, dependent way	+	
7.	Visits with her own family only	+	
8.	Leaves most family decisions to husband	+	
9.	Takes pleasure in things she and children do together	+	
10.	Takes pleasure in her children's adventures	+	
11.	Clings to her children	+	
12.	Can make decisions and take responsibility for them	—	
13.	Has at one time shown capacity to hold job	—	
14.	Complains of feeling neglected by parents	+	
15.	Seems to treat all adults as if they were parents	+	
16.	Frequently refers to opinions of, or quotes her mother	+	
17.	Frequently refers to opinions of, or quotes her father	+	
18.	Keeps insisting that interviewer give advice or intervene on her behalf	+	

VERBAL ACCESSIBILITY SCALE

Sequence Numbering	Item	Direction for Scoring Yes	No
1.	Evidences (verbalization) negative or discouraged attitude toward future accomplishments or attainments	+	
2.	Mentions she is aimless or getting nowhere	+	
3.	Says she enjoys living	+	
4.	Evidences excessive concern with religion or expresses some highly unusual religious ideas	+	
5.	Claims she is unable to perform at job or housework or get anything done	+	
6.	Speaks of herself as healthy, strong, energetic	+	
7.	It is hard for her to consider a new way of looking at same thing	−	
8.	From time to time becomes preoccupied or shows lapses of attention		+
9.	Speech is full of long pauses	−	
10.	Speaks in a faint voice or voice fades away at end of sentences	−	
11.	Talks comfortably with interviewer by the second contact	+	
12.	Usually states opinions reasonably direct	+	
13.	Talks in an ambiguous, obscure, vague, or cryptic manner	−	+
14.	Whines when she talks	−	
15.	Feels free to verbalize regarding hurts received	+	−

Sequence Numbering		Direction for Scoring	
		Yes	No
16.	Expresses ideas of revenge and wishes to retaliate	+	
17.	Evidences a sense of humor	+	
18.	Verbalizes embarrassment	+	
19.	Verbalizes shame	+	
20.	Verbalizes guilt	+	
21.	Enjoys talking about herself	+	
22.	Answers questions with single words or by phrases only	—	
23.	Talks of her situation with practically no outward sign of emotion	—	
24.	Shows warmth in voice much of time with interviewer	+	
25.	Shows warmth in tone in discussing her children	+	
26.	Shows warmth in tone in talking with her children	+	
27.	Can laugh at herself	+	
28.	Expresses boredom with her life	+	
29.	Shares problems with her husband	+	
30.	Shares plans with her husband	+	
31.	Shares plans for children with her husband	+	
32.	Shares conversation with her husband	+	
33.	Is able to say she enjoys sex	+	
34.	Shares family decision-making with husband	+	
35.	Discusses her children freely	+	

Sequence Numbering		Direction for Scoring	
		Yes	No
36.	Individualizes her children noticeably	+	
37.	Discusses her children's behavior as if from the outside	—	
38.	Discusses her children's assets	+	
39.	Discusses her children's liabilities	+	
40.	Speaks with pride of personal achievement or possession	+	
41.	Complains of feeling neglected by parents	+	
42.	Keeps eyes closed or averted	—	
43.	Expresses objection to interview or resentment at having to answer questions	—	
44.	Expresses awareness of complexities in others' decisions; that they have to weigh alternatives	+	
45.	Manner of response or failure to respond makes it uncertain whether or not many items are true (namely, subject incoherent, evasive, suggestible)	—	
46.	Frequently, and appropriately, expresses herself in abstractions	+	
47.	Uses figures or speech colorfully or amusingly	+	

NOTE: This VA scale from the MCS is scored so that a high + score means high verbal accessibility. In this way, the high score is different in meaning from those on the other two scales which are scored in the pathological direction.

C

Infantilization Scale

$\wp\wp\wp\wp\wp\wp\wp\wp\wp\wp\wp\wp\wp\wp\wp\wp$

Checklist	*Value in*
Number	*Scoring*

I. "You are an extension of mother."

    (a) *Amount of father's intervention when child was a baby*

  (1)   None, father reported never changing child's diapers, feeding, or giving the child a bath.   +

  (2)   Some, father reported changing child's diapers or feeding or giving the child a bath.   —

  (3)   Much, father reported changing child's diapers, feeding, and giving the child a bath.   —

    (b) *Mother's response to child's cry when he was a baby*

Checklist Number		Value in Scoring

| (4) | Mother let child cry if she knew he was not hungry for food or wet, occasionally checking; or child did not cry much: good baby. | — |
| (5) | Mother always checked to see why child was crying. | + |

(c) *Mother's response to child's demand for attention when she was busy*

| (6) | Mother indicates inconsistency in her reaction. | + |

(d) *Mother's reaction to leaving child at home*

(7)	Mother reports not having any problem.	—
(8)	Mother states they never go out or do not use babysitters.	+
(9)	Mother indicates she always takes the child with her or slips out.	+

(e) *Discipline of child by father*

| (10) | Father is strict—known. | — |
| (11) | Father disciplines "sometimes." | + |

II. "You are fragile."

(a) *Mother's report of child's accidents*

| (12) | Never, or usual falls and scratches. | — |
| (13) | Mother reports child hurts himself quite often. | + |

(b) *Child's control (spanking)*

| (14) | Mother says child should be spanked, but no indication child was ever spanked. | — |
| (15) | Mother reports child was not spanked in early childhood but later on got occasional spankings. | — |

Checklist Number		Value in Scoring

(16)   Mother reports child was never spanked because it does no good.   +

(17)   Mother reports child was never spanked because it is dangerous.   +

(c) *Mother's awareness of child's activities*

(18)   Mother keeps track of exactly where child is and checks on him often.   +

(19)   Mother reports not keeping track of where child is but checks occasionally.   —

(20)   Mother never keeps track or checks where child is.   —

(d) *Degree of freedom given to child*

(21)   Mother permits child to go to fixed location and in a familiar route.   —

(22)   Mother does not let child go outside the yard; must either hear or see child.   +

(e) *Mother's spanking practices*

(23)   Mother spanks occasionally.   —
(24)   Never spanked by both parents.   +
(25)   Never spanked, with justification related to handicap.   +

III.   "You are special."

(a) *Differences in rearing child and siblings*

(26)   Mother indicates no differences or only sex differences.   —

(27)   Mother indicates damaged child was harder to rear.   +

(b) *Mother's responses to child's demand for attention when she was busy*

(28)   Mother goes on with her business.   —

Checklist Number		*Value in Scoring*
(29)	Mother indicates that her reaction depends on what the child wants.	+
(30)	Mother responds promptly to child's demands or "gives in."	+
	(c) *Mother's differentiation between child and siblings*	
(31)	Unfavorable.	—
(32)	Favorable, unqualified.	+
	(d) *Mother threatens but does not follow through on punishment*	
(33)	Never.	+
(34)	Often or occasionally.	+
	(e) *Mother's reaction to child's behavior at table during meals*	
(35)	Mother describes child's table manners in a positive way.	+
(36)	Mother dwells on child's behavior.	—
(37)	Mother complains and/or gives examples of child's annoying eating habits.	—
	Miscellaneous Items.	
	(a) *Mother's attention to child as infant and ability to play with him*	
(38)	Mother answers positively but does not recall how or "played a little."	—
(39)	Mother answers vaguely, looks for excuses.	—
(40)	Mother indicates she did not play much.	+
	(b) *Parental attitude toward discipline of child*	
(41)	Mother indicates she has a set way of rewarding her child.	—
(42)	Mother indicates she rewards child occasionally.	+

NOTE: Add a constant to algebraic sum to eliminate minus scores for statistical analyses.

References

ADORNO, T. W., AND OTHERS. *The Authoritarian Personality*. New York: Harper and Row, 1950.

American Humane Association, Children's Division. "In the Interest of Children: A Century of Progress." Denver, Colo., 1966.

ARIETI, S. *Interpretation of Schizophrenia*. New York: Basic Books, 1955.

BALDWIN, A. L., KALHORN, J., AND BREESE, F. H. "The Appraisal of Parent Behavior." *Psychological Monographs; General and Applied*, 1949, 299.

BALL, R. A. "A Poverty Case: The Analgesic Culture of the Southern Appalachians." *American Sociological Review*, 1968, 33.

BANDLER, L. S. "Casework—A Process of Socialization: Gains, Limitations, Conclusions." In E. Pavenstedt (Ed.), *The Drifters: Children of Disorganized Lower-Class Families*. Boston: Little, Brown, 1967.

BANDURA, A., AND WALTERS, R. H. *Adolescent Aggression*. New York: Ronald Press, 1959.

BATESON, G., AND OTHERS. "Toward a Theory of Schizophrenia." *Behavioral Science*, 1956, 1.

BATTLE, E., AND ROTTER, J. B. "Children's Feelings of Personal Control

as Related to Social Class and Ethnic Group." *Journal of Personality,* 1963, *31.*

BAUMRIND, D. "Child Care Practices Anteceding Three Patterns of Preschool Behavior." *Genetic Psychology Monographs.* 1967, *75.*

BELCHER, J. "Evaluation and Restandardization of Sewell's Socioeconomic Scale." *Rural Sociology,* 1951, *16.*

BENDER, L. "Psychopathic Behavior Disorders in Children." In R. Lindner and R. V. Seliger (Eds.), *Handbook of Correctional Psychology.* New York: Philosophical Library, 1948.

BERNE, E. *Games People Play.* New York: Grove Press, 1964.

BERNSTEIN, B. "Social Class, Linguistic Codes, and Grammatical Elements."*Language and Speech,* 1962, *5.*

BOEHM, B. "The Community and the Social Agency Define Neglect." *Child Welfare,* 1964, *43.*

BONEM, G., AND RENO, P. "By Bread Alone and Little Bread." *Social Work,* 1968, *13.*

BORGMAN, R. D. "Intelligence and Maternal Inadequacy." *Child Welfare,* 1969, *48.*

BORGMAN, R. D. *Maternal Influences upon Development of Moral Reasoning in Retarded Children.* Unpublished Ph. D. dissertation. Raleigh, N.C.: North Carolina State University, 1972.

BOWLBY, J. *Forty-Four Juvenile Thieves.* London: Bailliere, Tindall, and Cox, 1946.

BOWLBY, J. "Separation Anxiety: A Critical Review of the Literature." New York: Child Welfare League of America, 1962.

BROWN, R. *Social Psychology.* New York: Free Press, 1965.

BUCKLEY, W. F. *Sociology and Modern Systems Theory.* Englewood Cliffs, N.J.: Prentice-Hall, 1967.

BURGESS, M. E., AND PRICE, D. O. *An American Dependency Challenge.* Chicago: American Public Welfare Association, 1963.

CAUDILL, H. M. *Night Comes to the Cumberlands.* Boston, Mass.: Little, Brown, 1962.

CHANSKY, N. "Mobility and the Rural School Drop-Out." Speech read at the annual meeting of The American Psychological Association, Sept., 1967.

COLLAZO-COLLAZO, J. M., AND RAMSEY, C. E. "Development of a Level of Living Scale For Puerto Rican Rural Families." Río Piedras, Puerto Rico: University of Puerto Rico Agricultural and Experimental Station Bulletin 156, 1960.

COSTIN, L. B. *Child Welfare: Policies and Practice.* New York: McGraw-Hill, 1972.

CUMMING, E., AND HENRY, W. E. *Growing Old: The Process of Disengagement.* New York: Basic Books, 1961.

DAVIS, W. A., AND HAVIGHURST, R. J. *Father of the Man.* Boston: Houghton-Mifflin, 1947.

DESPERT, J. L. *The Emotionally Disturbed Child—Then and Now.* New York: Vantage, 1965.

District of Columbia Dept. of Public Welfare. *Toward Social and Economic Independence: The First Three Years of the District of Columbia Training Center,* Washington, D.C., 1965.

DEUTSCH, M. "The Disadvantaged Child and the Learning Process." In L. A. Ferman (Ed.), *Poverty in America.* Ann Arbor, Mich. University of Michigan Press, 1961.

DOLLARD, J., AND OTHERS. *Frustration and Aggression.* New Haven, Conn.: Yale University Press, 1939.

EELLS, K., AND OTHERS. *Intelligence and Cultural Differences.* Chicago: University of Chicago Press, 1951.

ENELOW, A. J. "The Silent Patient." *Psychiatry,* 1960, *23.*

ERIKSON, E. H. *Childhood and Society.* New York: Norton, 1950.

FAIRBAIRN, W. R. D. *An Object-Relations Theory of the Personality.* New York: Basic Books, 1952.

FIERMAN, L. B. (Ed.) *Effective Psycho-therapy: The Contribution of Hellmuth Kaiser.* New York: Free Press, 1965.

FLANAGAN, J. C. "The Critical Incident Technique." *Psychological Bulletin,* 1954, *54.*

FORD, T. R. (Ed.) *The Southern Appalachian Region.* Lexington, Ky.: University of Kentucky Press, 1962.

FRANKL, V. E. *From Death Camp to Existentialism.* Boston, Mass.: Beacon Press, 1962.

FRANKL, V. E. *Man's Search for Meaning.* Boston, Mass.: Beacon Press, 1962.

FREUD, A. *The Ego and the Mechanisms of Defense.* New York: International Universities Press, 1946.

FREUD, S. "Mourning and Melancholia." In *Collected Papers,* Vol. 4. London: Hogarth, 1925.

GERTH, H. H., AND MILLS, C. W. *From Max Weber: Essays in Sociology.* New York: Oxford University Press, 1946.

GIL, D. G. *Violence Against Children: Physical Abuse in the United States.* Cambridge, Mass.: Harvard University Press, 1970.

GIL, T. D. "The Legal Nature of Neglect." *Crime and Delinquency,* 1960, *6.*

GINSBURG, L. "Social Problems in Rural America." In *Social Work Practice,* 1969. New York: Columbia University Press, 1969.

GOLDFARB, W. "Psychological Privation in Infancy and Psychological Adjustment." *American Journal of Ortho-psychiatry*, 1945, *15*.

GUNTRIP, H. *Schizoid Phenomena, Object Relations and the Self*. New York: International Universities Press, 1969.

HARING, J. *Freedom of Communication Between Parents and Adolescents with Problems*. Unpublished D. S. W. dissertation, Case Western Reserve University, 1965.

HARTMANN, H. *Ego Psychology and the Problem of Adaptation*. New York: International Universities Press, 1958.

HARTUP, W. W. "Dependence and Independence." In H. W. Stevenson (Ed.), *Sixty-Second Yearbook of the National Society for the Study of Education, Part I*, Chicago, 1963.

HEBER, R. *A Manual in Terminology and Classification in Mental Retardation*. Springfield, Ill.: American Association on Mental Deficiency, 1961.

HEPNER, R., AND MAIDEN, N. C. "Growth Rate, Nutrient Intake, and 'Mothering' as Determinants of Malnutrition in Disadvantaged Children." *Nutrition Reviews*, 1971, *29*.

HERZOG, E. "Social Stereotypes and Social Research." *Journal of Social Issues*, 1970, *26*.

HERZOG, E., AND SUDIA, C. E. "Family Structure and Composition." In R. Miller (Ed.), *Race, Research, and Reason: Social Work Perspectives*. New York: National Association of Social Workers, 1969.

HILL, L. B. "Infantile Personalities." *American Journal of Psychiatry*, 1952, *109*.

HOFFMAN, M. "Power Assertion by the Parent and its Impact on the Child." *Child Development*, 1960, *31*.

HOLLINGSHEAD, A. B. *Elmstown's Youth*. New York: Wiley, 1949.

HOLLINGSHEAD, A. B., AND REDLICH, F. C. *Social Class and Mental Illness*. New York: Appleton-Century-Crofts, 1958.

HOLLIS, F. *Development of a Casework Treatment Typology*. Unpublished Research Project Report, Columbia University School of Social Work, 1966.

HOWELLS, J. G., AND LAYNG, J. "Separation Experiences and Mental Health." *Lancet*, 1955, *269*.

HOWELLS, J. G. "The Psychopathogenesis of Hard-Core Families." *American Journal of Psychiatry*, 1966, *122*.

ISRAEL, J. *Alienation: From Marx to Modern Sociology*. Boston, Mass.: Allyn and Bacon, 1971.

JAFFEE, L. *An Investigation of Some Factors Related to Delinquency*

Proneness. Unpublished Master's Thesis. Columbus, Ohio: Ohio State University, Department of Sociology, 1959.

JAFFEE, L. D., AND POLANSKY, N. A. "Verbal Inaccessibility in Young Adolescents Showing Delinquent Trends." *Journal of Health and Human Behavior,* 1962, *3.*

JEFFERS, C. *Living Poor.* Ann Arbor, Mich.: Ann Arbor Science Publishers, 1967.

JETER, H. R. *Children, Problems, and Services in Child Welfare Programs.* Washington, D.C.: Children's Bureau, publication 403, 1963.

JONES, M. *The Therapeutic Community.* New York: Basic Books, 1964.

JOURARD, S. M. "Self-Disclosure Patterns in British and American College Females." *Journal of Social Psychology,* 1961, *54.*

KADUSHIN, A. "Introduction of New Orientations in Child Welfare Research." In M. Norris and B. Wallace (Eds.), *The Known and the Unknown in Child Welfare Research: An Appraisal.* New York: Child Welfare League of America, 1965.

KADUSHIN, A. *Child Welfare Services.* New York: Macmillan, 1967.

KAHN, A. J. "The Design of Research." In N. A. Polansky (Ed.), *Social Work Research.* Chicago: University of Chicago Press, 1960.

KARDINER, A. *The Psychological Frontiers of Society.* New York: Columbia University Press, 1945.

KAUFMAN, I. "Psychodynamics of Protective Casework." In H. J. Parad and R. R. Miller (Eds.), *Ego-Oriented Casework: Problems and Perspectives.* New York: Family Service Association of America, 1963.

KERNBERG, O. "Borderline Personality Organization." *Journal of the American Psychoanalytic Association,* 1967, *15.*

KLEIN, M., AND OTHERS. *Developments in Psychoanalysis.* London: Hogarth, 1952.

KOHLBERG, L. "Development of Moral Character and Moral Ideology." In M. and L. W. Hoffman (Eds.), *Review of Child Development Research.* Vol. 1. New York: Russell Sage Foundation, 1964.

KOUNIN, J. "Experimental Studies of Rigidity." *Character and Personality,* 1941, *9.*

LEVY, D. "Primary Affect Hunger." *American Journal of Psychiatry,* 1937, *94.*

LEVY, D. *Maternal Overprotection.* New York: Columbia University Press, 1943.

LEWIN, K. *Field Theory in Social Science.* New York: Harper and Row, 1951.

LEWIS, H. "Syndromes of Urban Poverty." In M. Greenblatt, P. E. Emery, and B. C. Glueck, Jr. (Eds.), *Poverty and Mental Health.* Washington, D.C.: American Psychiatric Association, 1967.

LIDZ, T., AND OTHERS. "The Intra-Familial Environment of Schizophrenic Patients." *American Journal of Psychiatry,* 1957, *114.*

LOOFF, D. H. *Appalachia's Children.* Lexington, Ky.: University Press of Kentucky, 1971.

LORR, M. "The Wittenborn Psychiatric Syndromes: An Oblique Rotation." *Journal of Consulting Psychology,* 1957, *21.*

LORR, M., AND JENKINS, R. "Patterns of Maladjustment in Children." *Journal of Clinical Psychology,* 1953, *9.*

LORR, M., JENKINS, R., AND O'CONNER, J. P. "Factors Descriptive of Psychopathology and Behavior of Hospitalized Psychotics." *Journal of Abnormal and Social Psychology,* 1955, *50.*

MAAS, H. "The Young-Adult Adjustment of Twenty Wartime Residential Nursery Children." *Child Welfare,* 1963, *42.*

MAAS, H. S., AND ENGLER, R. E., JR. *Children in Need of Parents.* New York: Columbia University Press, 1959.

MC GUIRE, C., AND WHITE, G. D. *The Measurement of Social Status.* Austin, Texas: University of Texas, Department of Sociology, 1955.

MECH, E. "Practice-Oriented Research on Separation in Child Welfare." In M. Norris and B. Wallace (Eds.), *The Known and Unknown in Child Welfare Research.* New York: Child Welfare League of America, 1965.

MERTON, R. K. "Social Structure and Anomie." In *Social Theory and Social Structure.* Glencoe, Ill.: Free Press, 1949.

MILLER, S. M. "Social Class and Projective Tests." *Journal of Projective Techniques,* 1958, *22.*

National Center for Social Statistics. *Child Welfare Statistics* 1969. Washington, D.C., 1969.

NOONEY, J. B., AND POLANSKY, N. A. "The Influence of Perceived Similarity and Personality on Verbal Accessibility." *Merrill-Palmer Quarterly,* 1962, *8.*

OLIVER, K., AND BARCLAY, A. "Stanford-Binet and Goodenough-Harris Test Performances of Head Start Children." *Psychological Reports,* 1967, *20.*

OZER, M. N. *Measure for Evaluation of School Age Children.* Unpub-

lished. Washington, D.C.: Children's Hospital of the District of Columbia, 1967.

PAVENSTEDT, E. (Ed.) *The Drifters: Children of Disorganized Lower-Class Families.* Boston: Little, Brown, 1967.

PECK, H. B., AND BELLSMITH, V. *Treatment of the Delinquent Adolescent.* New York: Family Service Association of America, 1954.

PETERSON, D. R. "Behavior Problems of Middle Childhood." *Journal of Consulting Psychology,* 1961, 25.

PHILLIPS, L. *Human Adaptation and Its Failures.* New York: Academic Press, 1968.

PHILLIPS, L., KADEN, S., AND WALDMAN, M. "Rorschach Indices of Developmental Level." *Journal of Genetic Psychology,* 1959, 94.

PHILLIPS, L., AND RABINOVITCH, M. S. "Social Role and Patterns of Symptomatic Behavior." *Journal of Abnormal and Social Psychology,* 1958, 57.

PIAGET, J. *Moral Judgment of the Child.* Glencoe, Ill.: Free Press, 1948.

PIAGET, J. *Origins of Intelligence.* Glencoe, Ill.: Free Press, 1950.

PLANT, J. S. *Personality and the Cultural Pattern.* New York: Commonwealth Fund, 1937.

PODELL, J. E., AND PHILLIPS, L. "A Developmental Analysis of Cognition as Observed in Dimensions of Rorschach and Objective Test Performances." *Journal of Personality,* 1959, 27.

POLANSKY, N. A. "Techniques for Ordering Cases." In N. A. Polansky (Ed.), *Social Work Research.* Chicago: University of Chicago Press, 1960.

POLANSKY, N. A. *Changing Services for Changing Clients.* New York: National Association of Social Workers, 1969.

POLANSKY, N. A. *Ego Psychology and Communication: Theory for the Interview.* Chicago: Aldine-Atherton, 1971.

POLANSKY, N. A., BOONE, D. R., DE SAIX, C., AND SHARLIN, S. A. "Pseudostoicism in Mothers of the Retarded." *Social Casework,* 1971, 51.

POLANSKY, N. A., AND BROWN, S. Q. "Verbal Accessibility and Fusion Fantasy in a Mountain Country." *American Journal of Orthopsychiatry,* 1967, 37.

POLANSKY, N. A., DE SAIX, C., AND SHARLIN, S. "Child Neglect in Appalachia." In *Social Work Practice,* 1971. New York: Columbia University Press, 1971.

POLANSKY, N. A., DE SAIX, C., AND SHARLIN, S. A. *Child Neglect: Under-*

standing and Reaching the Parent. New York: Child Welfare League of America, 1972.

POLANSKY, N. A., DE SAIX, C., WING, M. L., AND PATTON, J. D. "Child Neglect in a Rural Community." *Social Casework,* 1968, *49.*

POLANSKY, N. A., MILLER, S. C., AND WHITE, R. B. "Some Reservations Regarding Group Psychotherapy in In-Patient Psychiatric Treatment." *Group Psychotherapy,* 1955, *8.*

POLANSKY, N. A., AND POLANSKY, N. F. "The Current Status of Child Abuse and Child Neglect in This Country." Report to the Joint Commission on the Mental Health of Children. Washington, D.C., Feb. 1968.

President's National Advisory Commission on Rural Poverty. *The People Left Behind.* Washington, D.C.: Government Printing Office, 1967.

RAPAPORT, D. "Edward Bibring's Theory of Depression." In M. M. Gill (Ed.), *The Collected Papers of David Rapaport.* New York: Basic Books, 1967.

RAPAPORT, D. "Some Metapsychological Considerations Concerning Activity and Passivity." In M. M. Gill (Ed.), *The Collected Papers of David Rapaport.* New York: Basic Books, 1967.

REICH, C. A. *The Greening of America.* New York: Bantam, 1971.

REINER, B. S., AND KAUFMAN, I. *Character Disorders in Parents of Delinquents.* New York: Family Service Association of America, 1959.

REISSMAN, F., AND MILLER, S. M. "Social Class and Projective Tests." *Journal of Projective Techniques,* 1958, *22.*

Report of the National Advisory Commission on Civil Disorders. New York: Bantam Books, 1968.

RICKERS-OVSIANKINA, M. "Cross-Cultural Study of Social Accessibility." *Acta Psychologica,* 1961, *19.*

ROTTER, J. B., AND SEEMAN, M. *Powerlessness Scale.* Unpublished mimeograph. Columbus, Ohio: Ohio State University, Department of Sociology, 1959.

ROTTER, J. B., AND WILLERMAN, B. "The Incomplete Sentence Test." *Journal of Consulting Psychology,* 1947, *11.*

RUESCH, J. "The Infantile Personality: The Core Problem of Psychosomatic Medicine." *Psychosomatic Medicine,* 1948, *10.*

SCHACHTER, H. *A Review of Sociocultural Factors that Influence Work with Southern Appalachian Mountaineer Clients.* Unpublished Program for Advanced Study project. Smith College School for Social Work, 1962.

SCHLEIFFER, M. J., AND TEELE, J. E. "The Mother of the School Drop-Out: The Alienated Adult." Boston, Mass.: Judge Baker Guidance Center, 1964.

SEARS, R. R., MACCOBY, E. E., AND LEVIN, H. *Patterns of Child Rearing.* New York: Harper and Row, 1957.

SEEMAN, M. "On the Meaning of Alienation." *American Sociological Review,* 1959, 24.

SEEMAN, M. "Alienation, Membership, and Political Knowledge: A Comparative Study." *Public Opinion Quarterly,* 1966, 30.

SELLTIZ, C., JAHODA, M., DEUTSCH, M., AND COOK, S. W. *Research Methods in Social Relations.* New York: Holt, 1959.

SHARLIN, S. A. *Infantilization: A Study in Intrafamilial Communication.* Unpublished Ph.D. dissertation. Athens, Ga.: University of Georgia, Department of Sociology, 1971.

SHARLIN, S. A., AND POLANSKY, N. A. "The Process of Infantilization." *American Journal of Orthopsychiatry,* 1972, 42.

SHERIDAN, M. "The Intelligence of 100 Neglectful Mothers." *British Medical Journal,* 1956, 1.

SKEELS, H., AND FILLMORE, E. A. "Mental Development of Children from Underprivileged Homes." *Journal of Genetic Psychology,* 1937, 50.

SPITZ, R. "Hospitalism: An Inquiry into the Genesis of Psychiatric Conditions in Early Childhood." In *The Psychoanalytic Study of the Child.* Vol. 1. New York: International Universities Press, 1945.

SPITZ, R., AND WOLF, K. M. "Anaclitic Repression." In *The Psychoanalytic Study of the Child.* Vol. 2. New York: International Universities Press, 1946.

SPITZER, R. L., ENDICOTT, J., AND COHEN, G. M. *Psychiatric Status Schedule.* New York: Columbia University, Department of Psychiatry, 1963.

STANTON, A. H., AND SCHWARZ, M. S. *The Mental Hospital.* New York: Basic Books, 1954.

TERMAN, L. *Measurement of Intelligence.* Boston: Houghton-Mifflin, 1916.

TURIEL, E. "Experimental Test of the Sequentiality of Developmental Stages in the Child's Moral Judgments." *Journal of Personality and Social Psychology,* 1966, 3.

U.S. Department of Commerce, Bureau of the Census. *1970 Census of Population: Number of Inhabitants.* July 1971.

VYGOTSKY, L. S. *Thought and Language.* Cambridge, Mass.: MIT Press, 1962.

WASSERMAN, H. "Early Careers of Professional Social Workers in a Public Child Welfare Agency." *Social Work,* 1970, *15.*

WECHSLER, D. *The Measurement of Adult Intelligence.* Baltimore, Md.: Williams and Wilkins, 1958 (4th Ed.).

WEINSTEIN, E. A. *Self-Image of the Foster Child.* New York: Russell Sage Foundation, 1960.

WELLER, J. E. *Yesterday's People: Life in Contemporary Appalachia.* Lexington, Ky.: University of Kentucky Press, 1965.

WERNER, H. "The Concept of Development from a Comparative and Organismic Point of View." In D. B. Harris (Ed.), *The Concept of Development.* Minneapolis, Minn.: University of Minnesota Press, 1957.

WHITE, R., AND LIPPITT, R. *Autocracy and Democracy.* New York: Harper and Row, 1960.

WITTKE, C. *We Who Built America.* New York: Prentice-Hall, 1939.

WOLFF, K. H. *The Sociology of Georg Simmel.* Glencoe, Ill.: Free Press, 1950.

YARROW, M. R., CAMPBELL, J. D., AND BURTON, R. V. *Child Rearing: An Inquiry into Research and Methods.* San Francisco: Jossey-Bass, 1968.

YOUNG, L. *Wednesday's Children.* New York: McGraw-Hill, 1964.

ZBOROWSKI, M., AND HERZOG, E. *Life is with People.* New York: International Universities Press, 1952.

Index

267

C

D

E

F

Fathers: competency of matched with wives' competency, 117–118; as determining level of child caring, 118–120; in neglect situations, 19–20

FIERMAN, L. B., 78, 89, 259

FILLMORE, E. A., 126, 265

FLANAGAN, J., 36, 38, 259

FORD, T. R., 69, 176, 259

FRANKL, V. E., 259

FREUD, A., 129, 259

FREUD, S., 129, 259

Fusion fantasy: to explain group pressures toward verbal inaccessibility, 89–90; as regressive cultural theme, 78

Futility: in apathy-futility syndrome, 54; contagious effect of, 55, 189; group support of, 64–65; resulting from detachment, 60–64; treatment of, 218–225

G

"Games," client, 190–207

GERTH, H. H., 57, 259

GIL, D. G., 25, 210, 259

GILL, T. D., 51, 259

GINZBURG, L., 5, 39, 259

GOLDFARB, W., 126, 127, 260

GUNTRIP, H., 59, 60, 136, 260

H

HARING, J., 175, 260

HARKINS, E. B., 38, 239

HARTMAN, B. H., 146

HARTMANN, H., 56, 260

HARTUP, W. W., 144, 260

HAVIGHURST, R. J., 157, 259

HEBER, R., 147, 260

HENRY, W. E., 61, 259

HEPNER, R., 33, 260

HERRELL, H. G., 15

HERZOG, E., 74, 79, 89, 122, 214, 260, 266

HILL, L. B., 19, 260

HOFFMAN, M., 123, 130, 260

HOLLINGSHEAD, A. B., 147, 157, 260

HOLLIS, F., 169, 260

HOWELLS, J. G., 17, 125, 260

I

Identification hypothesis, 129–130

Immaturity: in conception of maternal role, 111–114; as depressing level of child care, 107–120; marginal child caring related to, 108–120; as measured by child-rearing conceptualization, 159–161; and moral reasoning, 155–164; reflected in Rorschach results, 110–111

Impulsivity: client "games" associated with, 198–207; in client manipulation, 198–207; as defense against depressive core, 66–67; among eruptive mothers, 20–21

Infantile personality and child neglect, 18

Infantilism: coordination as reflection of, 150; and self-regarding attitudes, 145–146

Infantilization: cycle of, 143; intellectual decrement as reflection of, 150; and maternal communications, 145–155; of southern Appalachian male, 75–76

Infantilization Scale (Appendix C), 252–256; description of, 151

Institutionalized treatment, 221–224

Intelligence: of child as determined by level of care, 140; as lowered by infantilization, 149–151; of mother as affecting care of child, 108–110; of mother as affecting child's intelligence, 140

Intergenerational transmission of futility, theories regarding, 124–131

ISRAEL, J., 58, 260

J

JAFFEE, L., 90, 260, 261

JAHODA, M., 36, 265

JEFFERS, C., 55, 176, 261

JENKINS, R., 262